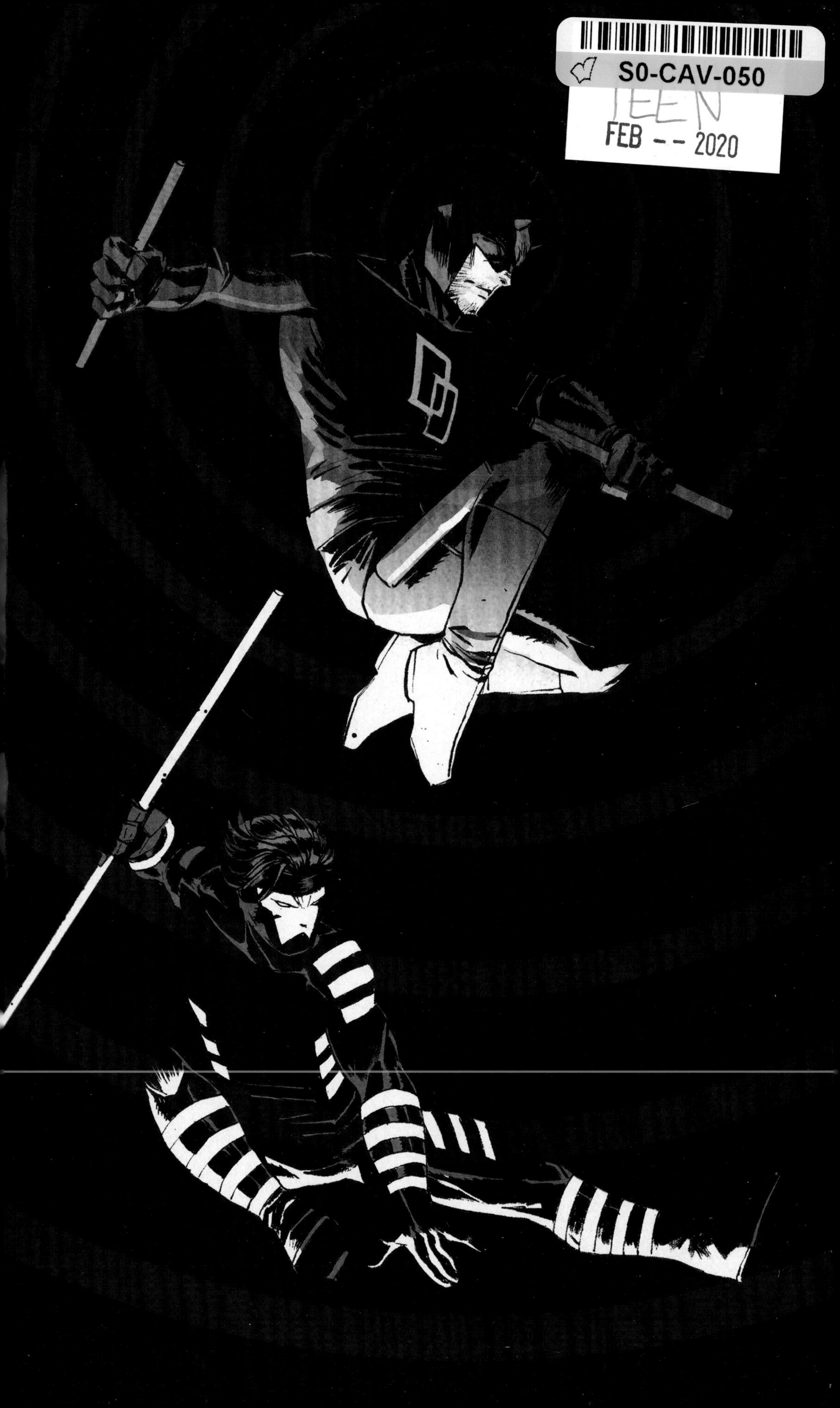

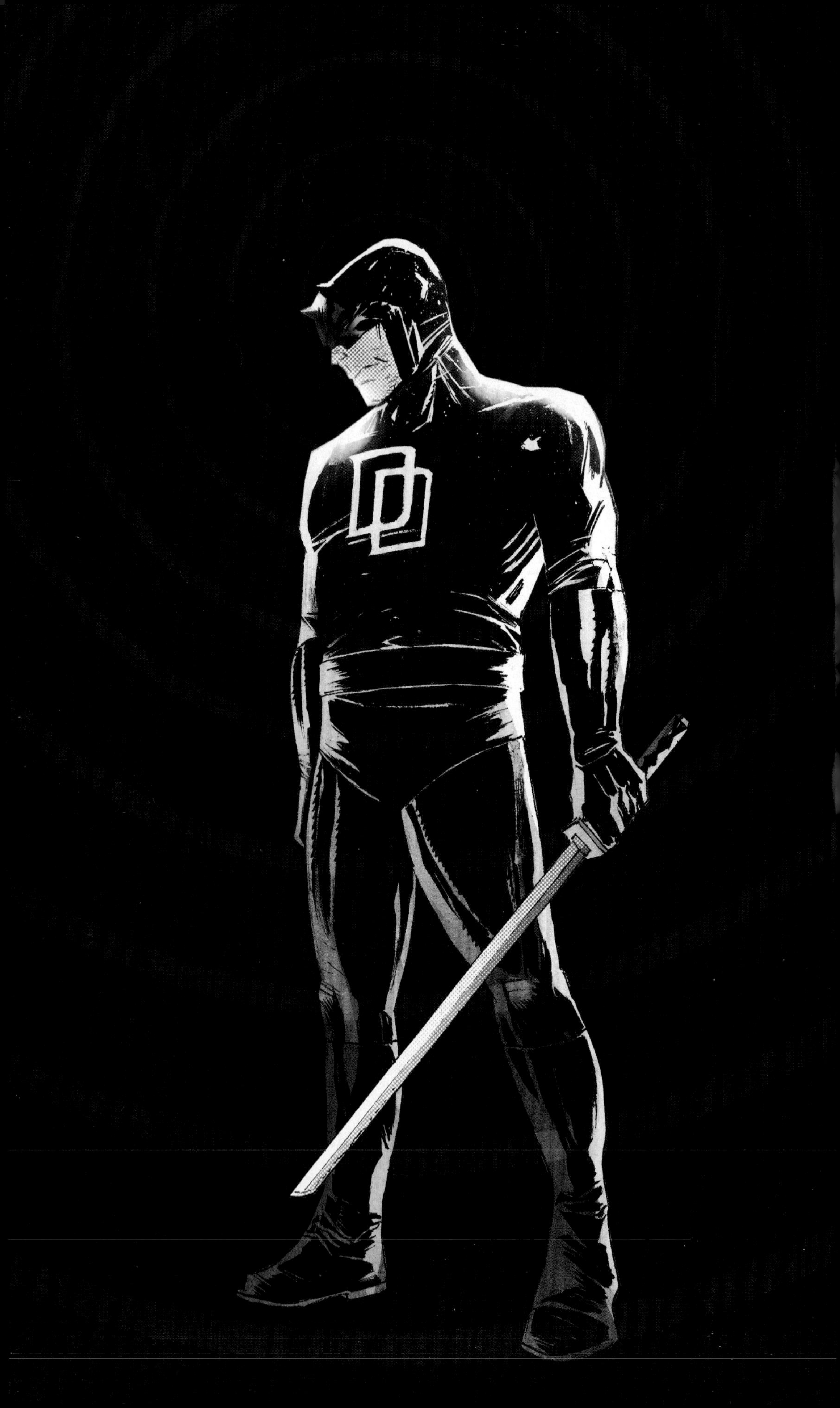

WHEN MATT MURDOCK WAS A KID, HE LOST HIS SIGHT IN AN ACCIDENT INVOLVING A TRUCK CARRYING RADIOACTIVE CHEMICALS. THOUGH HE COULD NO LONGER SEE, THE CHEMICALS HEIGHTENED MURDOCK'S OTHER SENSES AND IMBUED HIM WITH AN AMAZING 360-DEGREE RADAR SENSE. NOW MATT USES HIS ABILITIES TO FIGHT FOR HIS CITY. HE IS THE *MAN WITHOUT FEAR*. HE

DAREDEVIL

MAYOR MURDOCK

WILSON FISK, A.K.A. THE KINGPIN, HAS USED HIS POWER AS MAYOR OF NEW YORK TO OUTLAW SUPER HEROES. SEEKING TO KEEP HIS ENEMIES CLOSE, FISK MADE MATT MURDOCK HIS DEPUTY MAYOR.

AS DAREDEVIL, MATT ASSEMBLED A TEAM OF HEROES TO EXPOSE FISK'S ILLICIT DEALINGS. BUT WHILE STAKING OUT A MEET-UP OF THE CITY'S MOST NOTORIOUS CRIMINALS ARRANGED BY THE KINGPIN, THE HEROES WERE CAPTURED IN A STING BY FISK'S FORCES. DAREDEVIL MANAGED TO ESCAPE AND CONFRONT FISK, ONLY TO BE DECEIVED AGAIN AND BRUTALLY SUBDUED.

TO MAKE MATTERS WORSE, THE HAND HAS ATTACKED! THEIR FIRST TARGET: THE KINGPIN! WITH FISK DOWN FOR THE COUNT, AND DUE TO A RECENT CHANGE IN THE ORDER OF SUCCESSION, MATT MURDOCK IS NOW THE MAYOR OF NEW YORK CITY!

CHARLES SOULE
WRITER

MIKE HENDERSON
ARTIST

MATT MILLA
COLOR ARTIST

VC's CLAYTON COWLES
LETTERER

CHRIS SPROUSE, KARL STORY & JORDIE BELLAIRE (*No. 601*),
CHRIS SPROUSE, KARL STORY & MARTE GRACIA (*Nos. 602-605*)
COVER ART

ANNALISE BISSA, TOM GRONEMAN, EMILY NEWCOMEN & LAUREN AMARO
ASSISTANT EDITORS

DEVIN LEWIS & JORDAN WHITE
EDITORS

COLLECTION EDITOR MARK D. BEAZLEY
ASSISTANT EDITOR CAITLIN O'CONNELL
ASSOCIATE MANAGING EDITOR KATERI WOODY
SENIOR EDITOR, SPECIAL PROJECTS JENNIFER GRÜNWALD

VP PRODUCTION & SPECIAL PROJECTS JEFF YOUNGQUIST
SVP PRINT, SALES & MARKETING DAVID GABRIEL
BOOK DESIGNER ADAM DEL RE

EDITOR IN CHIEF C.B. CEBULSKI
CHIEF CREATIVE OFFICER JOE QUESADA
PRESIDENT DAN BUCKLEY
EXECUTIVE PRODUCER ALAN FINE

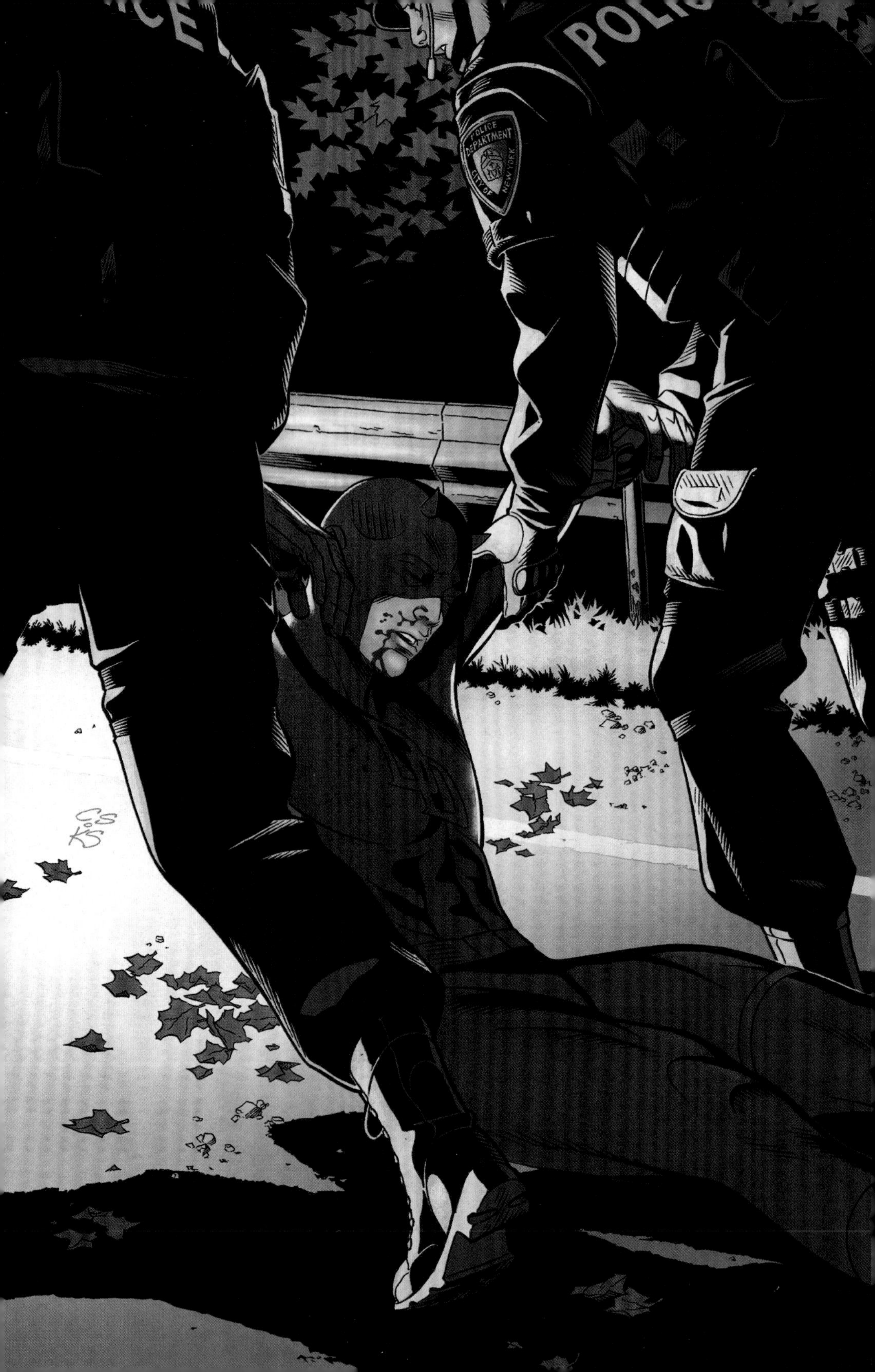

POLICE
DEPARTMENT
CITY OF NEW YORK

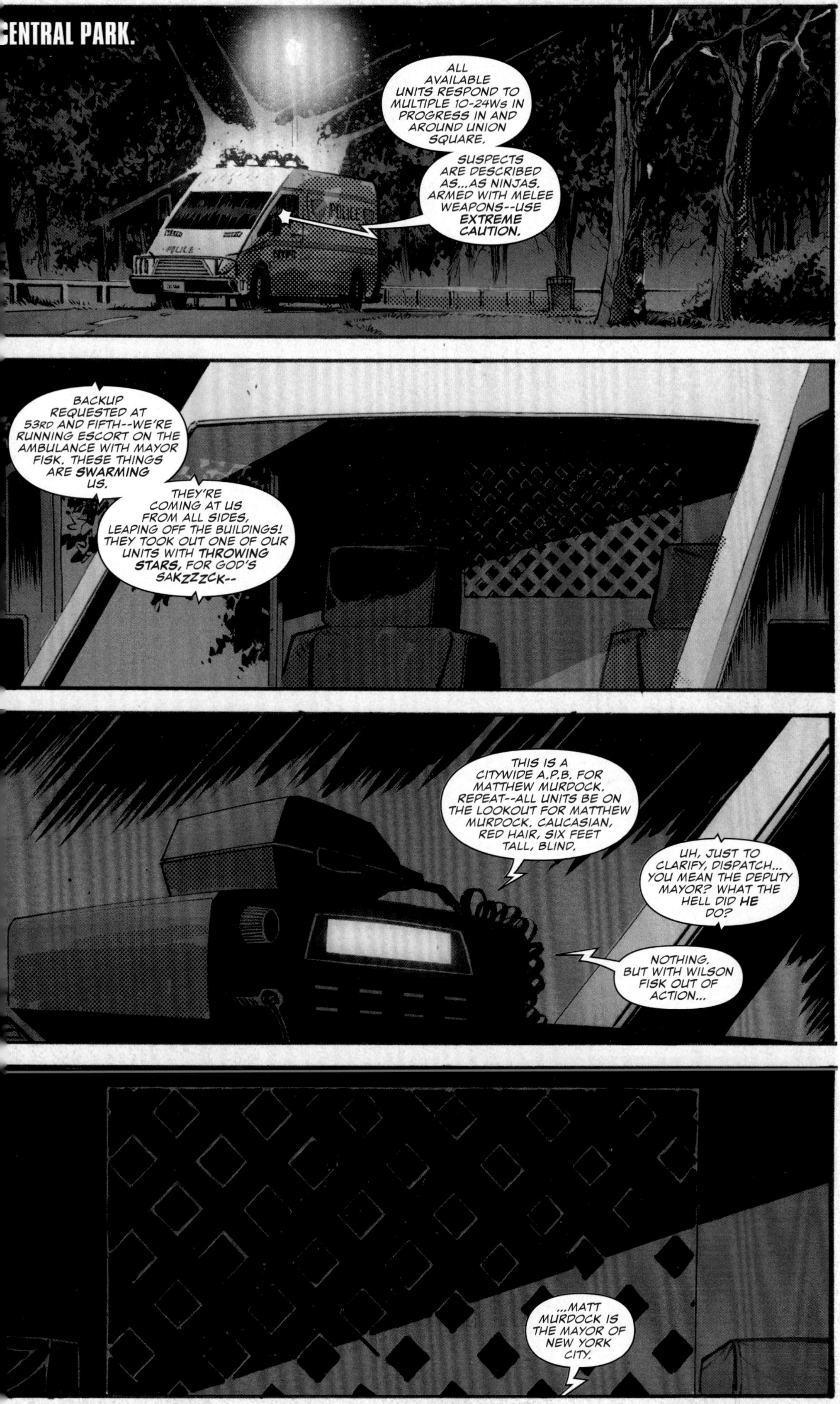

CENTRAL PARK.
ALL AVAILABLE UNITS RESPOND TO MULTIPLE 10-24Ws IN PROGRESS IN AND AROUND UNION SQUARE.
SUSPECTS ARE DESCRIBED AS...AS NINJAS. ARMED WITH MELEE WEAPONS--USE EXTREME CAUTION.
POLICE
BACKUP REQUESTED AT 53RD AND FIFTH--WE'RE RUNNING ESCORT ON THE AMBULANCE WITH MAYOR FISK. THESE THINGS ARE SWARMING US.
THEY'RE COMING AT US FROM ALL SIDES, LEAPING OFF THE BUILDINGS! THEY TOOK OUT ONE OF OUR UNITS WITH THROWING STARS, FOR GOD'S SAKZZZCK--
THIS IS A CITYWIDE A.P.B. FOR MATTHEW MURDOCK. REPEAT--ALL UNITS BE ON THE LOOKOUT FOR MATTHEW MURDOCK. CAUCASIAN, RED HAIR, SIX FEET TALL, BLIND.
UH, JUST TO CLARIFY, DISPATCH... YOU MEAN THE DEPUTY MAYOR? WHAT THE HELL DID HE DO?
NOTHING. BUT WITH WILSON FISK OUT OF ACTION...
...MATT MURDOCK IS THE MAYOR OF NEW YORK CITY.

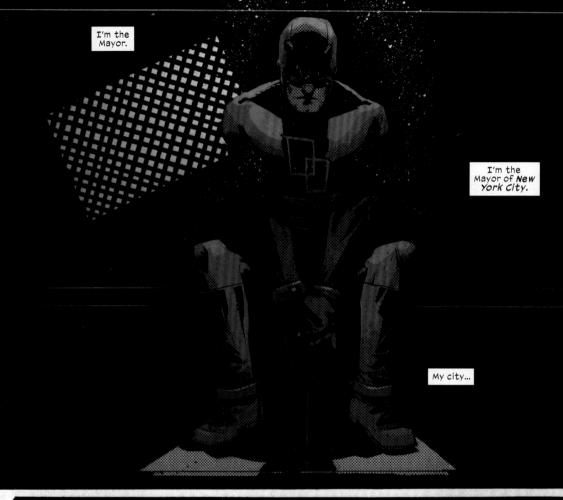

The Mayor.

I'm the Mayor.

I'm the Mayor of *New York City*.

My city...

...is *my* city.

I have to get out of here.

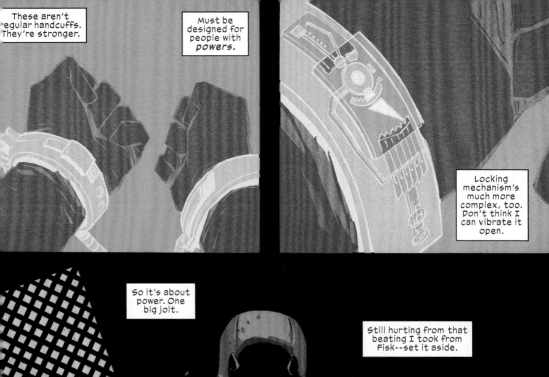

These aren't regular handcuffs. They're stronger.

Must be designed for people with *powers.*

Locking mechanism's much more complex, too. Don't think I can vibrate it open.

So it's about power. One big jolt.

Still hurting from that beating I took from Fisk--set it aside.

Focus.

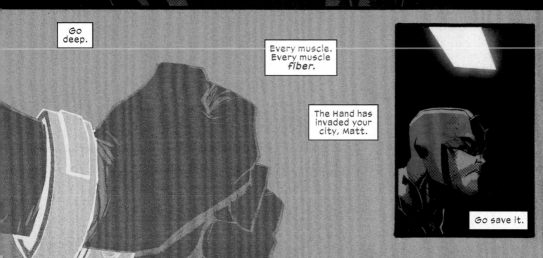

Go deep.

Every muscle. Every muscle *fiber.*

The Hand has invaded your city, Matt.

Go save it.

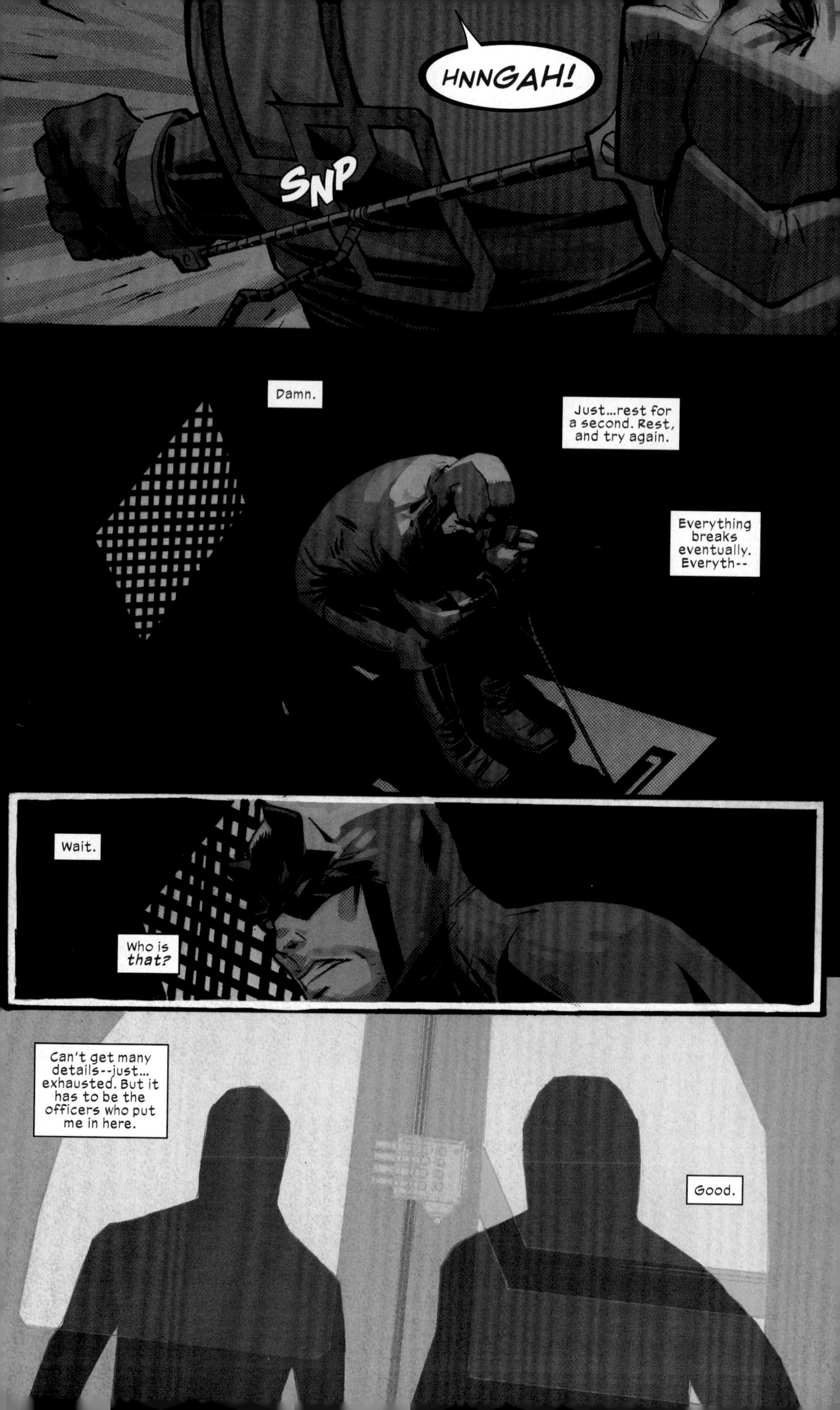
HNNGAH!
SNP
Damn.
Just...rest for a second. Rest, and try again.
Everything breaks eventually. Everyth--
Wait.
Who is *that?*
Can't get many details--just... exhausted. But it has to be the officers who put me in here.
Good.

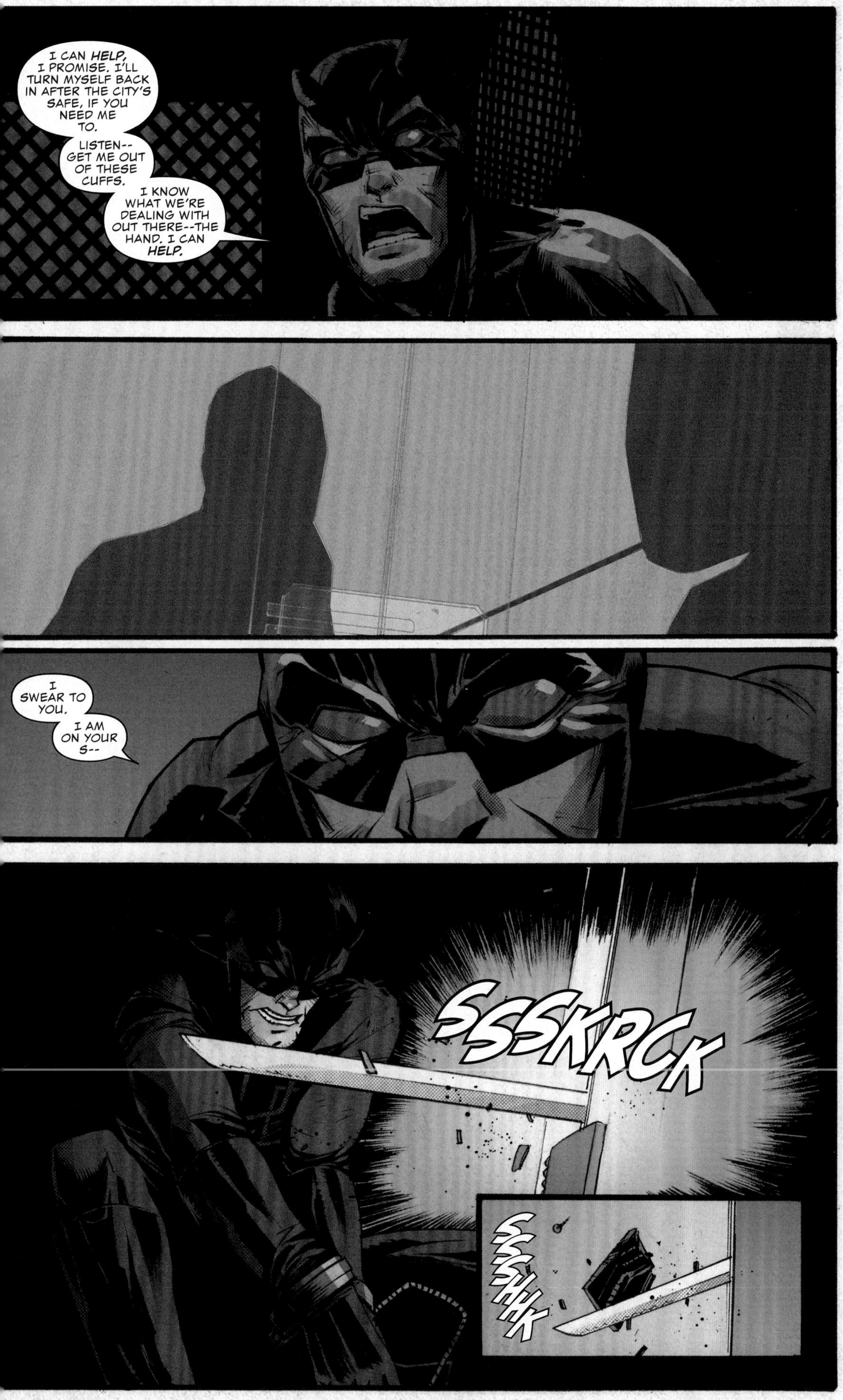
I CAN HELP, I PROMISE. I'LL TURN MYSELF BACK IN AFTER THE CITY'S SAFE, IF YOU NEED ME TO.
LISTEN-- GET ME OUT OF THESE CUFFS.
I KNOW WHAT WE'RE DEALING WITH OUT THERE--THE HAND. I CAN HELP.
I SWEAR TO YOU.
I AM ON YOUR S--
SSSKRCK
SSSHHK

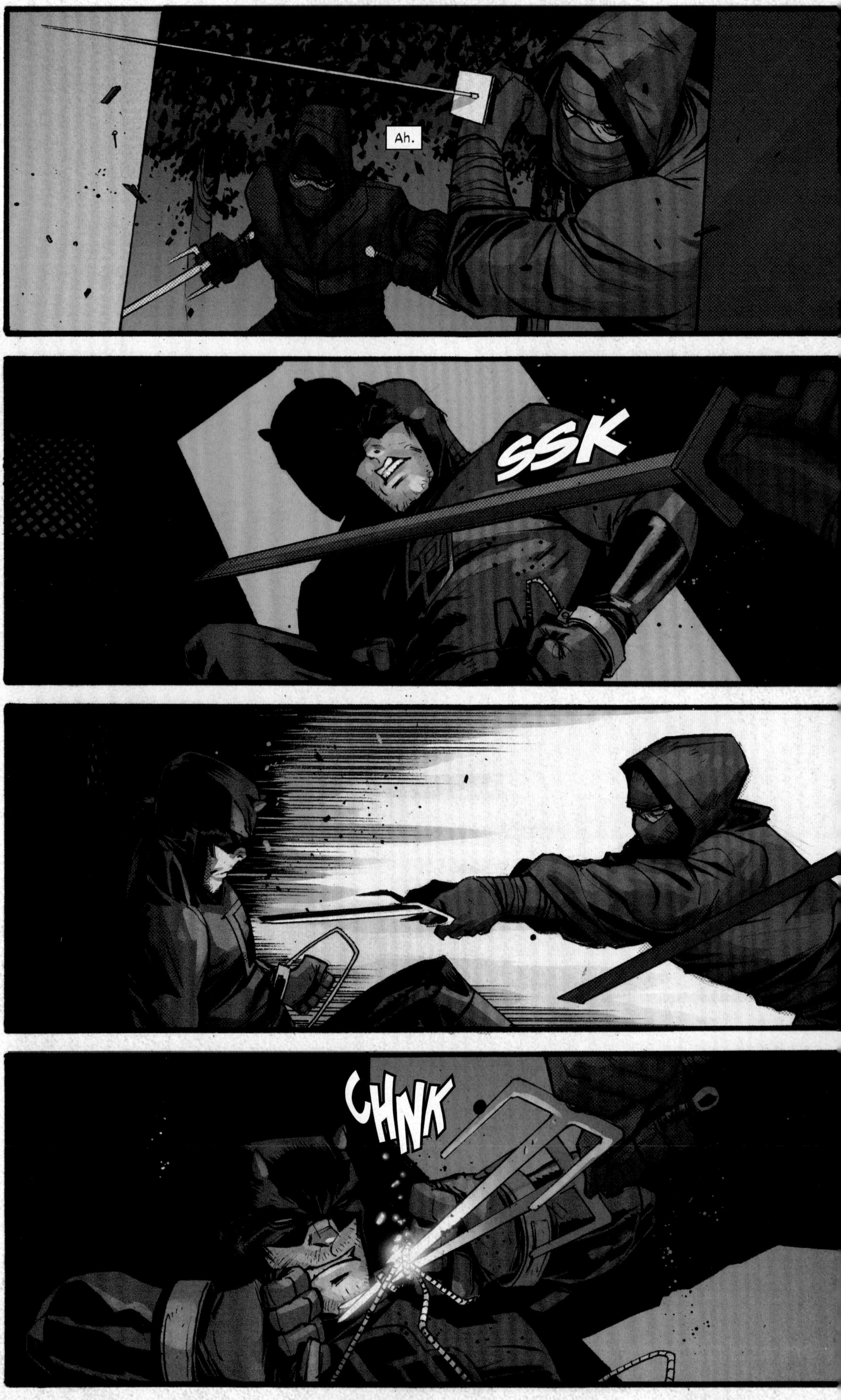
Ah.
SSK
CHNK

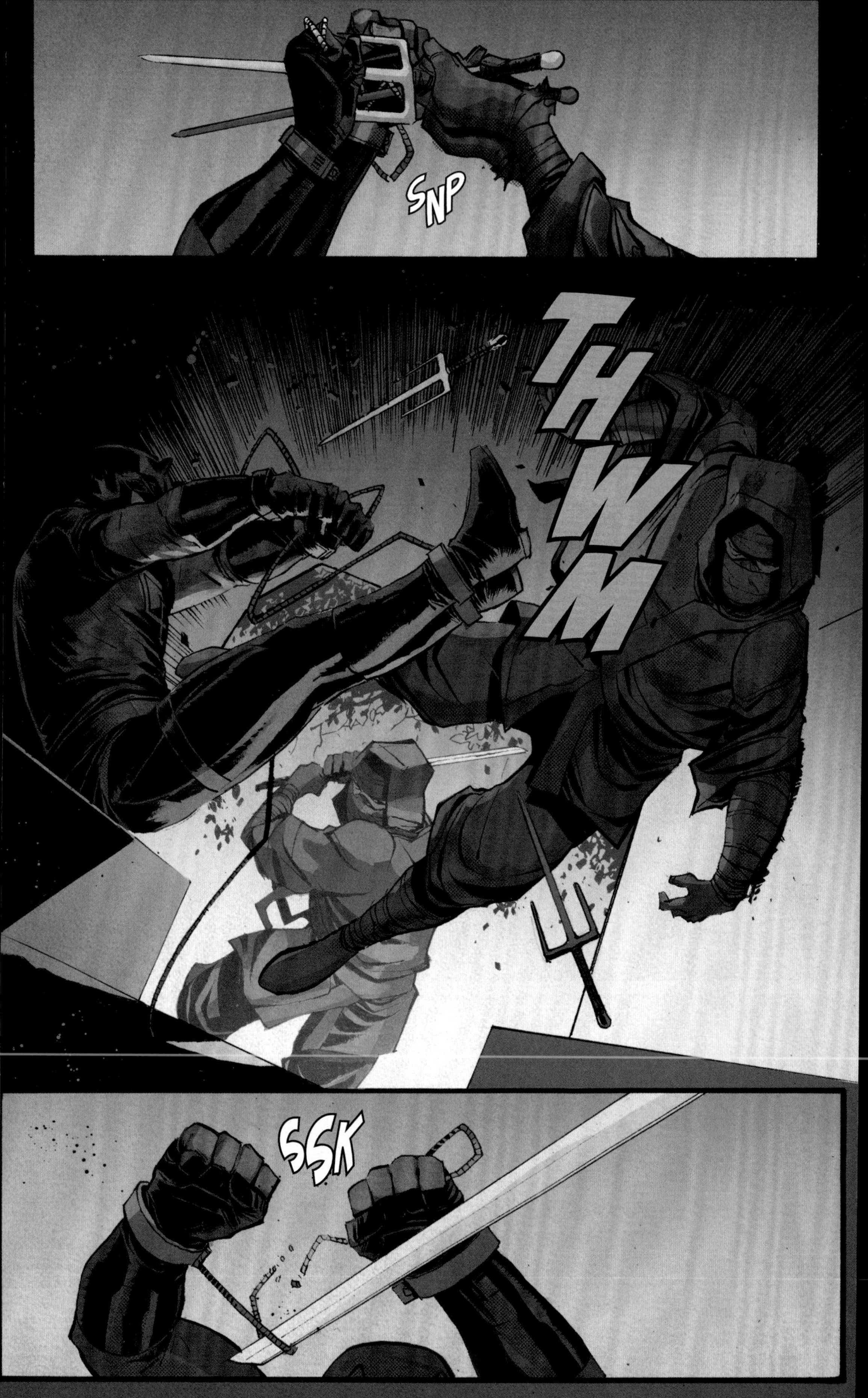

SNP
THWM
SSK

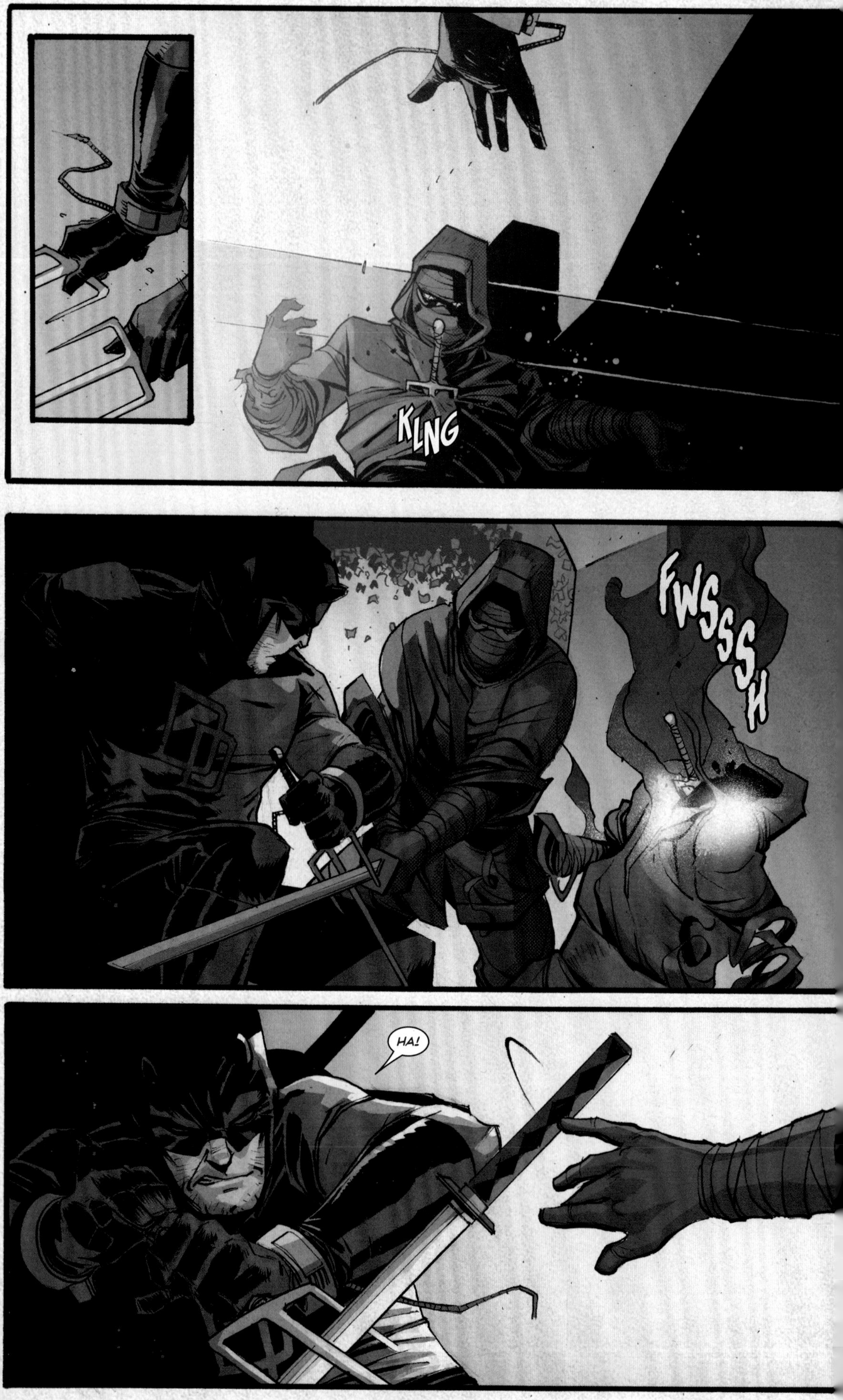
KLNG
FWSSSH
HA!

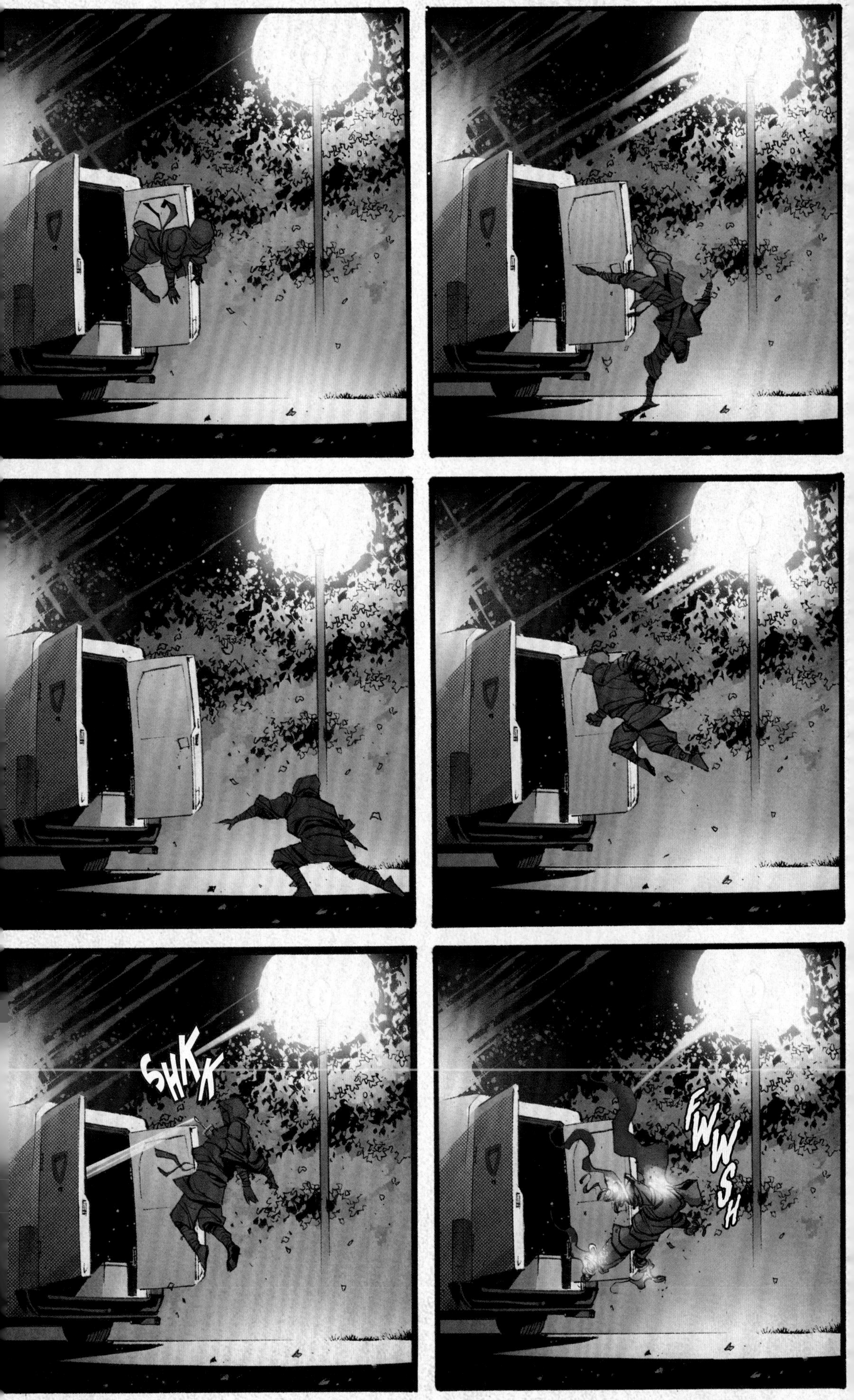
SHKK
FWWSH

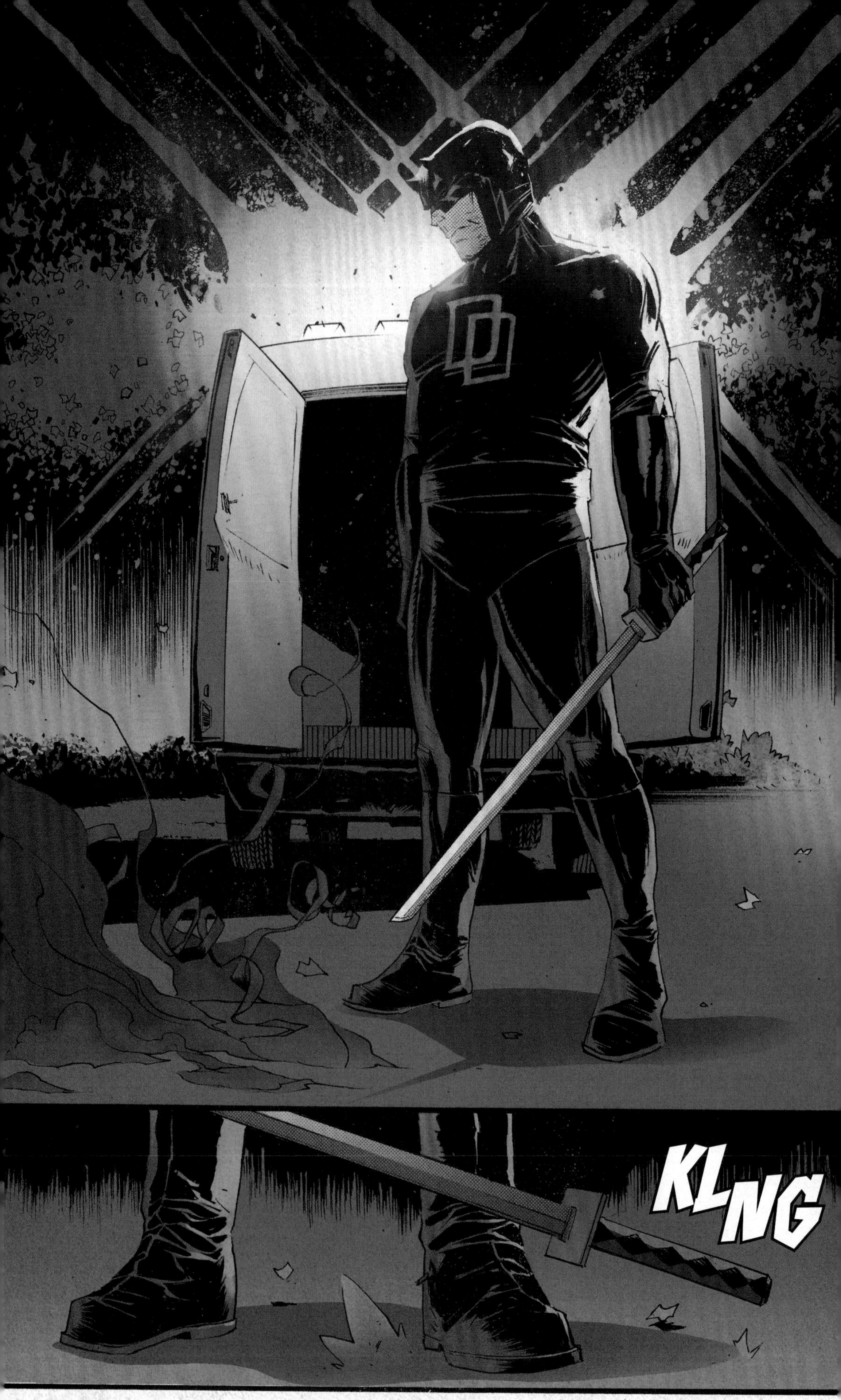
KLNG

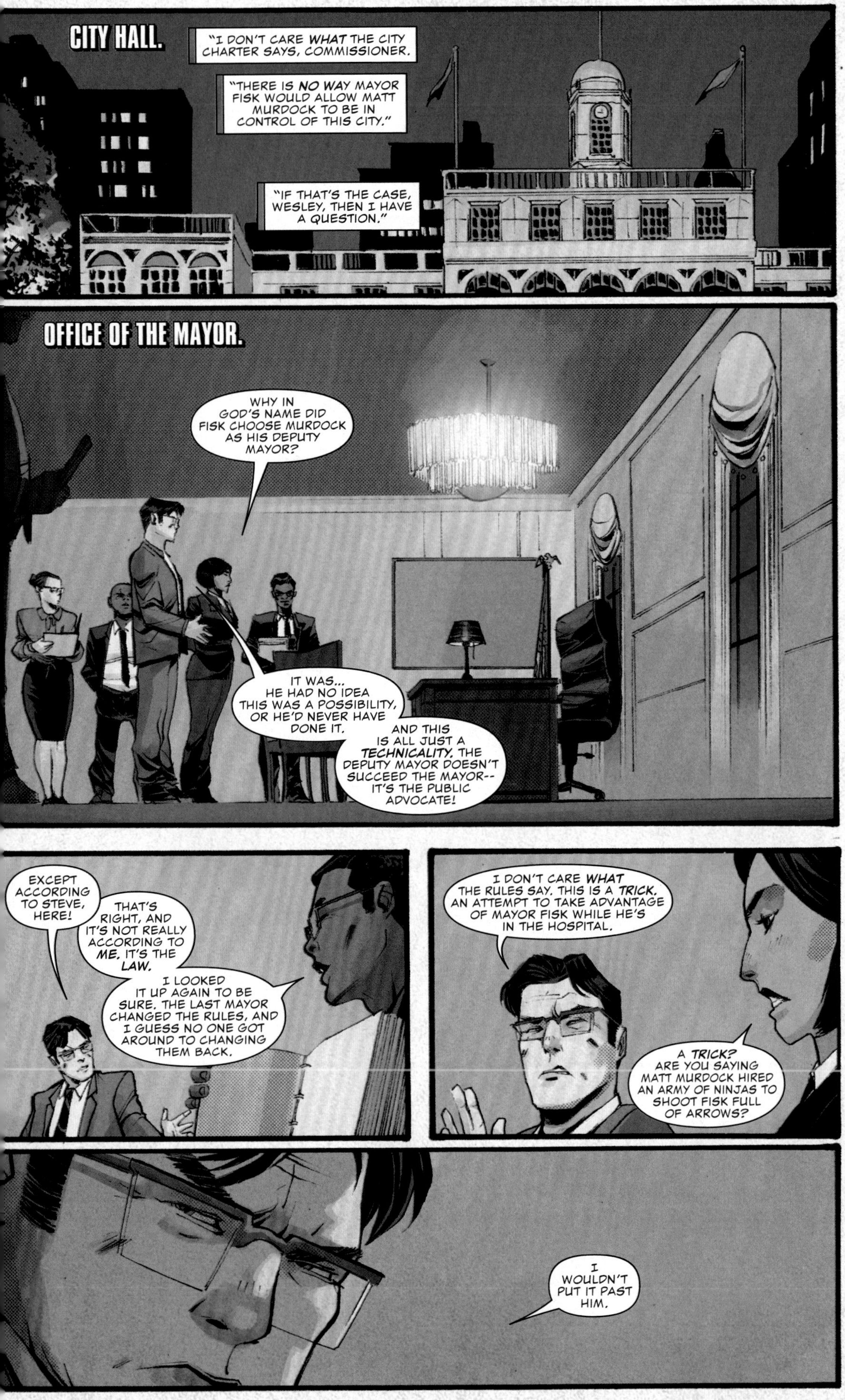
CITY HALL.
"I DON'T CARE WHAT THE CITY CHARTER SAYS, COMMISSIONER.
"THERE IS NO WAY MAYOR FISK WOULD ALLOW MATT MURDOCK TO BE IN CONTROL OF THIS CITY."
"IF THAT'S THE CASE, WESLEY, THEN I HAVE A QUESTION."
OFFICE OF THE MAYOR.
WHY IN GOD'S NAME DID FISK CHOOSE MURDOCK AS HIS DEPUTY MAYOR?
IT WAS... HE HAD NO IDEA THIS WAS A POSSIBILITY, OR HE'D NEVER HAVE DONE IT.
AND THIS IS ALL JUST A TECHNICALITY. THE DEPUTY MAYOR DOESN'T SUCCEED THE MAYOR-- IT'S THE PUBLIC ADVOCATE!
EXCEPT ACCORDING TO STEVE, HERE!
THAT'S RIGHT, AND IT'S NOT REALLY ACCORDING TO ME. IT'S THE LAW.
I LOOKED IT UP AGAIN TO BE SURE. THE LAST MAYOR CHANGED THE RULES, AND I GUESS NO ONE GOT AROUND TO CHANGING THEM BACK.
I DON'T CARE WHAT THE RULES SAY. THIS IS A TRICK. AN ATTEMPT TO TAKE ADVANTAGE OF MAYOR FISK WHILE HE'S IN THE HOSPITAL.
A TRICK? ARE YOU SAYING MATT MURDOCK HIRED AN ARMY OF NINJAS TO SHOOT FISK FULL OF ARROWS?
I WOULDN'T PUT IT PAST HIM.

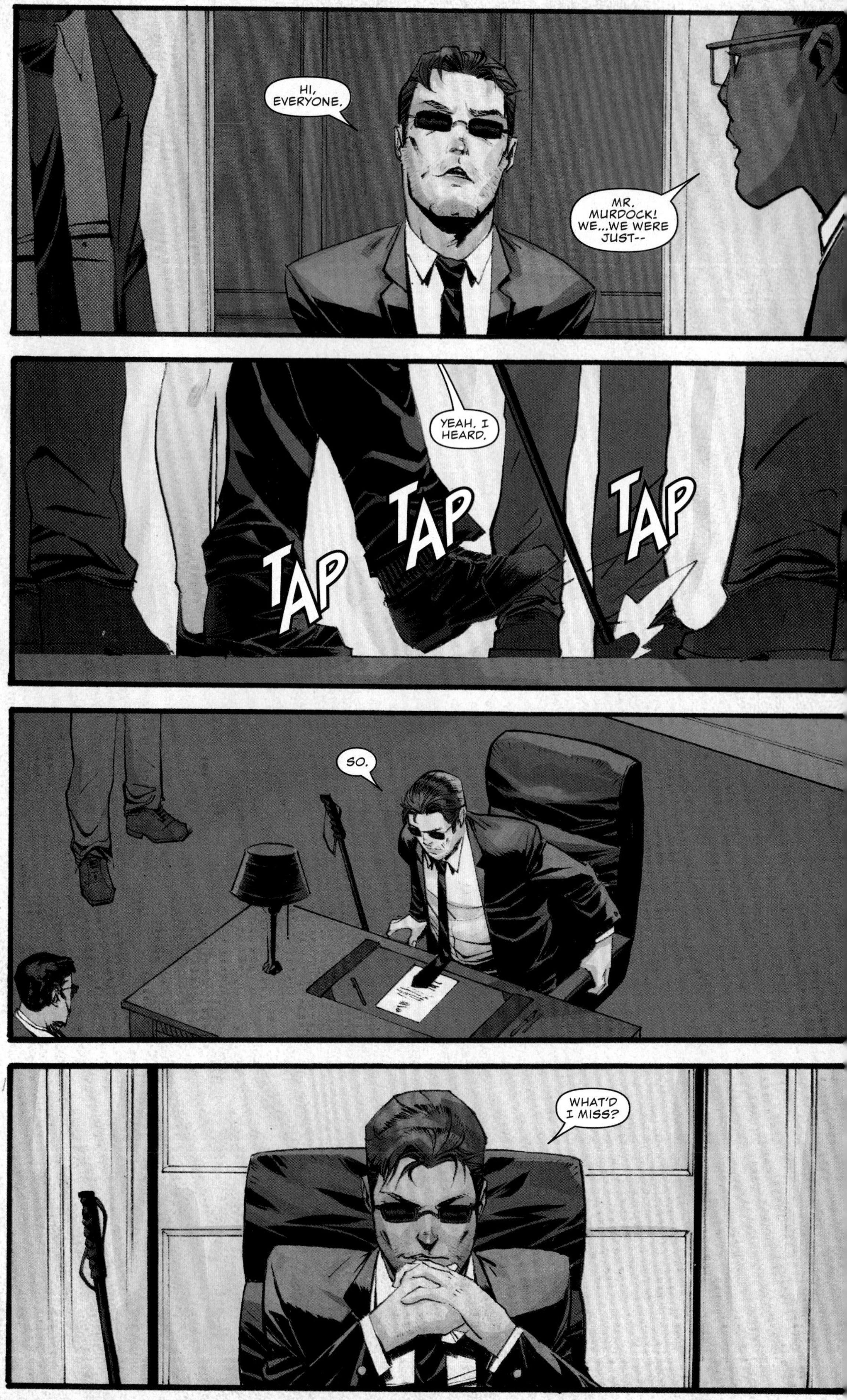
HI, EVERYONE.
MR. MURDOCK! WE...WE WERE JUST--
YEAH, I HEARD.
TAP
TAP
TAP
SO.
WHAT'D I MISS?

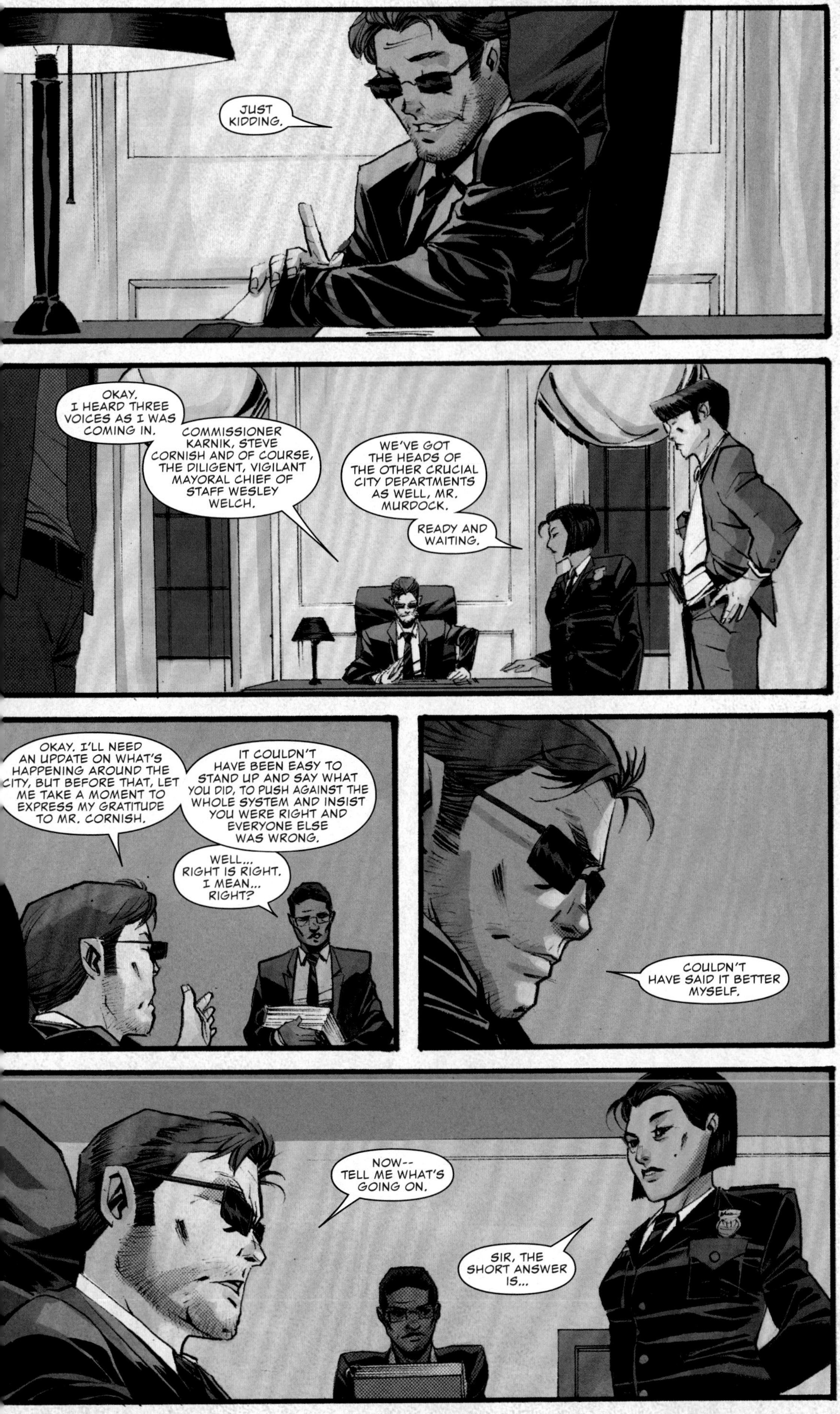
JUST KIDDING.
OKAY. I HEARD THREE VOICES AS I WAS COMING IN.
COMMISSIONER KARNIK, STEVE CORNISH AND OF COURSE, THE DILIGENT, VIGILANT MAYORAL CHIEF OF STAFF WESLEY WELCH.
WE'VE GOT THE HEADS OF THE OTHER CRUCIAL CITY DEPARTMENTS AS WELL, MR. MURDOCK.
READY AND WAITING.
OKAY. I'LL NEED AN UPDATE ON WHAT'S HAPPENING AROUND THE CITY, BUT BEFORE THAT, LET ME TAKE A MOMENT TO EXPRESS MY GRATITUDE TO MR. CORNISH.
IT COULDN'T HAVE BEEN EASY TO STAND UP AND SAY WHAT YOU DID, TO PUSH AGAINST THE WHOLE SYSTEM AND INSIST YOU WERE RIGHT AND EVERYONE ELSE WAS WRONG.
WELL... RIGHT IS RIGHT. I MEAN... RIGHT?
COULDN'T HAVE SAID IT BETTER MYSELF.
NOW-- TELL ME WHAT'S GOING ON.
SIR, THE SHORT ANSWER IS...

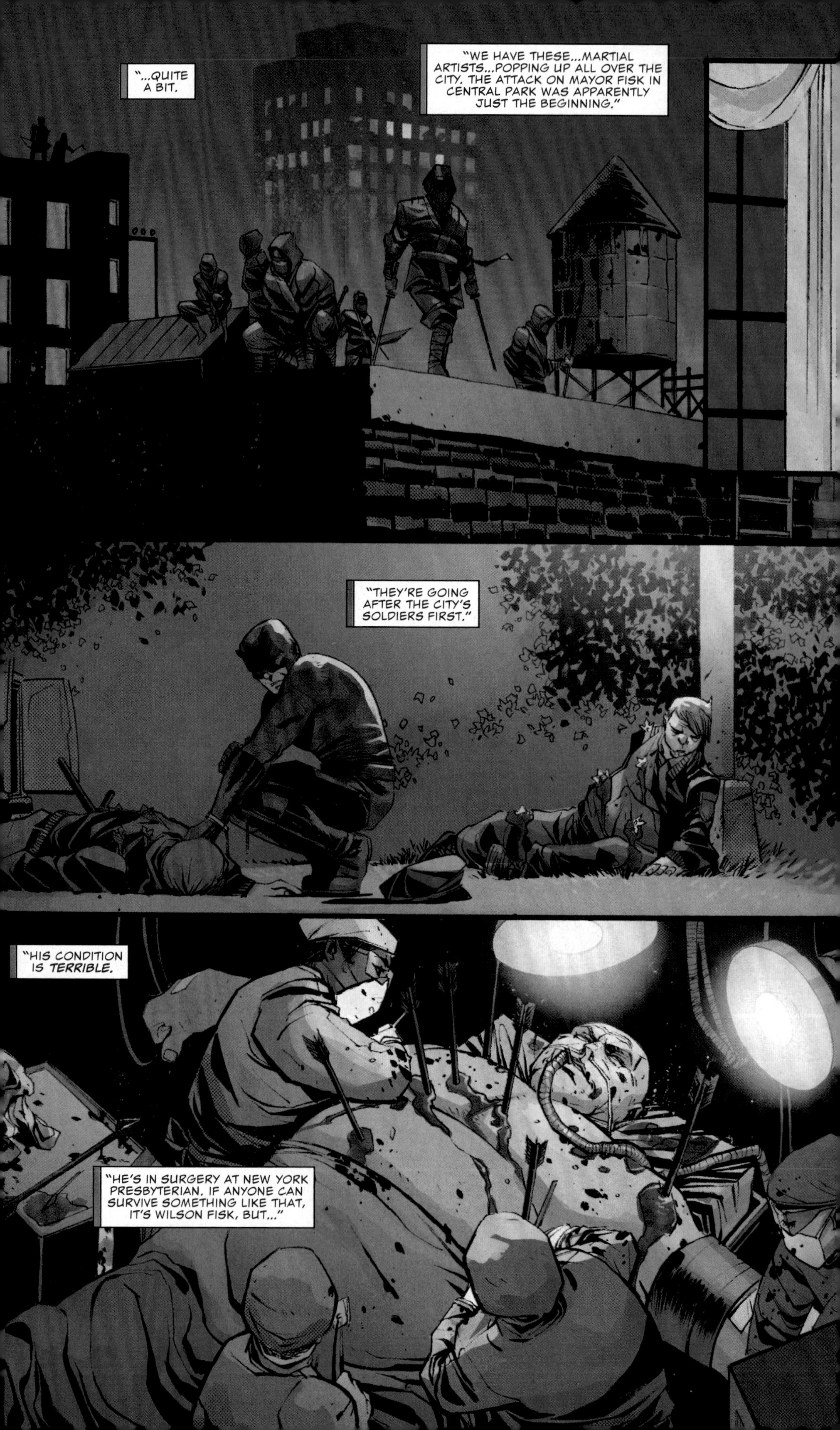
"...QUITE A BIT.
"WE HAVE THESE...MARTIAL ARTISTS...POPPING UP ALL OVER THE CITY. THE ATTACK ON MAYOR FISK IN CENTRAL PARK WAS APPARENTLY JUST THE BEGINNING."
"THEY'RE GOING AFTER THE CITY'S SOLDIERS FIRST."
"HIS CONDITION IS TERRIBLE.
"HE'S IN SURGERY AT NEW YORK PRESBYTERIAN. IF ANYONE CAN SURVIVE SOMETHING LIKE THAT, IT'S WILSON FISK, BUT..."

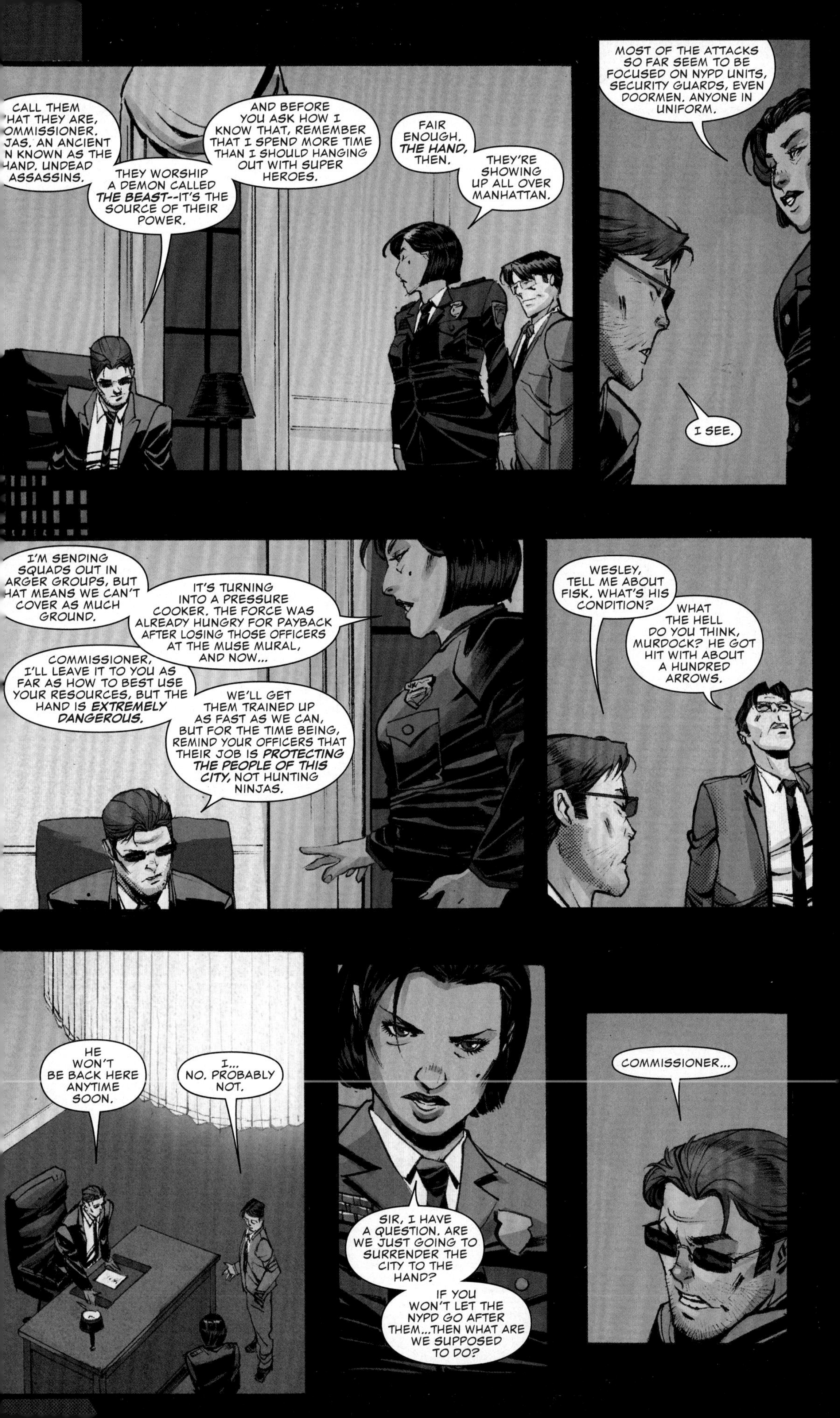
CALL THEM 'HAT THEY ARE, OMMISSIONER. JAS. AN ANCIENT N KNOWN AS THE HAND. UNDEAD ASSASSINS.
THEY WORSHIP A DEMON CALLED *THE BEAST*--IT'S THE SOURCE OF THEIR POWER.
AND BEFORE YOU ASK HOW I KNOW THAT, REMEMBER THAT I SPEND MORE TIME THAN I SHOULD HANGING OUT WITH SUPER HEROES.
FAIR ENOUGH. *THE HAND,* THEN.
THEY'RE SHOWING UP ALL OVER MANHATTAN.
MOST OF THE ATTACKS SO FAR SEEM TO BE FOCUSED ON NYPD UNITS, SECURITY GUARDS, EVEN DOORMEN. ANYONE IN UNIFORM.
I SEE.
I'M SENDING SQUADS OUT IN ARGER GROUPS, BUT HAT MEANS WE CAN'T COVER AS MUCH GROUND.
IT'S TURNING INTO A PRESSURE COOKER. THE FORCE WAS ALREADY HUNGRY FOR PAYBACK AFTER LOSING THOSE OFFICERS AT THE MUSE MURAL, AND NOW...
COMMISSIONER, I'LL LEAVE IT TO YOU AS FAR AS HOW TO BEST USE YOUR RESOURCES, BUT THE HAND IS *EXTREMELY DANGEROUS.*
WE'LL GET THEM TRAINED UP AS FAST AS WE CAN, BUT FOR THE TIME BEING, REMIND YOUR OFFICERS THAT THEIR JOB IS *PROTECTING THE PEOPLE OF THIS CITY,* NOT HUNTING NINJAS.
WESLEY, TELL ME ABOUT FISK. WHAT'S HIS CONDITION?
WHAT THE HELL DO YOU THINK, MURDOCK? HE GOT HIT WITH ABOUT A HUNDRED ARROWS.
HE WON'T BE BACK HERE ANYTIME SOON.
I... NO. PROBABLY NOT.
SIR, I HAVE A QUESTION. ARE WE JUST GOING TO SURRENDER THE CITY TO THE HAND?
IF YOU WON'T LET THE NYPD GO AFTER THEM...THEN WHAT ARE WE SUPPOSED TO DO?
COMMISSIONER...

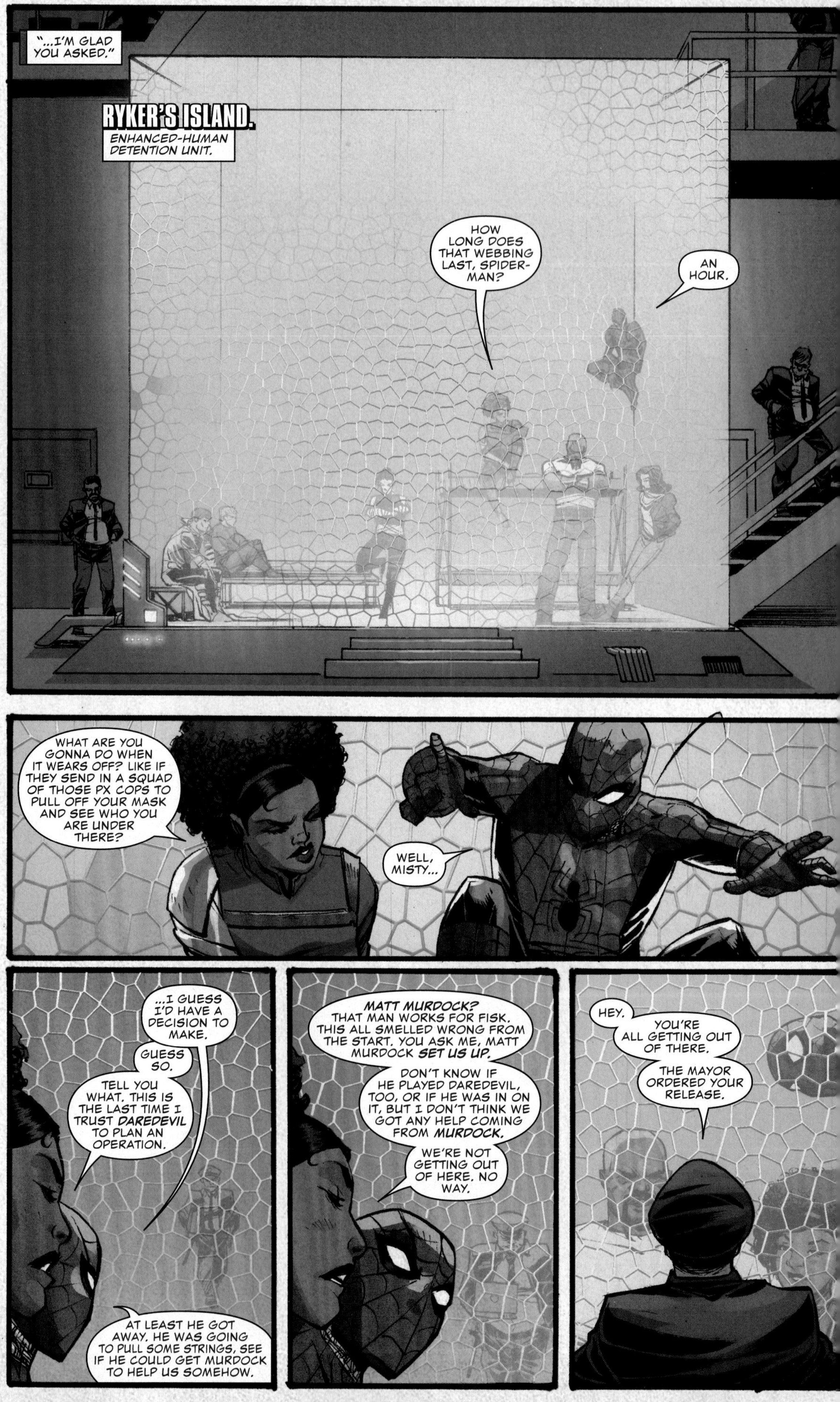
"...I'M GLAD YOU ASKED."
RYKER'S ISLAND.
ENHANCED-HUMAN DETENTION UNIT.
HOW LONG DOES THAT WEBBING LAST, SPIDER-MAN?
AN HOUR.
WHAT ARE YOU GONNA DO WHEN IT WEARS OFF? LIKE IF THEY SEND IN A SQUAD OF THOSE PX COPS TO PULL OFF YOUR MASK AND SEE WHO YOU ARE UNDER THERE?
WELL, MISTY...
...I GUESS I'D HAVE A DECISION TO MAKE.
GUESS SO.
TELL YOU WHAT. THIS IS THE LAST TIME I TRUST DAREDEVIL TO PLAN AN OPERATION.
AT LEAST HE GOT AWAY. HE WAS GOING TO PULL SOME STRINGS, SEE IF HE COULD GET MURDOCK TO HELP US SOMEHOW.
MATT MURDOCK? THAT MAN WORKS FOR FISK. THIS ALL SMELLED WRONG FROM THE START. YOU ASK ME, MATT MURDOCK SET US UP.
DON'T KNOW IF HE PLAYED DAREDEVIL, TOO, OR IF HE WAS IN ON IT, BUT I DON'T THINK WE GOT ANY HELP COMING FROM MURDOCK.
WE'RE NOT GETTING OUT OF HERE. NO WAY.
HEY.
YOU'RE ALL GETTING OUT OF THERE.
THE MAYOR ORDERED YOUR RELEASE.

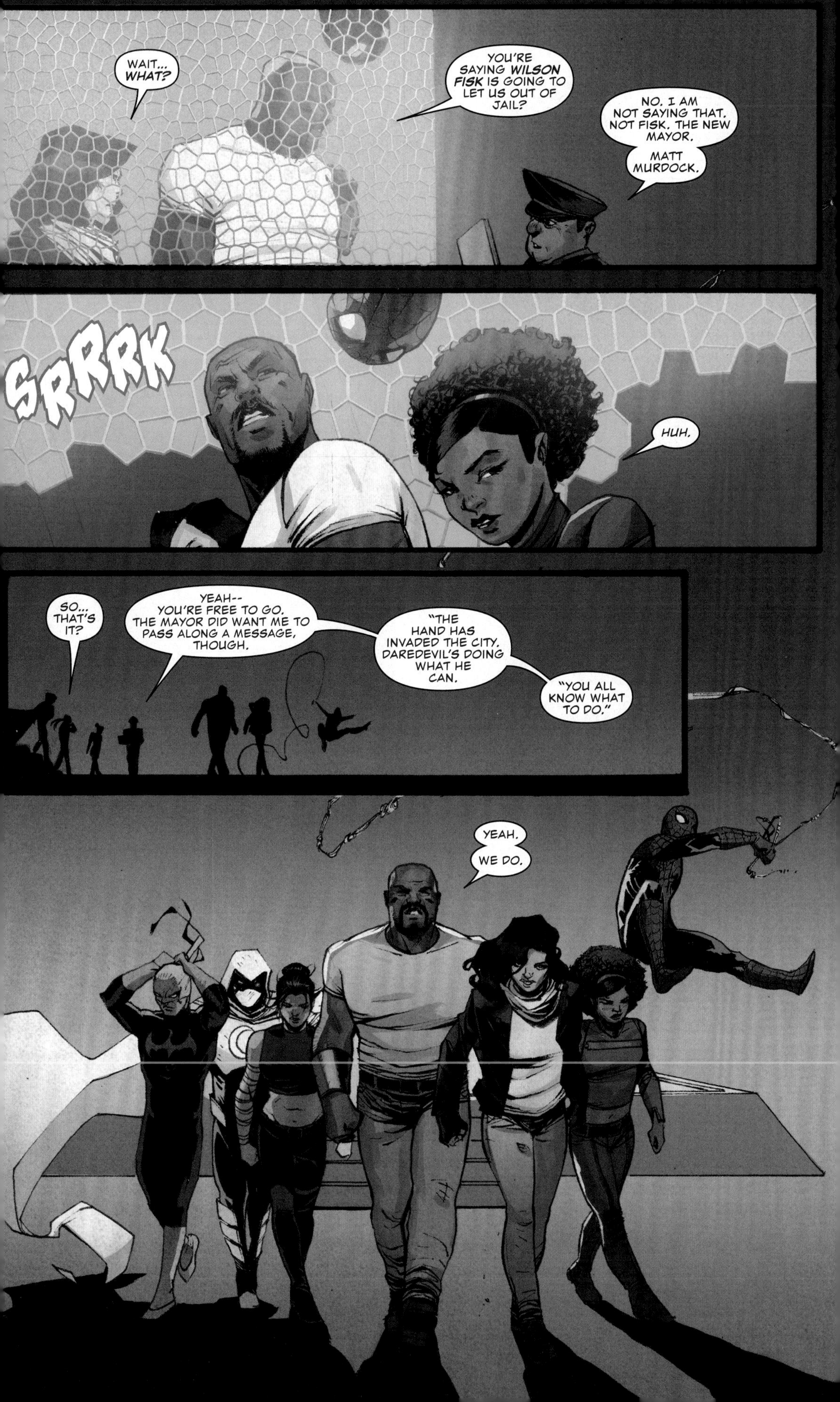
WAIT... WHAT?
YOU'RE SAYING WILSON FISK IS GOING TO LET US OUT OF JAIL?
NO. I AM NOT SAYING THAT. NOT FISK. THE NEW MAYOR.
MATT MURDOCK.
SRRRK
HUH.
SO... THAT'S IT?
YEAH-- YOU'RE FREE TO GO. THE MAYOR DID WANT ME TO PASS ALONG A MESSAGE, THOUGH.
"THE HAND HAS INVADED THE CITY. DAREDEVIL'S DOING WHAT HE CAN.
"YOU ALL KNOW WHAT TO DO."
YEAH.
WE DO.

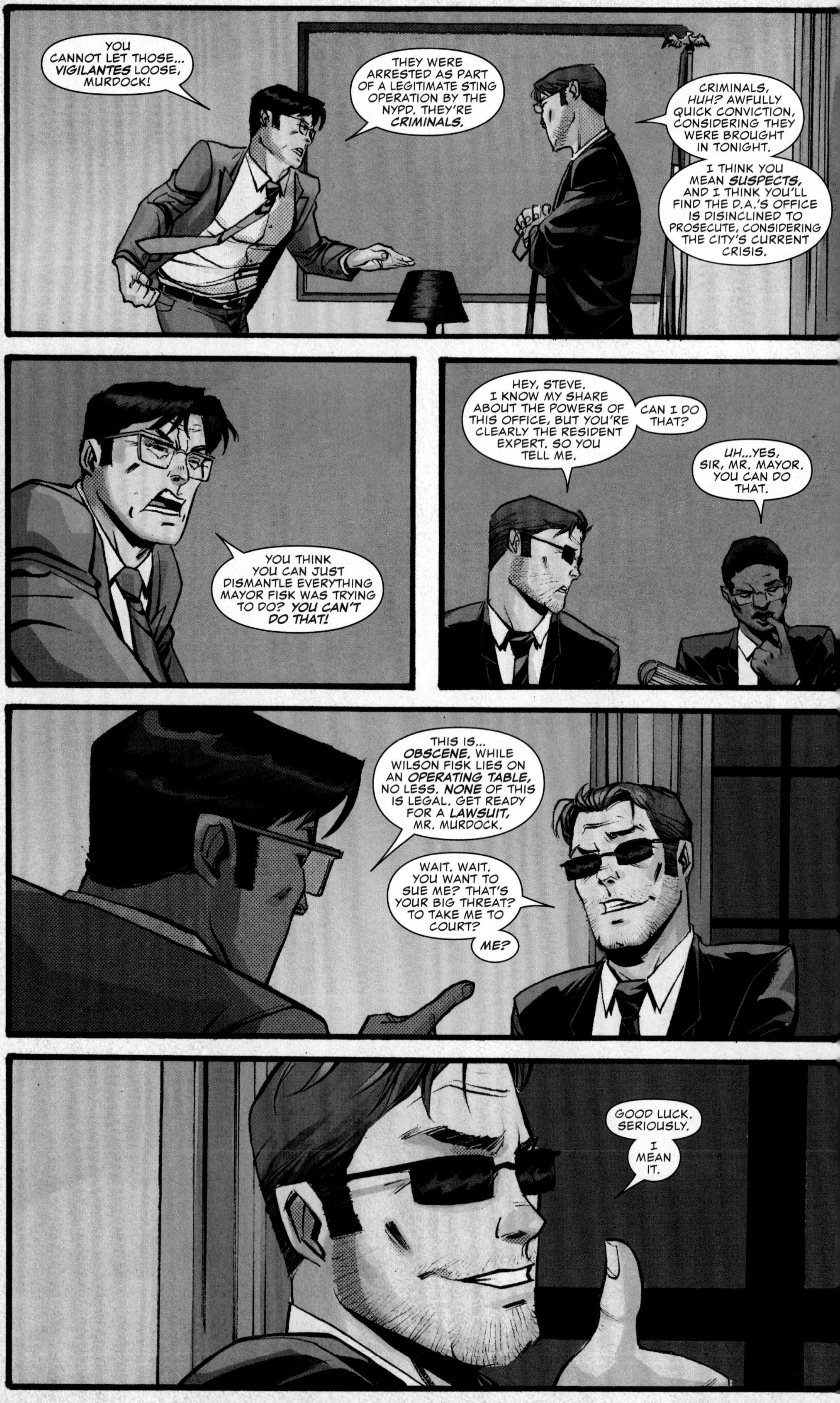
YOU CANNOT LET THOSE... VIGILANTES LOOSE, MURDOCK!
THEY WERE ARRESTED AS PART OF A LEGITIMATE STING OPERATION BY THE NYPD. THEY'RE CRIMINALS.
CRIMINALS, HUH? AWFULLY QUICK CONVICTION, CONSIDERING THEY WERE BROUGHT IN TONIGHT.
I THINK YOU MEAN SUSPECTS, AND I THINK YOU'LL FIND THE D.A.'S OFFICE IS DISINCLINED TO PROSECUTE, CONSIDERING THE CITY'S CURRENT CRISIS.
YOU THINK YOU CAN JUST DISMANTLE EVERYTHING MAYOR FISK WAS TRYING TO DO? YOU CAN'T DO THAT!
HEY, STEVE. I KNOW MY SHARE ABOUT THE POWERS OF THIS OFFICE, BUT YOU'RE CLEARLY THE RESIDENT EXPERT. SO YOU TELL ME.
CAN I DO THAT?
UH...YES, SIR, MR. MAYOR. YOU CAN DO THAT.
THIS IS... OBSCENE. WHILE WILSON FISK LIES ON AN OPERATING TABLE, NO LESS. NONE OF THIS IS LEGAL. GET READY FOR A LAWSUIT, MR. MURDOCK.
WAIT. WAIT. YOU WANT TO SUE ME? THAT'S YOUR BIG THREAT? TO TAKE ME TO COURT?
ME?
GOOD LUCK. SERIOUSLY.
I MEAN IT.

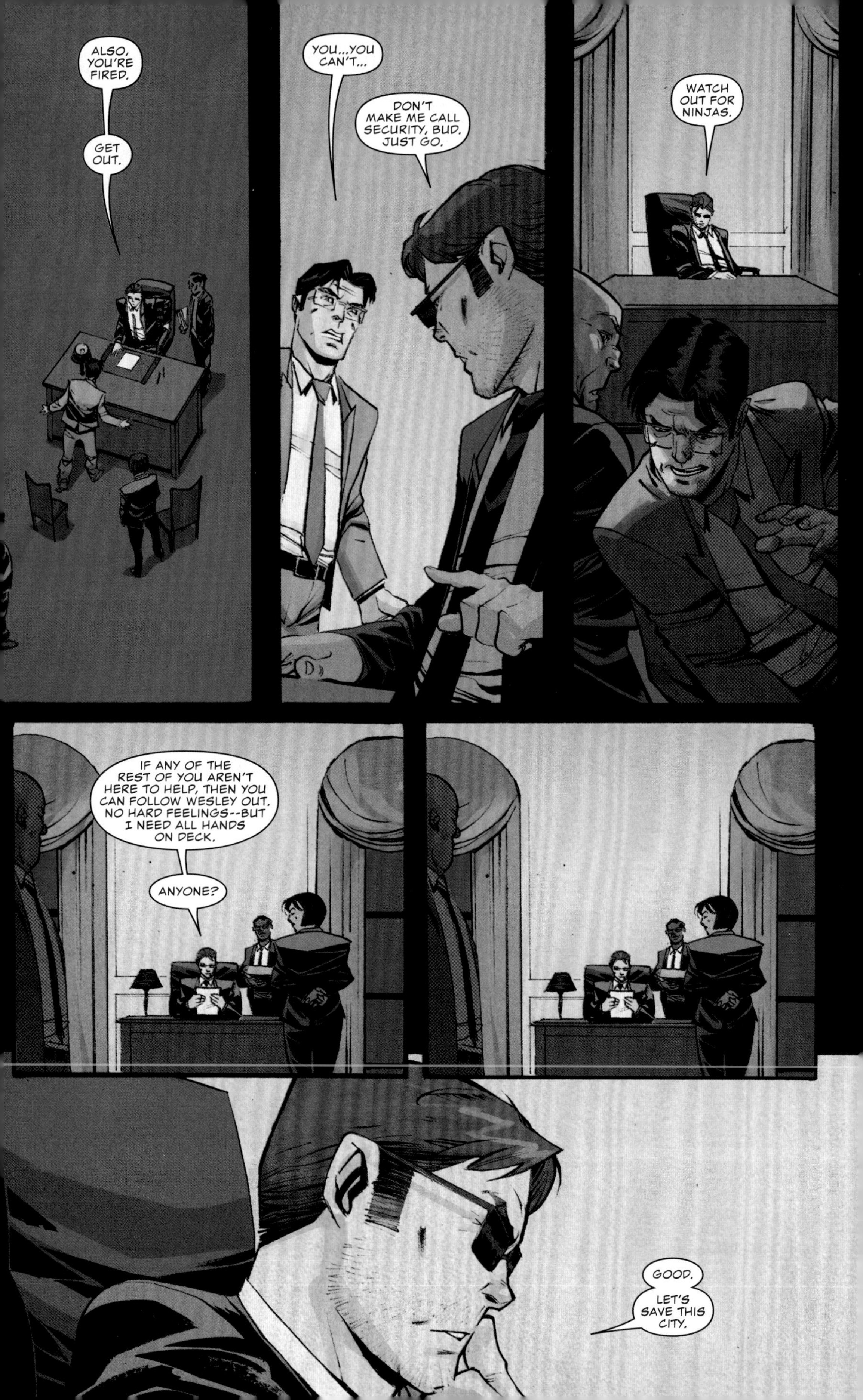
ALSO, YOU'RE FIRED.
GET OUT.
YOU...YOU CAN'T...
DON'T MAKE ME CALL SECURITY, BUD. JUST GO.
WATCH OUT FOR NINJAS.
IF ANY OF THE REST OF YOU AREN'T HERE TO HELP, THEN YOU CAN FOLLOW WESLEY OUT. NO HARD FEELINGS--BUT I NEED ALL HANDS ON DECK.
ANYONE?
GOOD.
LET'S SAVE THIS CITY.

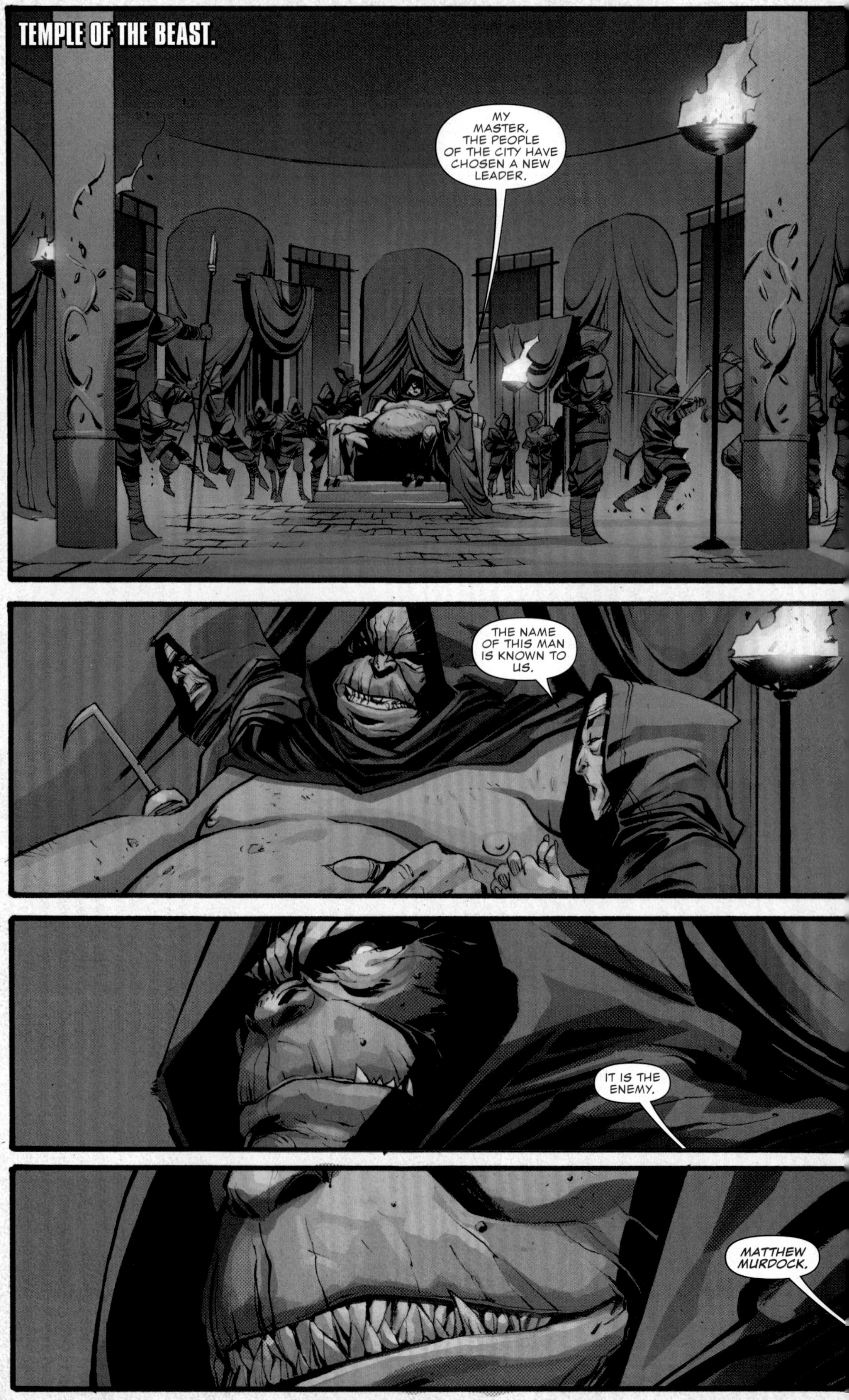

TEMPLE OF THE BEAST.
MY MASTER, THE PEOPLE OF THE CITY HAVE CHOSEN A NEW LEADER.
THE NAME OF THIS MAN IS KNOWN TO US.
IT IS THE ENEMY.
MATTHEW MURDOCK.

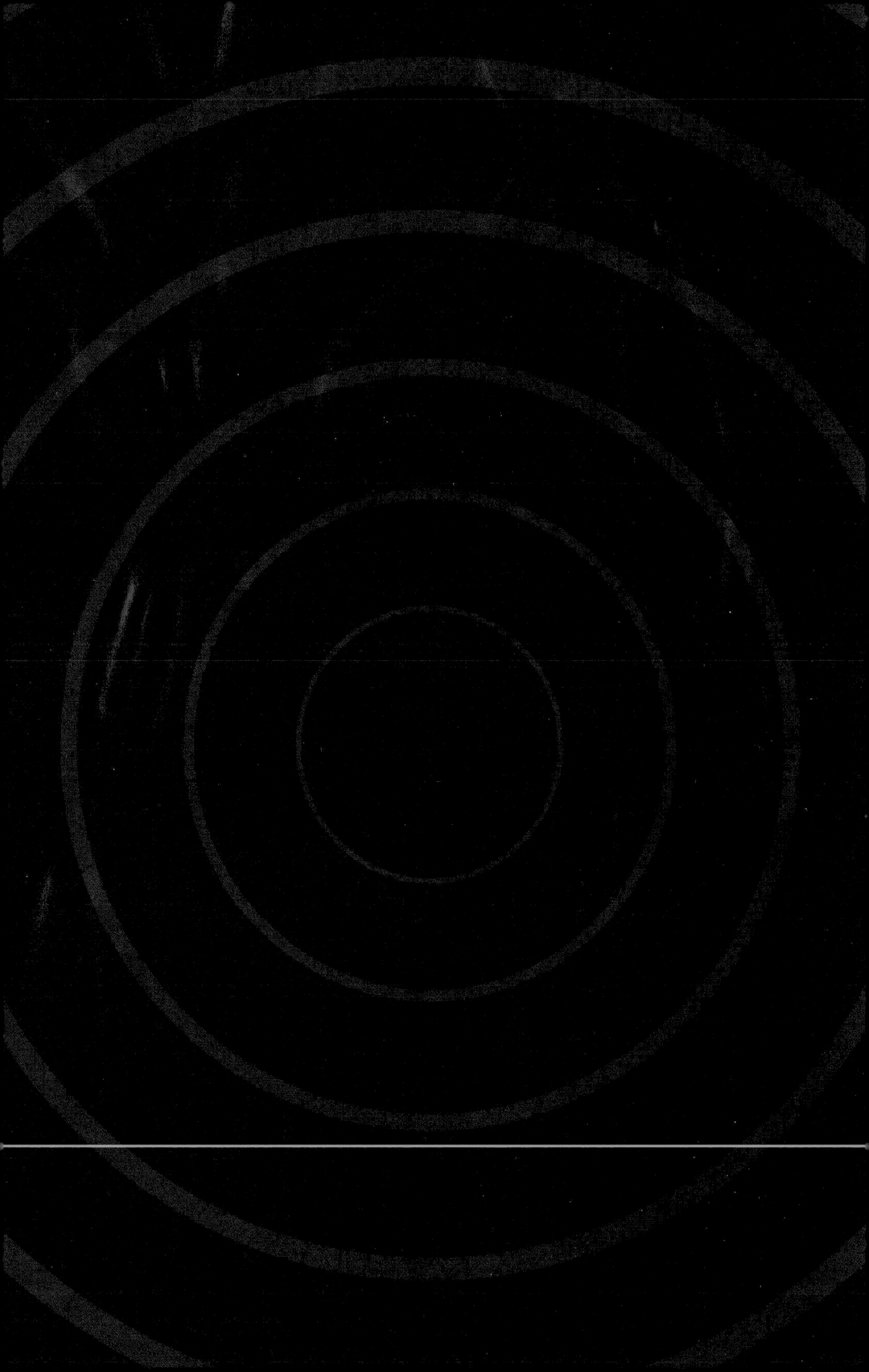

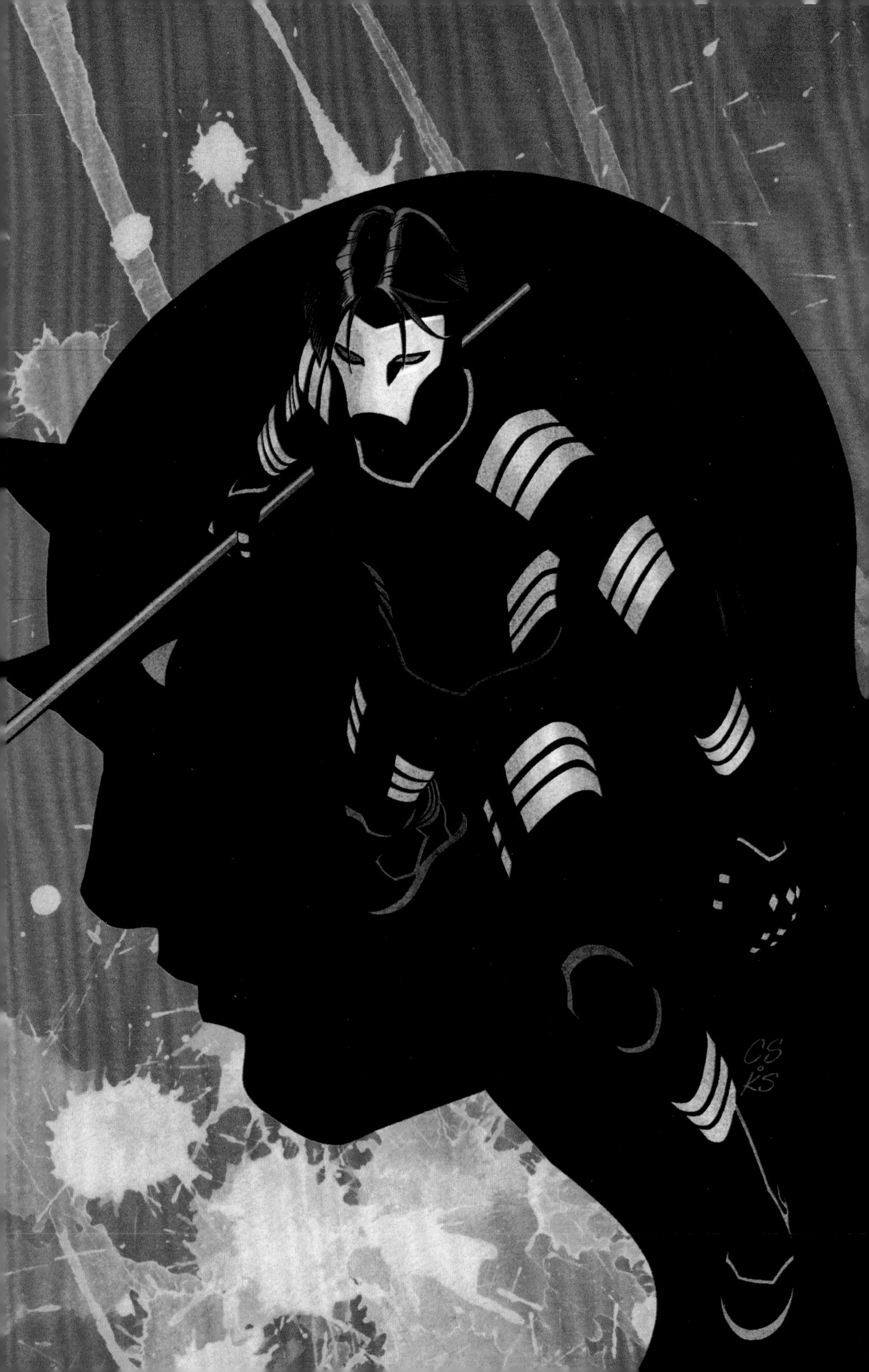
CS
KS

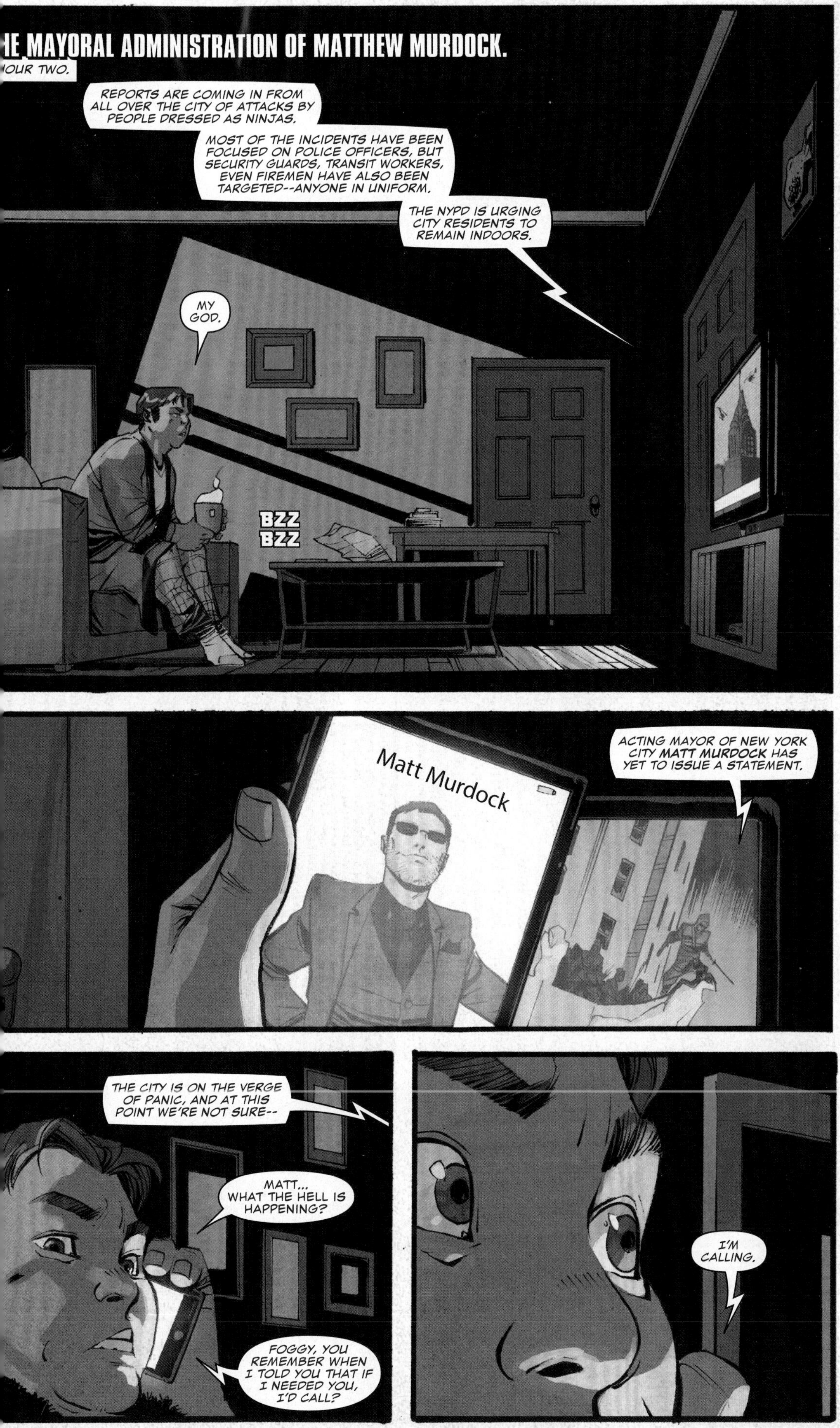

IE MAYORAL ADMINISTRATION OF MATTHEW MURDOCK.
OUR TWO.
REPORTS ARE COMING IN FROM ALL OVER THE CITY OF ATTACKS BY PEOPLE DRESSED AS NINJAS.
MOST OF THE INCIDENTS HAVE BEEN FOCUSED ON POLICE OFFICERS, BUT SECURITY GUARDS, TRANSIT WORKERS, EVEN FIREMEN HAVE ALSO BEEN TARGETED--ANYONE IN UNIFORM.
THE NYPD IS URGING CITY RESIDENTS TO REMAIN INDOORS.
MY GOD.
BZZ BZZ
Matt Murdock
ACTING MAYOR OF NEW YORK CITY MATT MURDOCK HAS YET TO ISSUE A STATEMENT.
THE CITY IS ON THE VERGE OF PANIC, AND AT THIS POINT WE'RE NOT SURE--
MATT... WHAT THE HELL IS HAPPENING?
FOGGY, YOU REMEMBER WHEN I TOLD YOU THAT IF I NEEDED YOU, I'D CALL?
I'M CALLING.

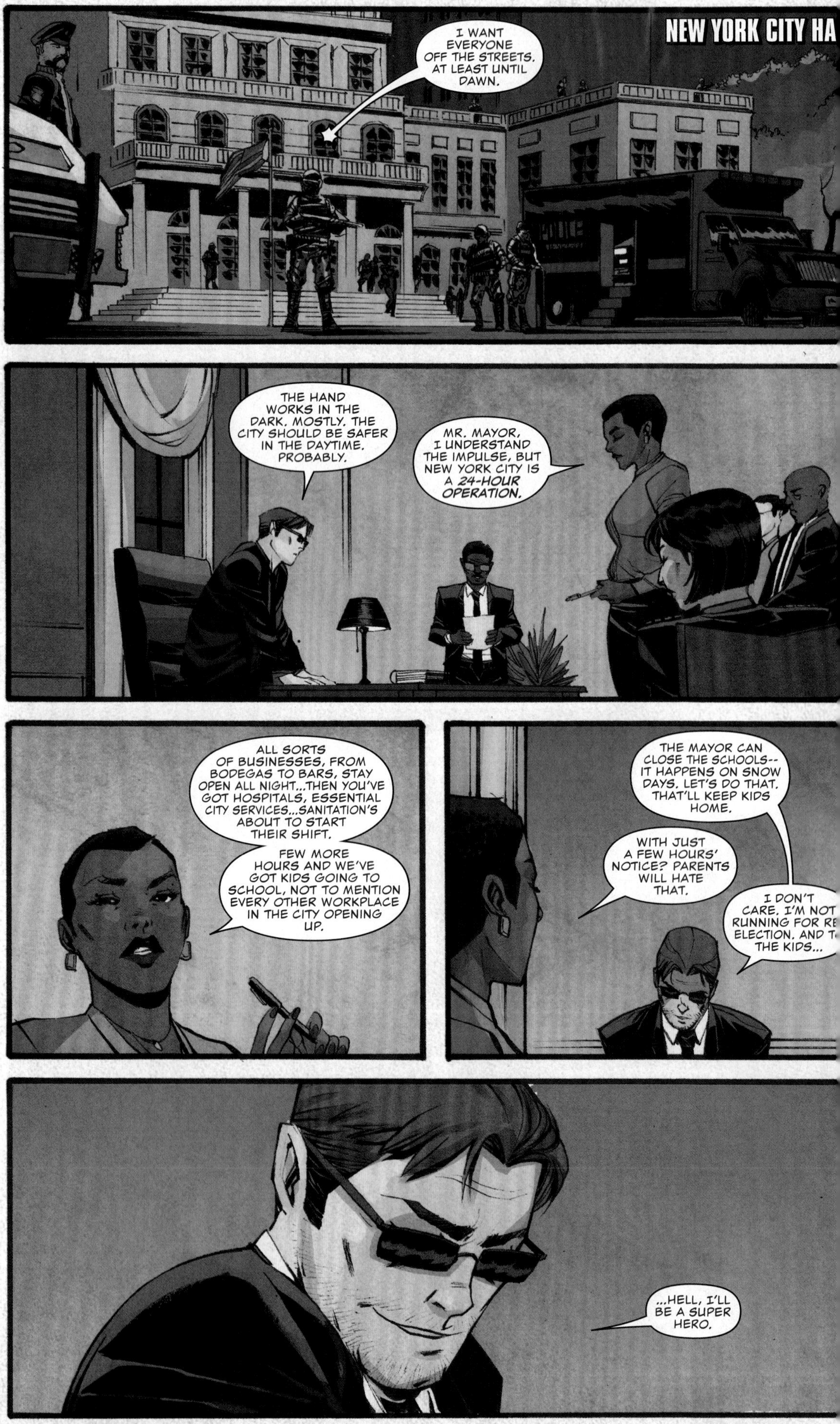
NEW YORK CITY HA
I WANT EVERYONE OFF THE STREETS. AT LEAST UNTIL DAWN.
THE HAND WORKS IN THE DARK. MOSTLY. THE CITY SHOULD BE SAFER IN THE DAYTIME. PROBABLY.
MR. MAYOR, I UNDERSTAND THE IMPULSE, BUT NEW YORK CITY IS A 24-HOUR OPERATION.
ALL SORTS OF BUSINESSES, FROM BODEGAS TO BARS, STAY OPEN ALL NIGHT...THEN YOU'VE GOT HOSPITALS, ESSENTIAL CITY SERVICES...SANITATION'S ABOUT TO START THEIR SHIFT.
FEW MORE HOURS AND WE'VE GOT KIDS GOING TO SCHOOL, NOT TO MENTION EVERY OTHER WORKPLACE IN THE CITY OPENING UP.
THE MAYOR CAN CLOSE THE SCHOOLS--IT HAPPENS ON SNOW DAYS. LET'S DO THAT. THAT'LL KEEP KIDS HOME.
WITH JUST A FEW HOURS' NOTICE? PARENTS WILL HATE THAT.
I DON'T CARE. I'M NOT RUNNING FOR RE ELECTION, AND T THE KIDS...
...HELL, I'LL BE A SUPER HERO.

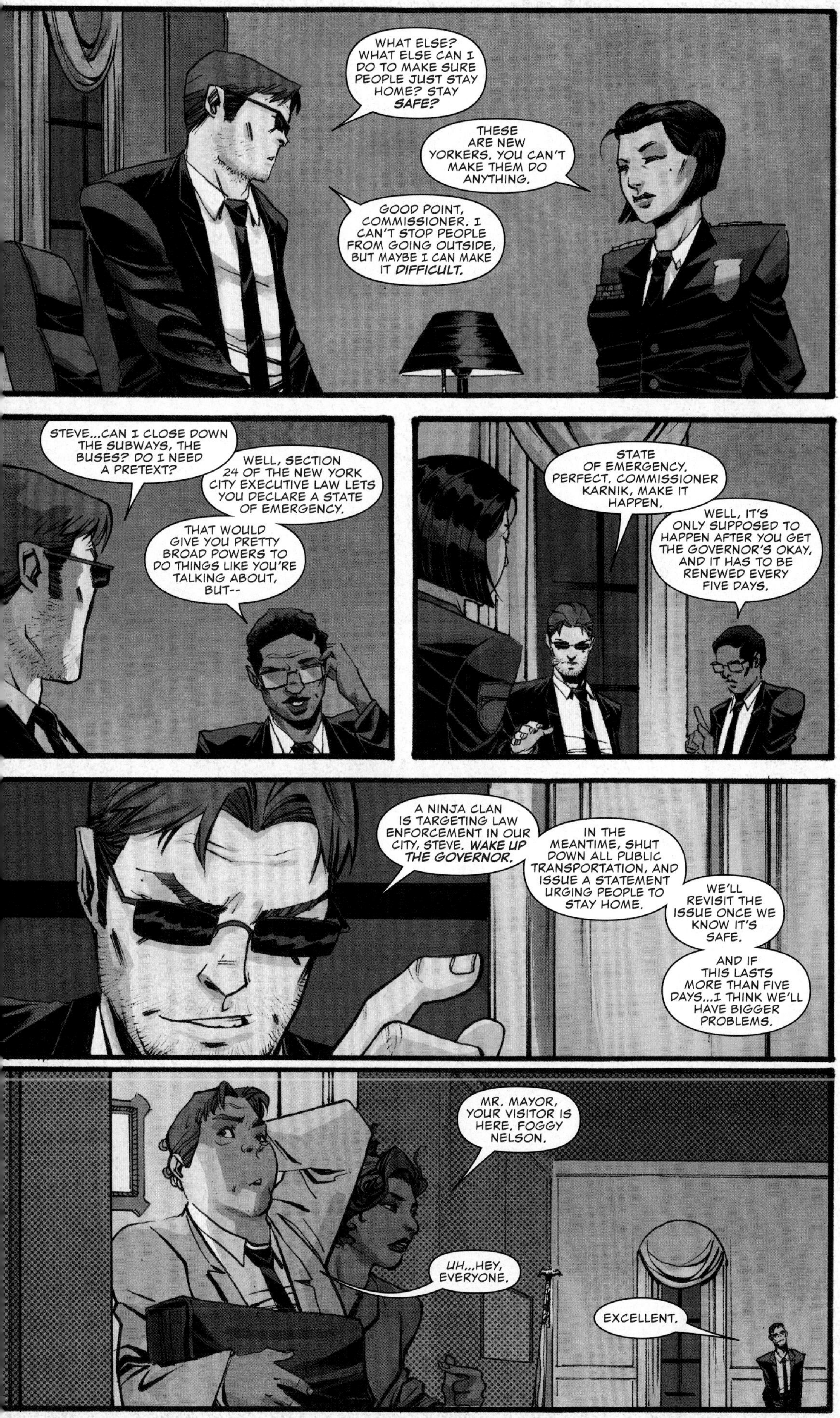
WHAT ELSE? WHAT ELSE CAN I DO TO MAKE SURE PEOPLE JUST STAY HOME? STAY SAFE?
THESE ARE NEW YORKERS. YOU CAN'T MAKE THEM DO ANYTHING.
GOOD POINT, COMMISSIONER. I CAN'T STOP PEOPLE FROM GOING OUTSIDE, BUT MAYBE I CAN MAKE IT DIFFICULT.
STEVE...CAN I CLOSE DOWN THE SUBWAYS, THE BUSES? DO I NEED A PRETEXT?
WELL, SECTION 24 OF THE NEW YORK CITY EXECUTIVE LAW LETS YOU DECLARE A STATE OF EMERGENCY.
THAT WOULD GIVE YOU PRETTY BROAD POWERS TO DO THINGS LIKE YOU'RE TALKING ABOUT, BUT--
STATE OF EMERGENCY. PERFECT. COMMISSIONER KARNIK, MAKE IT HAPPEN.
WELL, IT'S ONLY SUPPOSED TO HAPPEN AFTER YOU GET THE GOVERNOR'S OKAY, AND IT HAS TO BE RENEWED EVERY FIVE DAYS.
A NINJA CLAN IS TARGETING LAW ENFORCEMENT IN OUR CITY, STEVE. WAKE UP THE GOVERNOR.
IN THE MEANTIME, SHUT DOWN ALL PUBLIC TRANSPORTATION, AND ISSUE A STATEMENT URGING PEOPLE TO STAY HOME.
WE'LL REVISIT THE ISSUE ONCE WE KNOW IT'S SAFE.
AND IF THIS LASTS MORE THAN FIVE DAYS...I THINK WE'LL HAVE BIGGER PROBLEMS.
MR. MAYOR, YOUR VISITOR IS HERE. FOGGY NELSON.
UH...HEY, EVERYONE.
EXCELLENT.

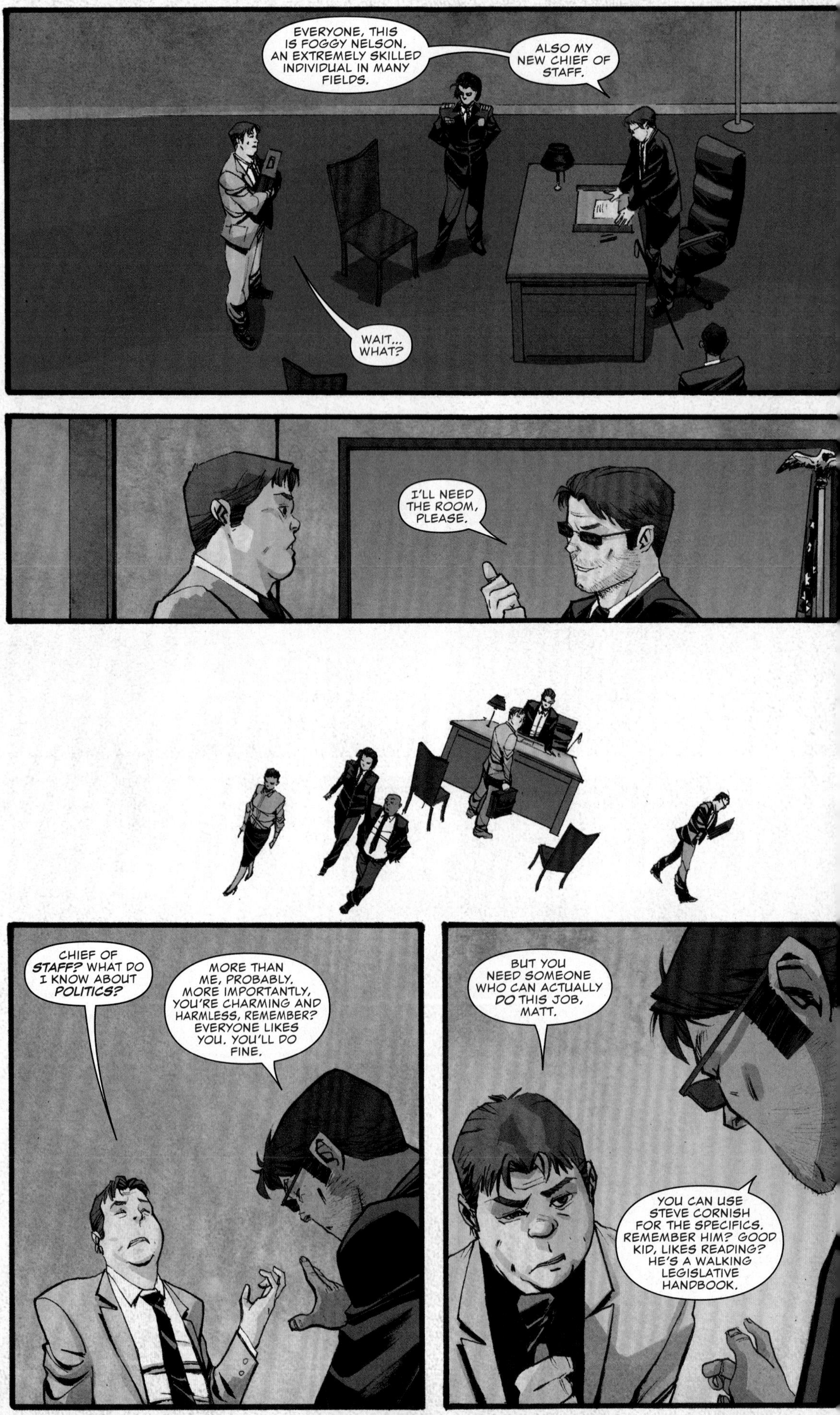
EVERYONE, THIS IS FOGGY NELSON. AN EXTREMELY SKILLED INDIVIDUAL IN MANY FIELDS.
ALSO MY NEW CHIEF OF STAFF.
WAIT... WHAT?
I'LL NEED THE ROOM, PLEASE.
CHIEF OF STAFF? WHAT DO I KNOW ABOUT POLITICS?
MORE THAN ME, PROBABLY. MORE IMPORTANTLY, YOU'RE CHARMING AND HARMLESS, REMEMBER? EVERYONE LIKES YOU. YOU'LL DO FINE.
BUT YOU NEED SOMEONE WHO CAN ACTUALLY DO THIS JOB, MATT.
YOU CAN USE STEVE CORNISH FOR THE SPECIFICS. REMEMBER HIM? GOOD KID, LIKES READING? HE'S A WALKING LEGISLATIVE HANDBOOK.

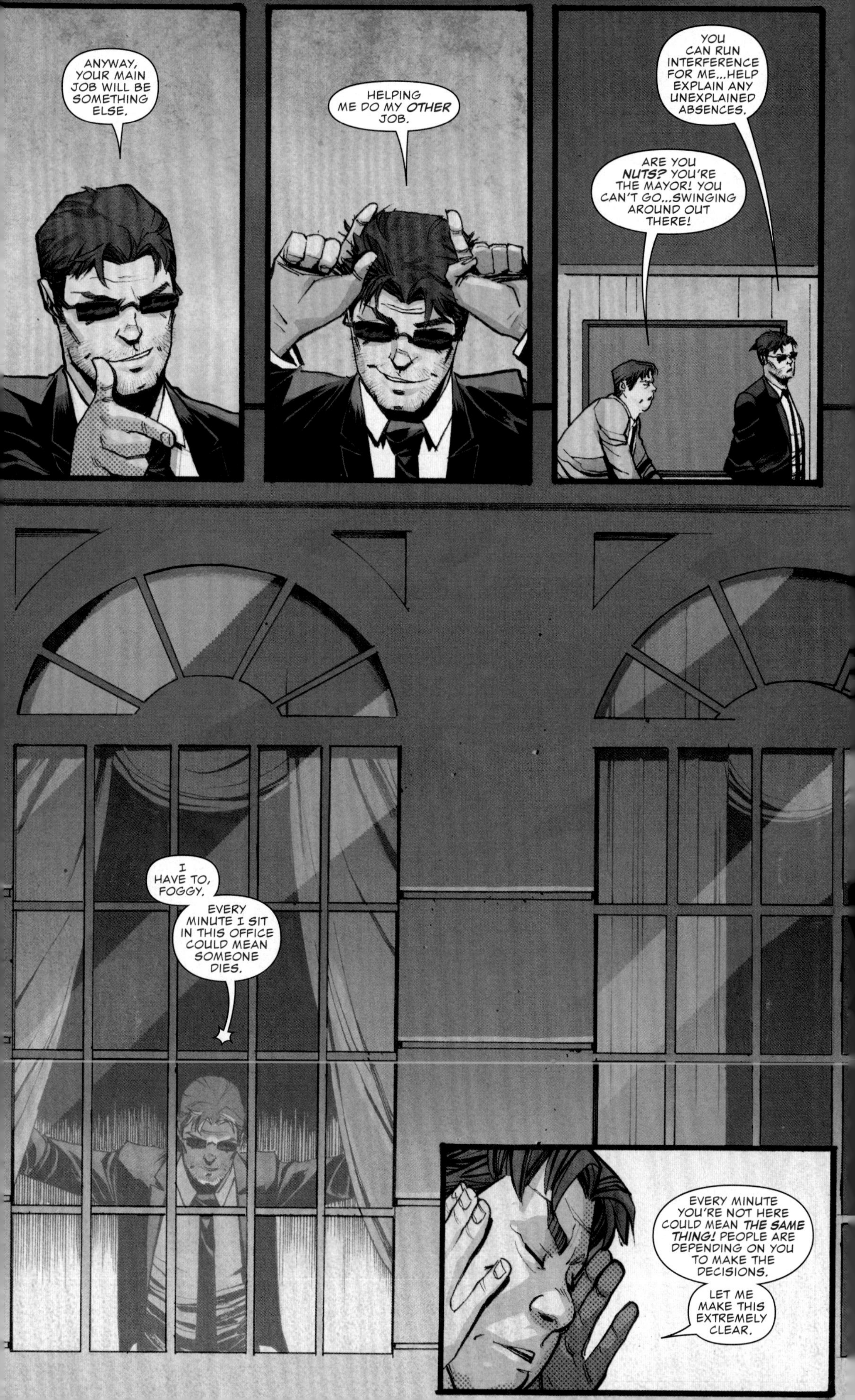
ANYWAY, YOUR MAIN JOB WILL BE SOMETHING ELSE.
HELPING ME DO MY OTHER JOB.
YOU CAN RUN INTERFERENCE FOR ME...HELP EXPLAIN ANY UNEXPLAINED ABSENCES.
ARE YOU NUTS? YOU'RE THE MAYOR! YOU CAN'T GO...SWINGING AROUND OUT THERE!
I HAVE TO, FOGGY.
EVERY MINUTE I SIT IN THIS OFFICE COULD MEAN SOMEONE DIES.
EVERY MINUTE YOU'RE NOT HERE COULD MEAN THE SAME THING! PEOPLE ARE DEPENDING ON YOU TO MAKE THE DECISIONS.
LET ME MAKE THIS EXTREMELY CLEAR.

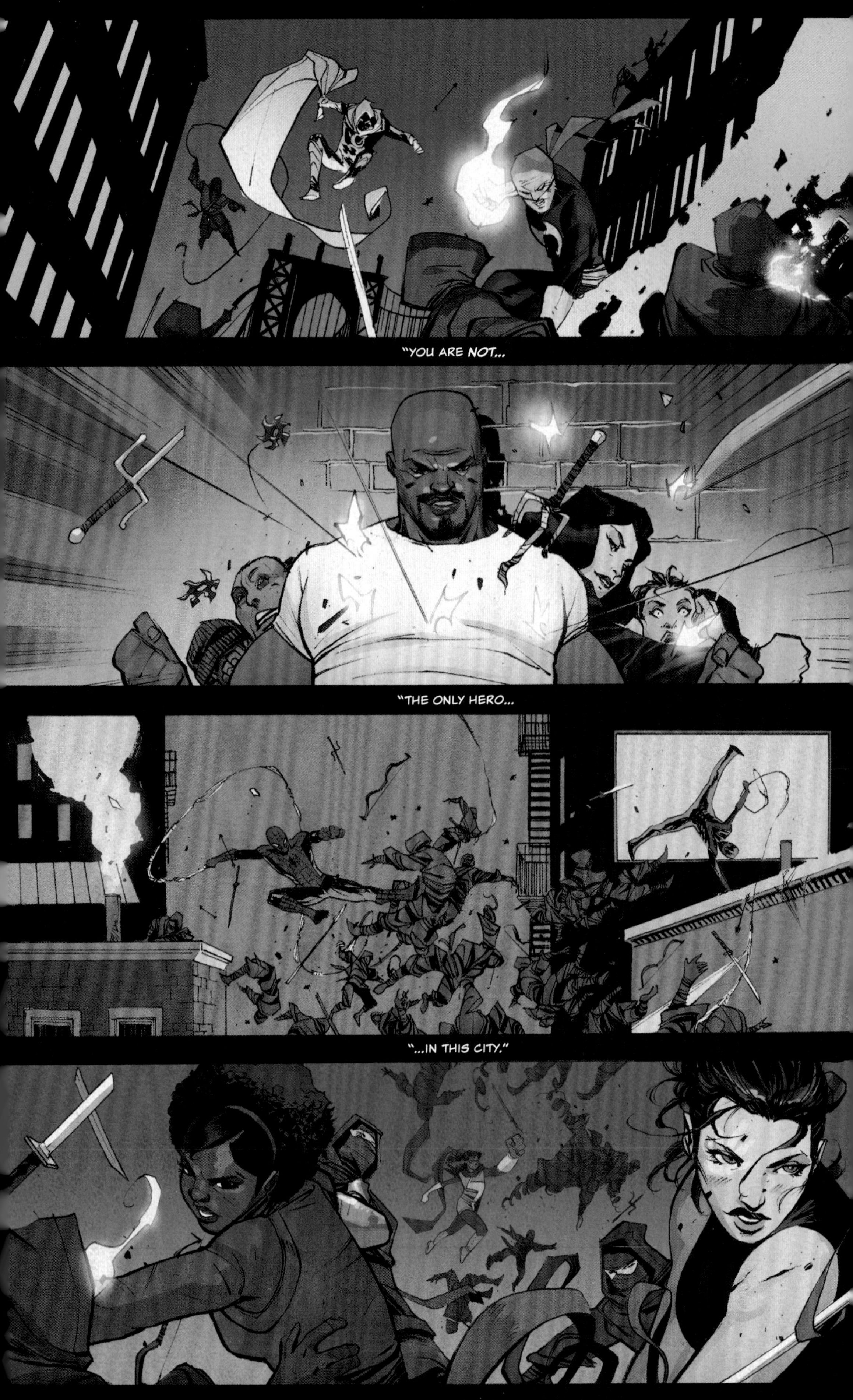
"YOU ARE NOT...
"THE ONLY HERO...
"...IN THIS CITY."

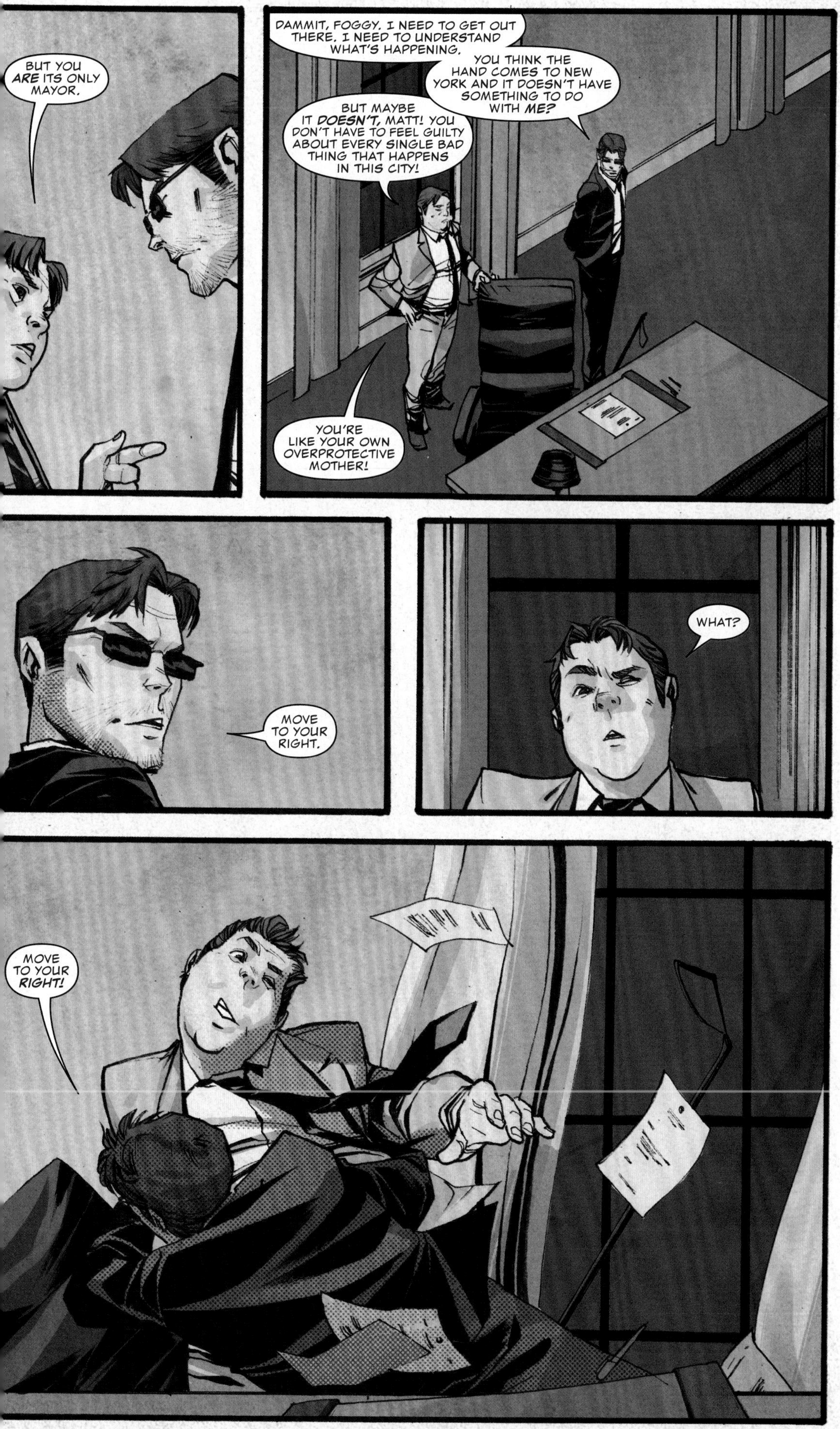
BUT YOU *ARE* ITS ONLY MAYOR.
DAMMIT, FOGGY. I NEED TO GET OUT THERE. I NEED TO UNDERSTAND WHAT'S HAPPENING.
YOU THINK THE HAND COMES TO NEW YORK AND IT DOESN'T HAVE SOMETHING TO DO WITH *ME?*
BUT MAYBE IT *DOESN'T,* MATT! YOU DON'T HAVE TO FEEL GUILTY ABOUT EVERY SINGLE BAD THING THAT HAPPENS IN THIS CITY!
YOU'RE LIKE YOUR OWN OVERPROTECTIVE MOTHER!
MOVE TO YOUR RIGHT.
WHAT?
MOVE TO YOUR *RIGHT!*

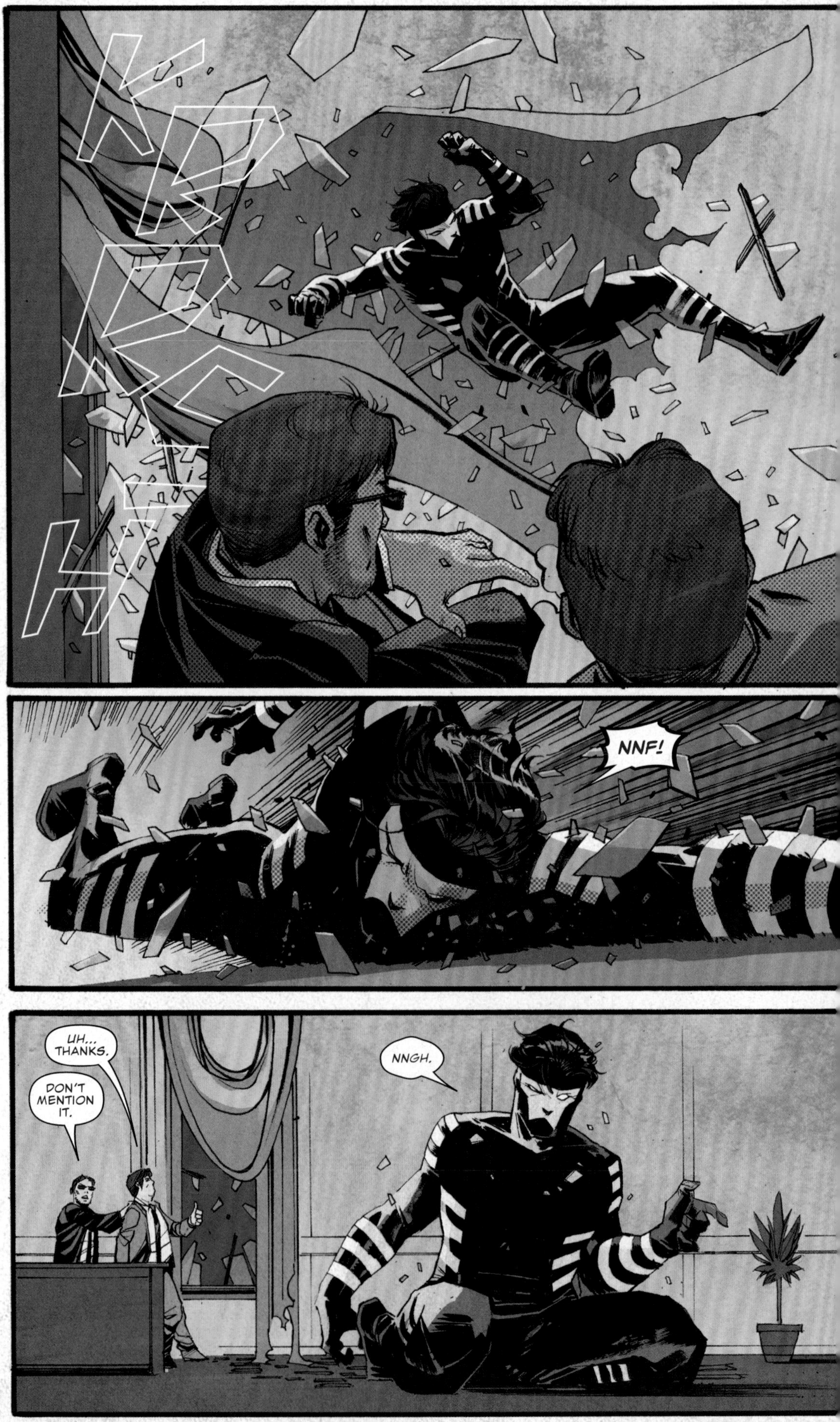
KRASH
NNF!
UH... THANKS.
DON'T MENTION IT.
NNGH.

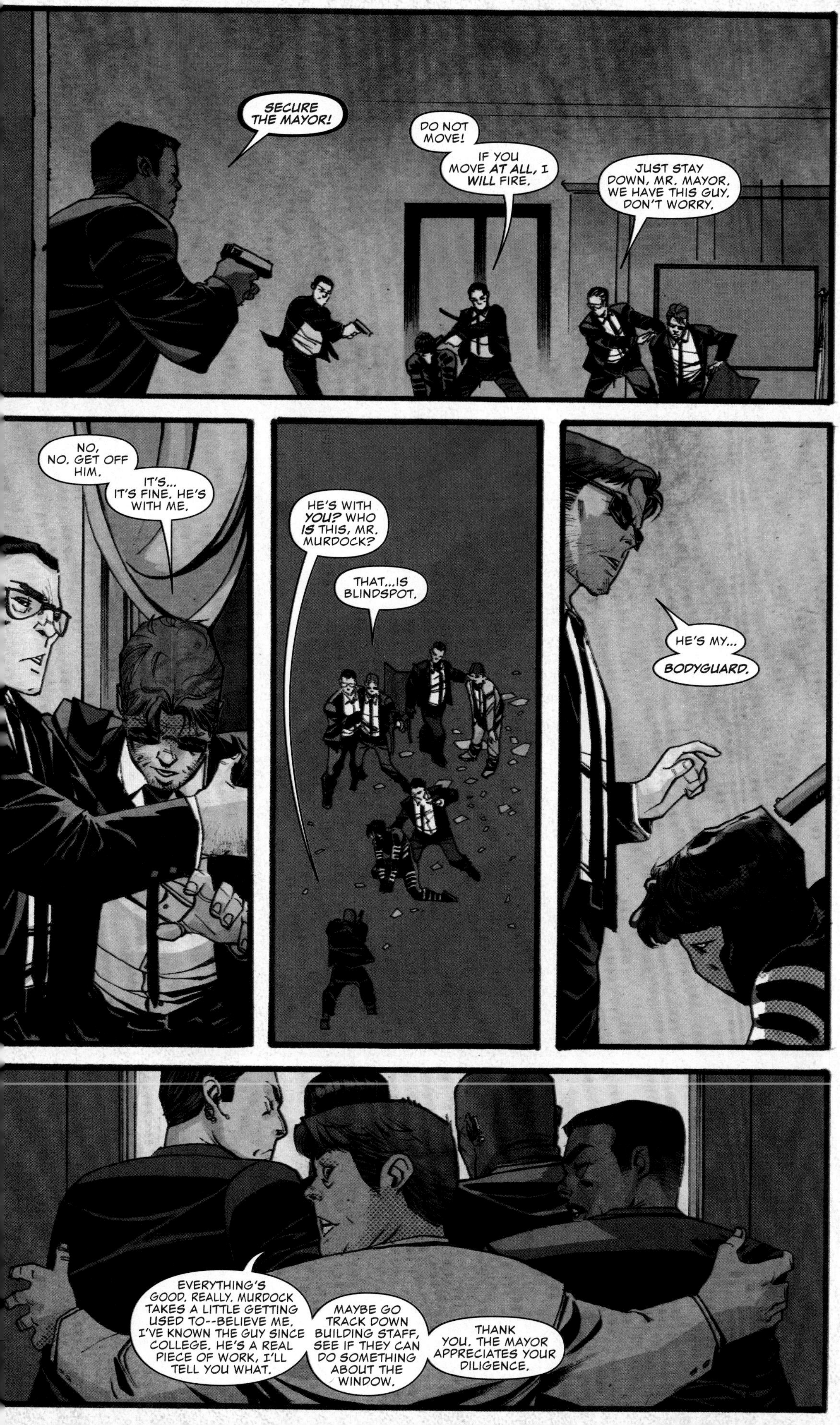
SECURE THE MAYOR!
DO NOT MOVE!
IF YOU MOVE AT ALL, I WILL FIRE.
JUST STAY DOWN, MR. MAYOR. WE HAVE THIS GUY. DON'T WORRY.
NO, NO. GET OFF HIM.
IT'S... IT'S FINE. HE'S WITH ME.
HE'S WITH YOU? WHO IS THIS, MR. MURDOCK?
THAT...IS BLINDSPOT.
HE'S MY...
BODYGUARD.
EVERYTHING'S GOOD, REALLY. MURDOCK TAKES A LITTLE GETTING USED TO--BELIEVE ME. I'VE KNOWN THE GUY SINCE COLLEGE. HE'S A REAL PIECE OF WORK, I'LL TELL YOU WHAT.
MAYBE GO TRACK DOWN BUILDING STAFF, SEE IF THEY CAN DO SOMETHING ABOUT THE WINDOW.
THANK YOU. THE MAYOR APPRECIATES YOUR DILIGENCE.

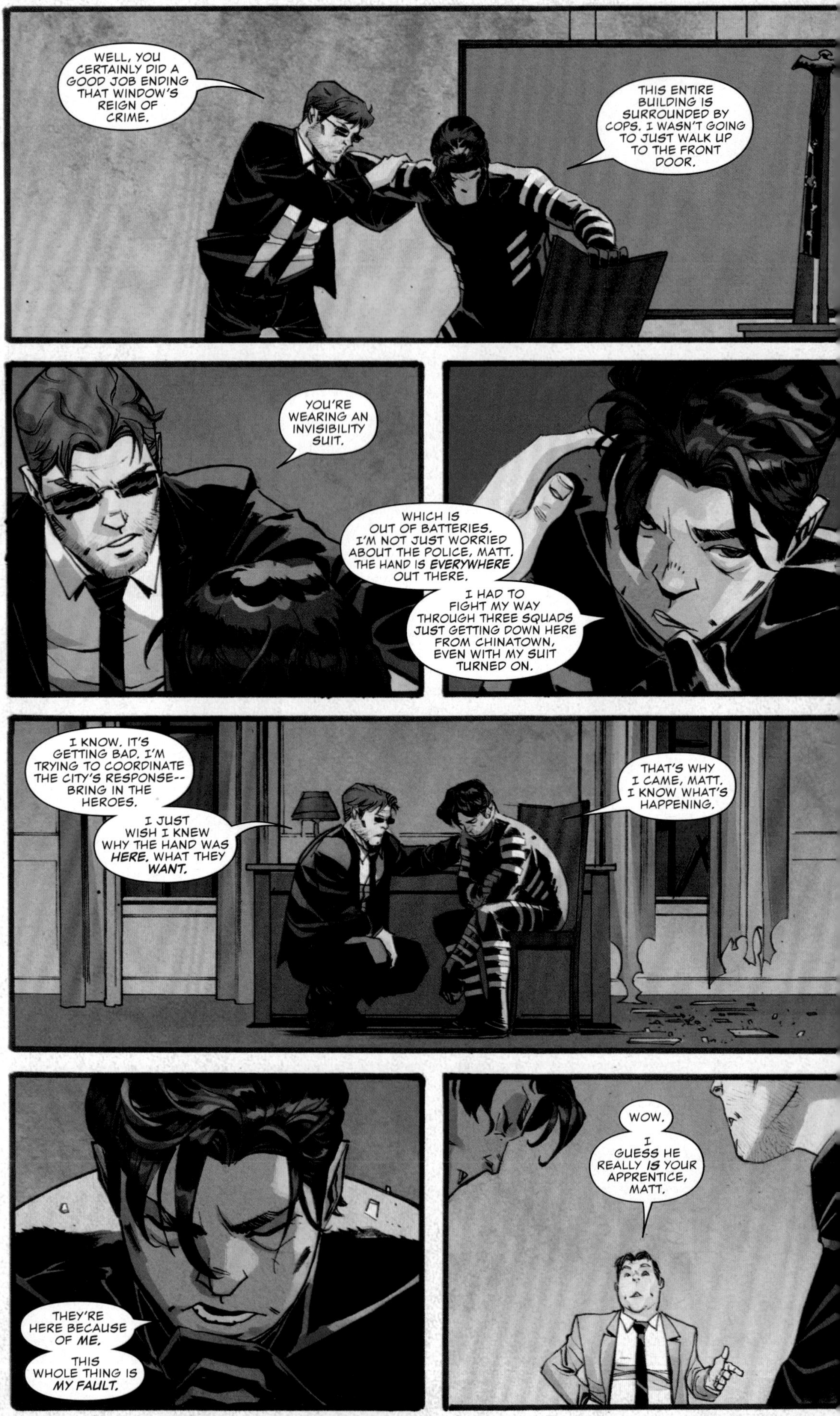
WELL, YOU CERTAINLY DID A GOOD JOB ENDING THAT WINDOW'S REIGN OF CRIME.
THIS ENTIRE BUILDING IS SURROUNDED BY COPS. I WASN'T GOING TO JUST WALK UP TO THE FRONT DOOR.
YOU'RE WEARING AN INVISIBILITY SUIT.
WHICH IS OUT OF BATTERIES. I'M NOT JUST WORRIED ABOUT THE POLICE, MATT. THE HAND IS EVERYWHERE OUT THERE.
I HAD TO FIGHT MY WAY THROUGH THREE SQUADS JUST GETTING DOWN HERE FROM CHINATOWN, EVEN WITH MY SUIT TURNED ON.
I KNOW. IT'S GETTING BAD. I'M TRYING TO COORDINATE THE CITY'S RESPONSE-- BRING IN THE HEROES.
I JUST WISH I KNEW WHY THE HAND WAS HERE, WHAT THEY WANT.
THAT'S WHY I CAME, MATT. I KNOW WHAT'S HAPPENING.
THEY'RE HERE BECAUSE OF ME.
THIS WHOLE THING IS MY FAULT.
WOW.
I GUESS HE REALLY IS YOUR APPRENTICE, MATT.

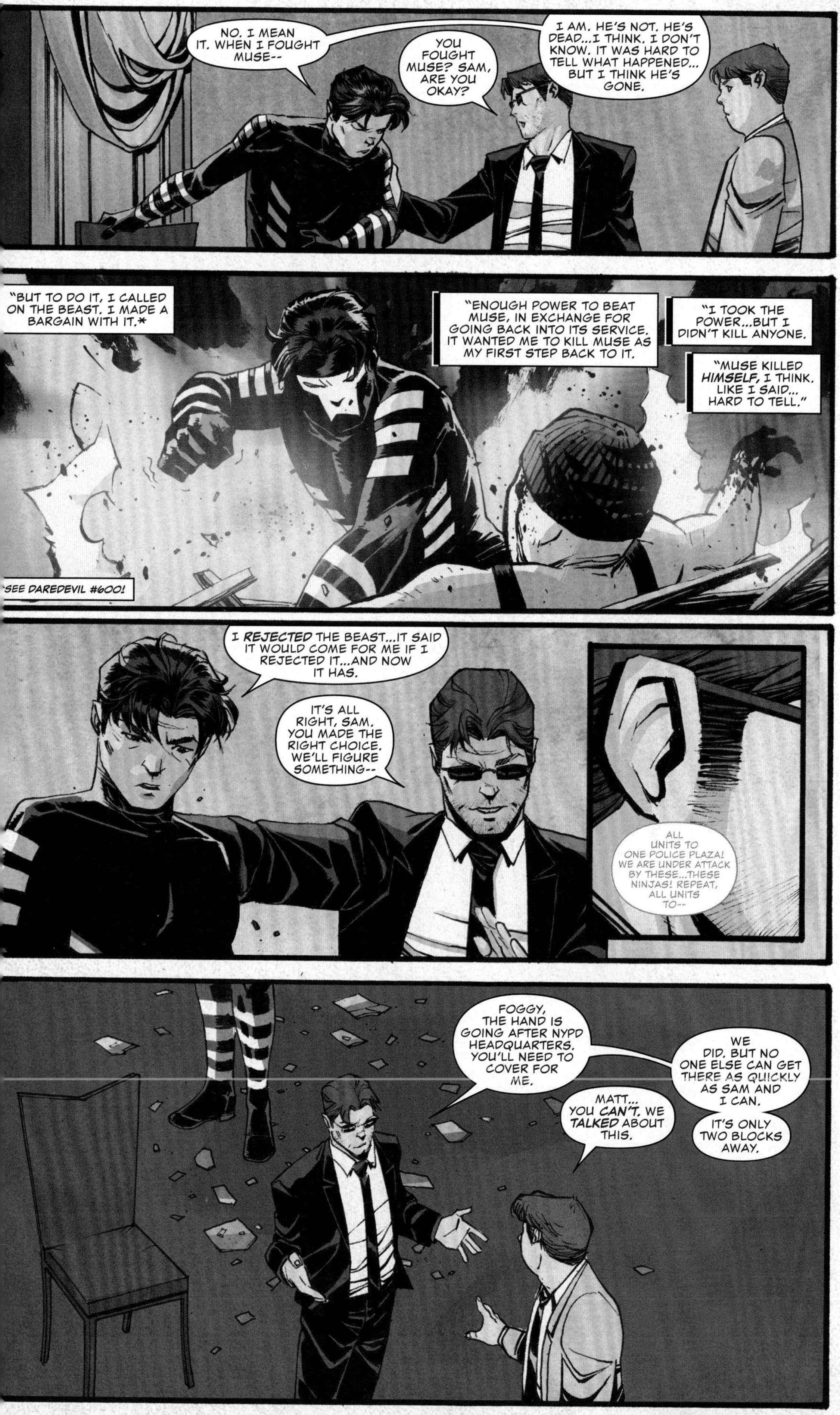
NO. I MEAN IT. WHEN I FOUGHT MUSE--
YOU FOUGHT MUSE? SAM, ARE YOU OKAY?
I AM. HE'S NOT. HE'S DEAD...I THINK. I DON'T KNOW. IT WAS HARD TO TELL WHAT HAPPENED... BUT I THINK HE'S GONE.
"BUT TO DO IT, I CALLED ON THE BEAST. I MADE A BARGAIN WITH IT.*
"ENOUGH POWER TO BEAT MUSE, IN EXCHANGE FOR GOING BACK INTO ITS SERVICE. IT WANTED ME TO KILL MUSE AS MY FIRST STEP BACK TO IT.
"I TOOK THE POWER...BUT I DIDN'T KILL ANYONE.
"MUSE KILLED *HIMSELF*, I THINK. LIKE I SAID... HARD TO TELL."
*SEE *DAREDEVIL #600!*
I *REJECTED* THE BEAST...IT SAID IT WOULD COME FOR ME IF I REJECTED IT...AND NOW IT HAS.
IT'S ALL RIGHT, SAM. YOU MADE THE RIGHT CHOICE. WE'LL FIGURE SOMETHING--
ALL UNITS TO ONE POLICE PLAZA! WE ARE UNDER ATTACK BY THESE...THESE NINJAS! REPEAT, ALL UNITS TO--
FOGGY, THE HAND IS GOING AFTER NYPD HEADQUARTERS. YOU'LL NEED TO COVER FOR ME.
MATT... YOU *CAN'T*. WE *TALKED* ABOUT THIS.
WE DID. BUT NO ONE ELSE CAN GET THERE AS QUICKLY AS SAM AND I CAN.
IT'S ONLY TWO BLOCKS AWAY.

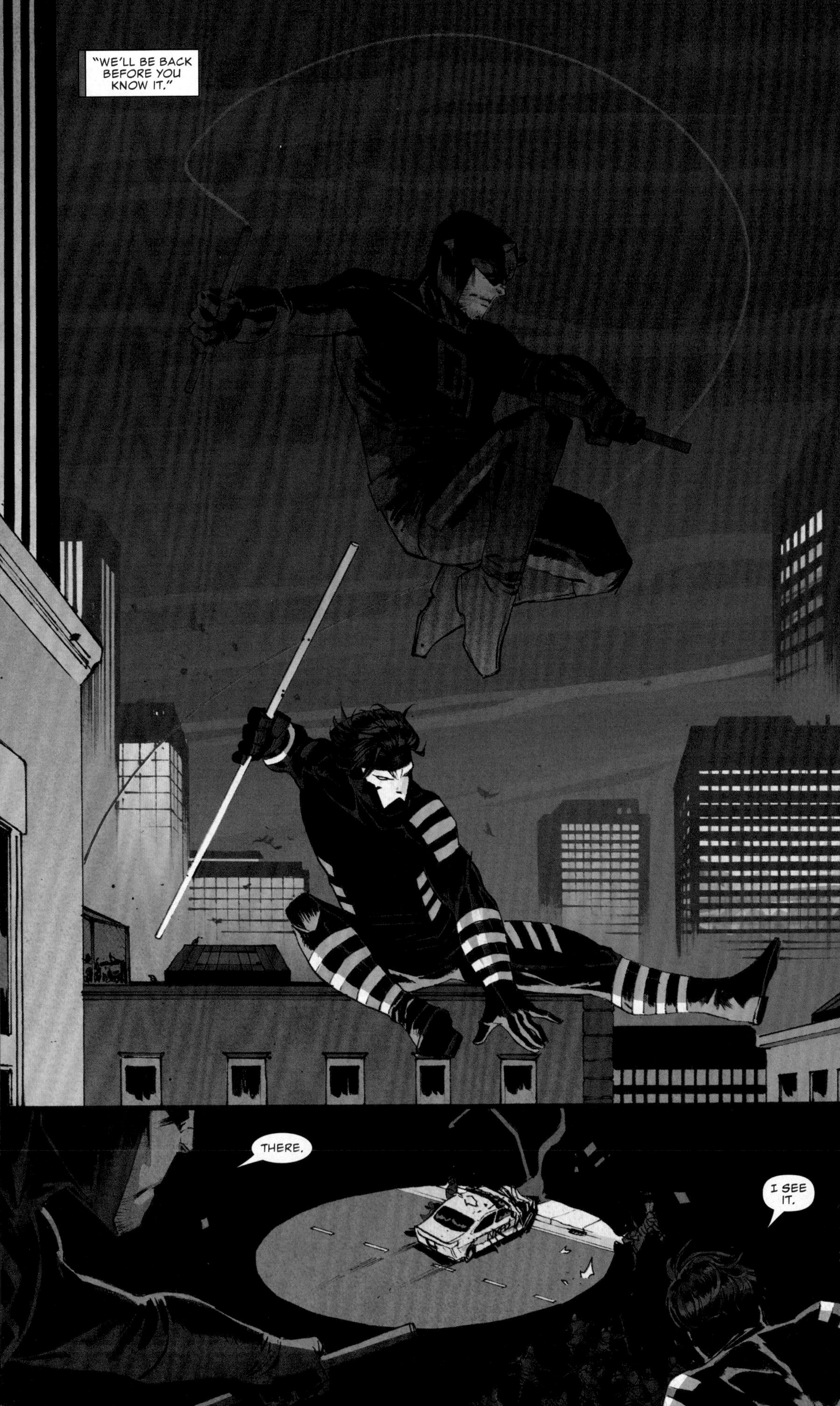
"WE'LL BE BACK BEFORE YOU KNOW IT."
THERE.
I SEE IT.

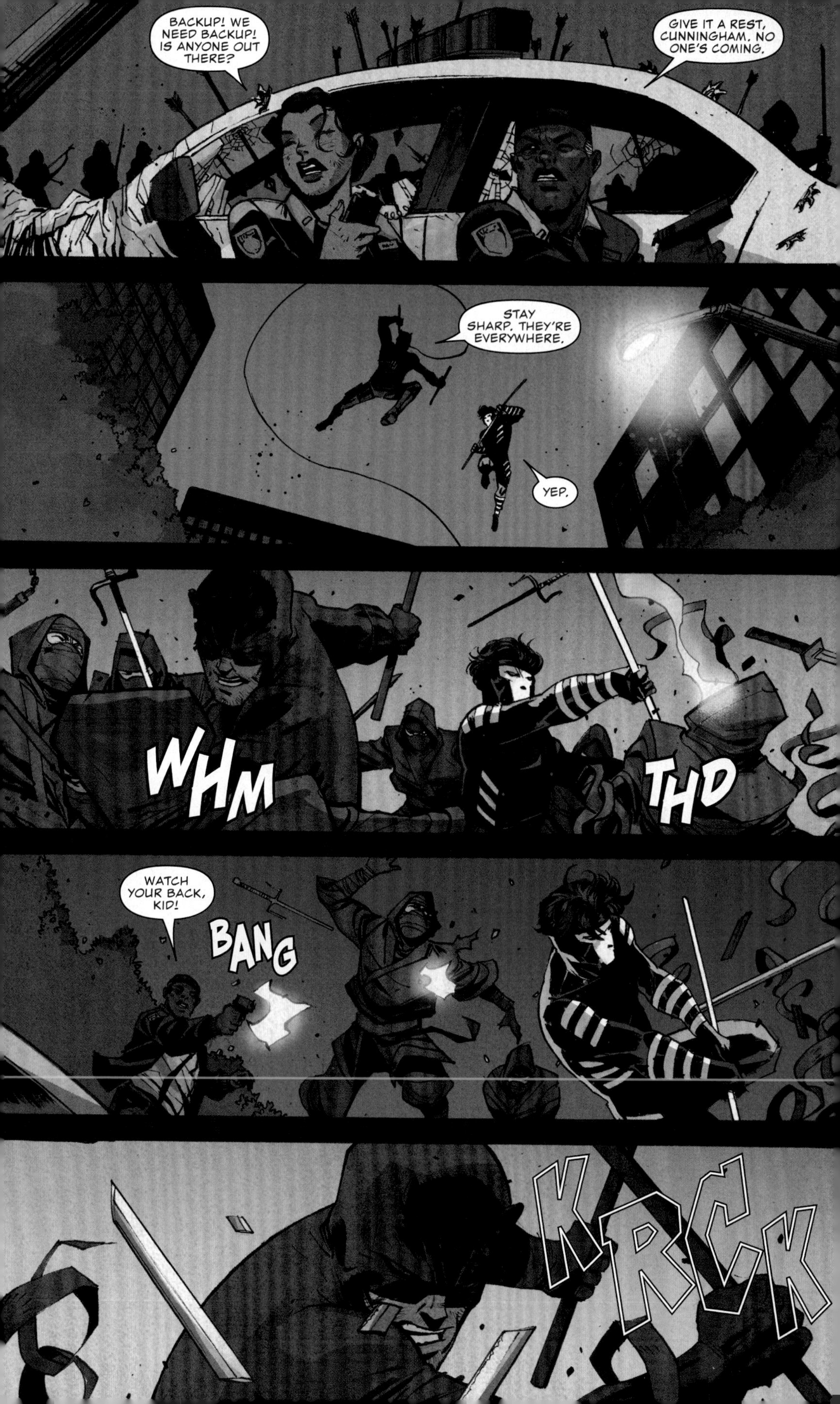
BACKUP! WE NEED BACKUP! IS ANYONE OUT THERE?
GIVE IT A REST, CUNNINGHAM. NO ONE'S COMING.
STAY SHARP. THEY'RE EVERYWHERE.
YEP.
WHM
THD
WATCH YOUR BACK, KID!
BANG
KRCK

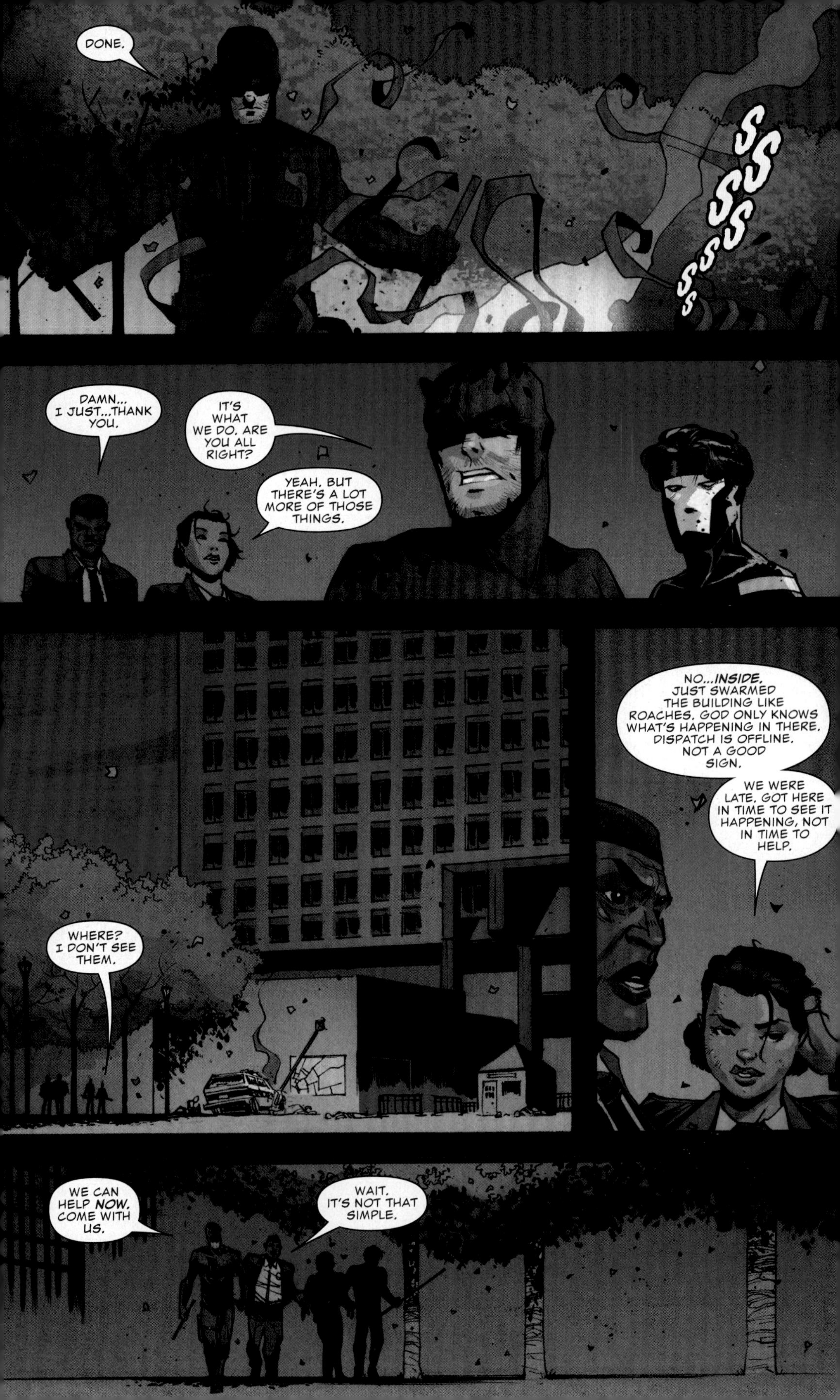
DONE.
SSSSSSS
DAMN... I JUST...THANK YOU.
IT'S WHAT WE DO. ARE YOU ALL RIGHT?
YEAH, BUT THERE'S A LOT MORE OF THOSE THINGS.
WHERE? I DON'T SEE THEM.
NO...INSIDE. JUST SWARMED THE BUILDING LIKE ROACHES. GOD ONLY KNOWS WHAT'S HAPPENING IN THERE. DISPATCH IS OFFLINE. NOT A GOOD SIGN.
WE WERE LATE. GOT HERE IN TIME TO SEE IT HAPPENING, NOT IN TIME TO HELP.
WE CAN HELP NOW. COME WITH US.
WAIT. IT'S NOT THAT SIMPLE.

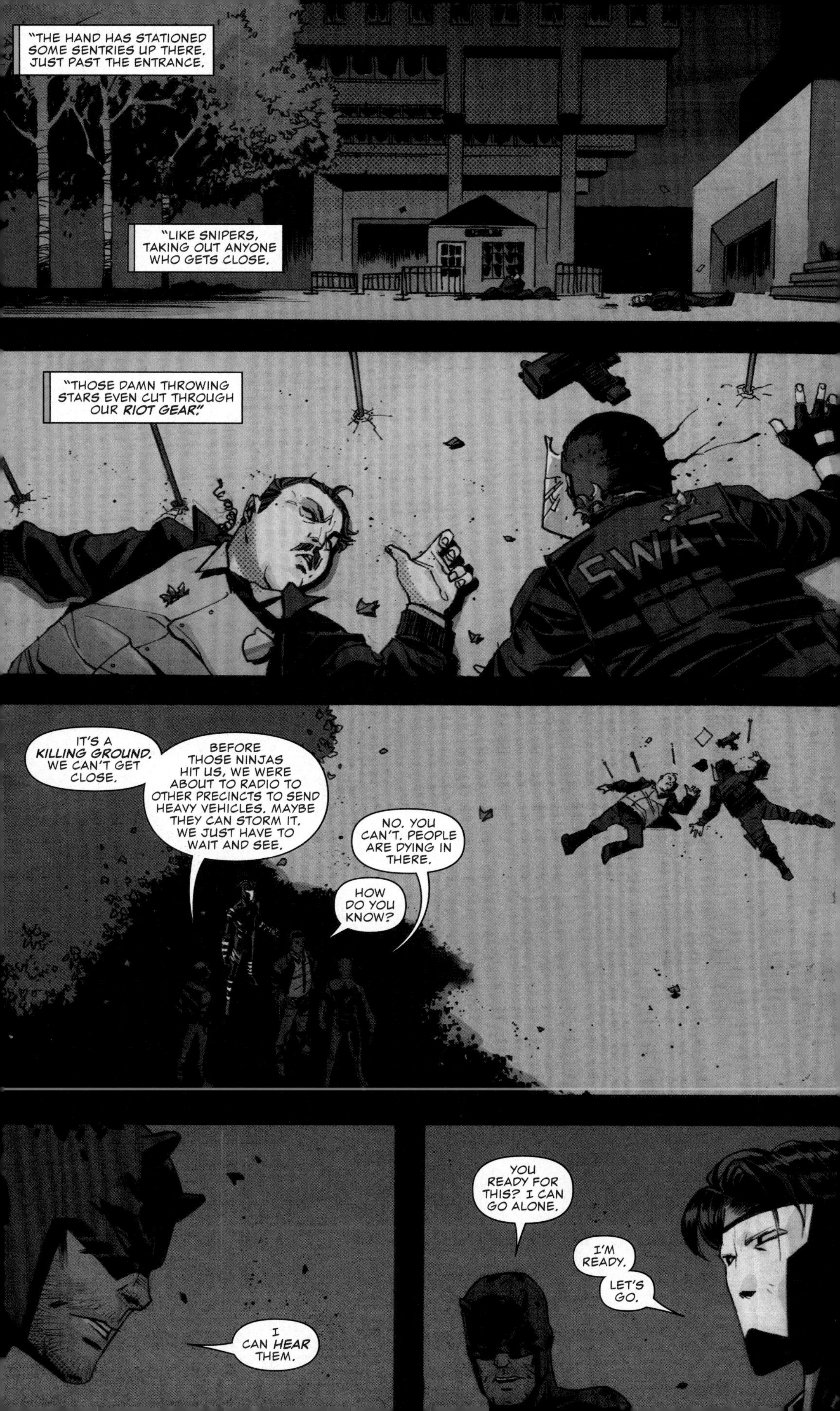
"THE HAND HAS STATIONED SOME SENTRIES UP THERE, JUST PAST THE ENTRANCE.
"LIKE SNIPERS, TAKING OUT ANYONE WHO GETS CLOSE.
"THOSE DAMN THROWING STARS EVEN CUT THROUGH OUR RIOT GEAR."
SWAT
IT'S A KILLING GROUND. WE CAN'T GET CLOSE.
BEFORE THOSE NINJAS HIT US, WE WERE ABOUT TO RADIO TO OTHER PRECINCTS TO SEND HEAVY VEHICLES. MAYBE THEY CAN STORM IT. WE JUST HAVE TO WAIT AND SEE.
NO, YOU CAN'T. PEOPLE ARE DYING IN THERE.
HOW DO YOU KNOW?
I CAN HEAR THEM.
YOU READY FOR THIS? I CAN GO ALONE.
I'M READY.
LET'S GO.

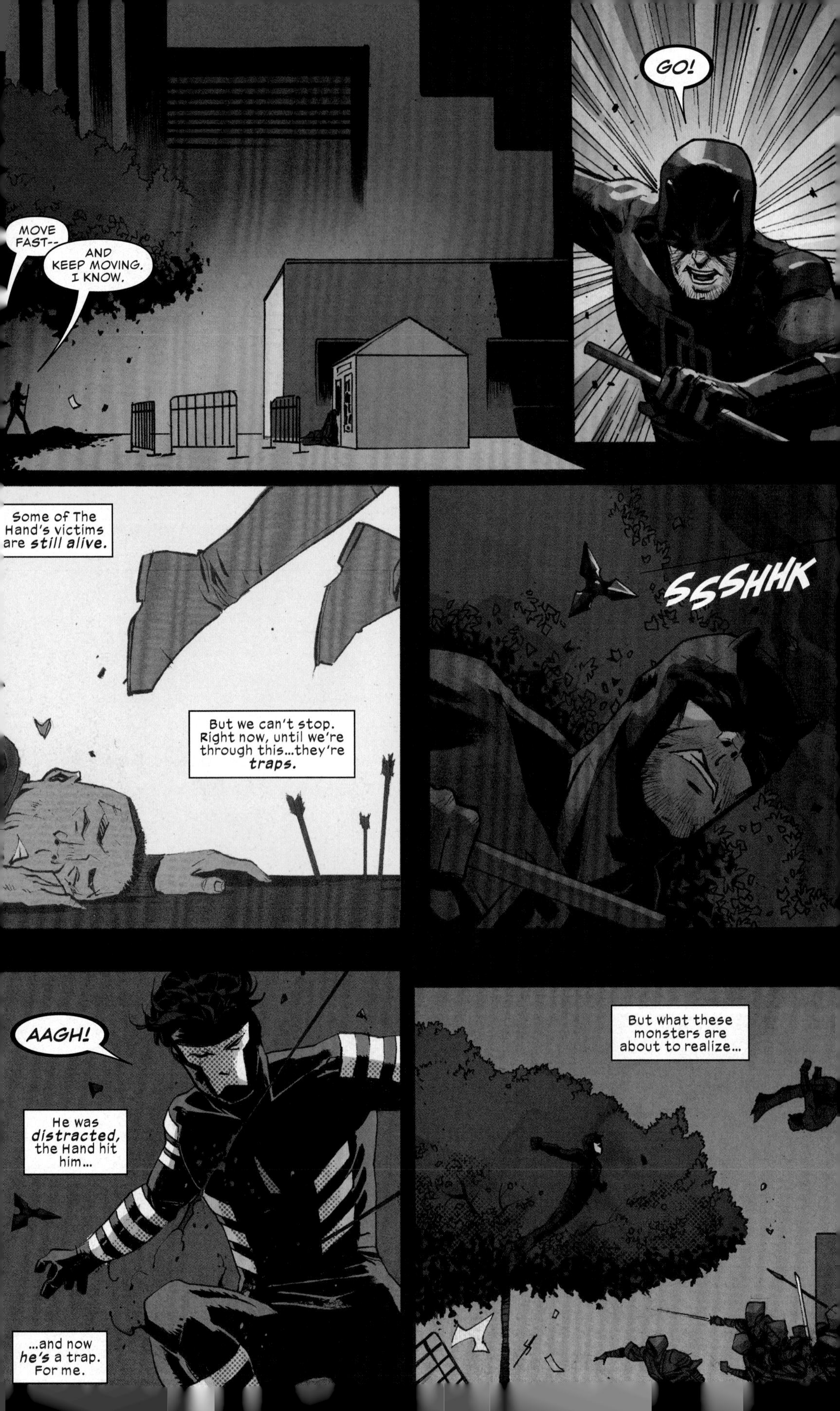
MOVE FAST--
AND KEEP MOVING. I KNOW.
GO!
Some of The Hand's victims are *still alive*.
But we can't stop. Right now, until we're through this...they're *traps*.
SSSHHK
AAGH!
He was *distracted*, the Hand hit him...
...and now *he's* a trap. For me.
But what these monsters are about to realize...

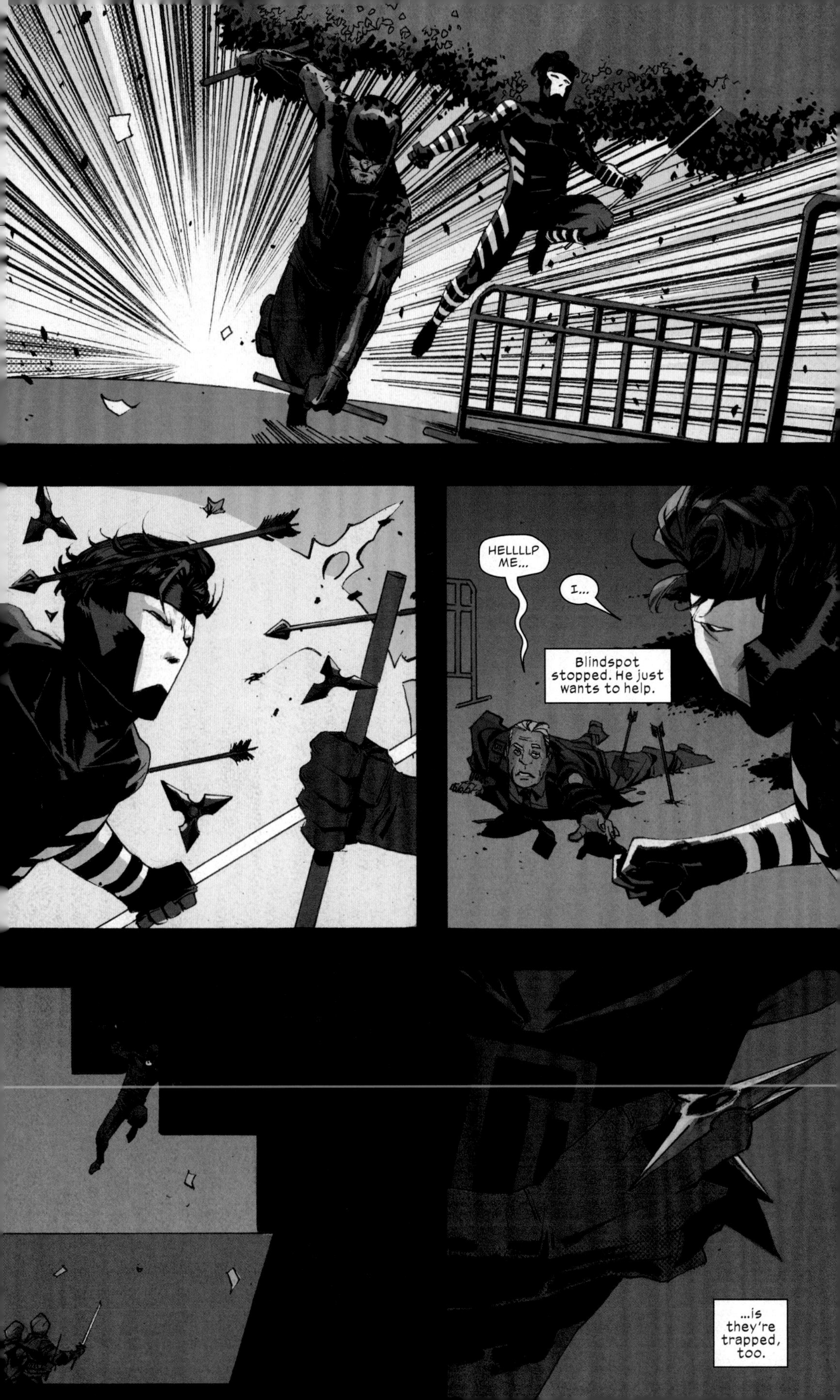
HELLLLP ME...
I...
Blindspot stopped. He just wants to help.
...is they're trapped, too.

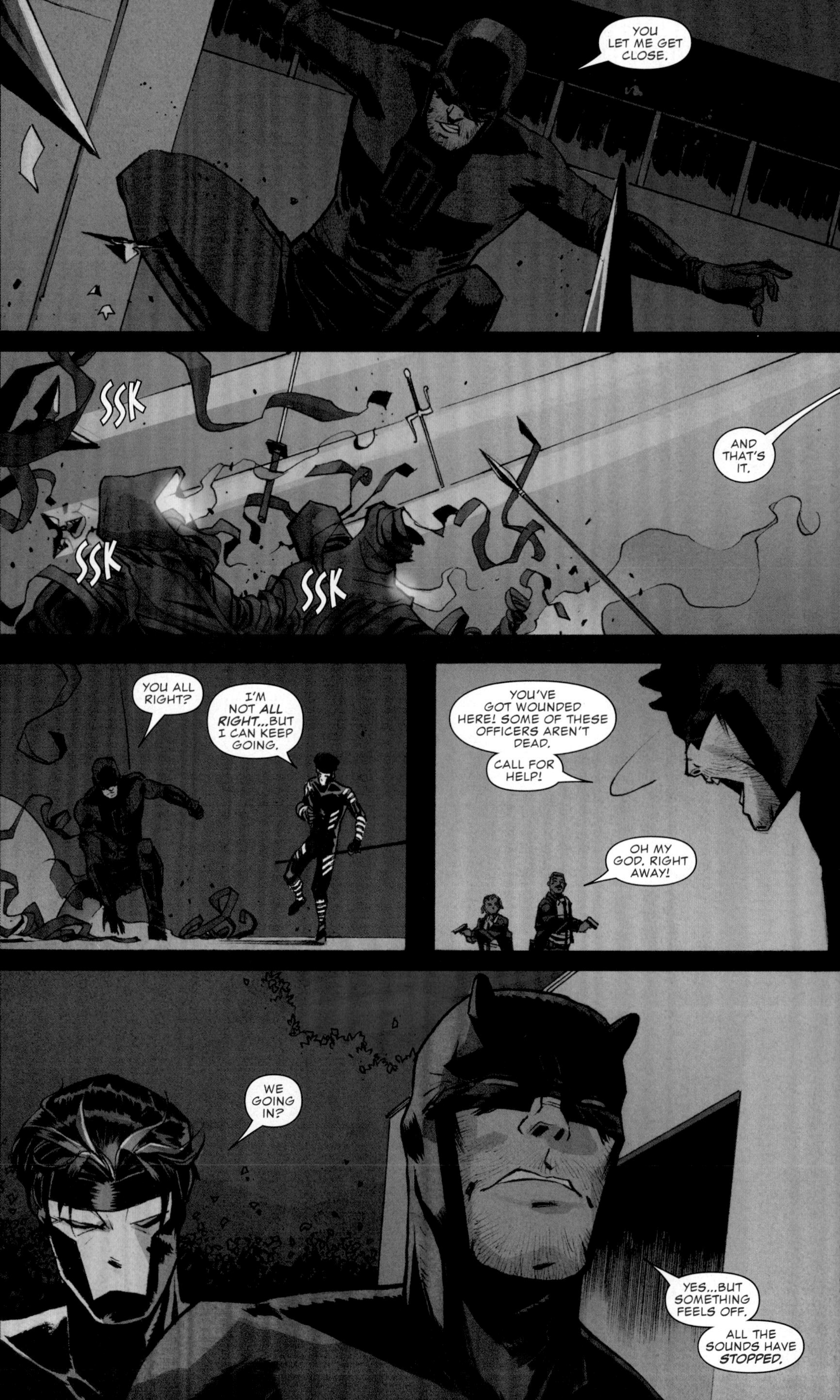
YOU LET ME GET CLOSE.
SSK
AND THAT'S IT.
SSK
SSK
YOU ALL RIGHT?
I'M NOT ALL RIGHT...BUT I CAN KEEP GOING.
YOU'VE GOT WOUNDED HERE! SOME OF THESE OFFICERS AREN'T DEAD.
CALL FOR HELP!
OH MY GOD. RIGHT AWAY!
WE GOING IN?
YES...BUT SOMETHING FEELS OFF.
ALL THE SOUNDS HAVE STOPPED.

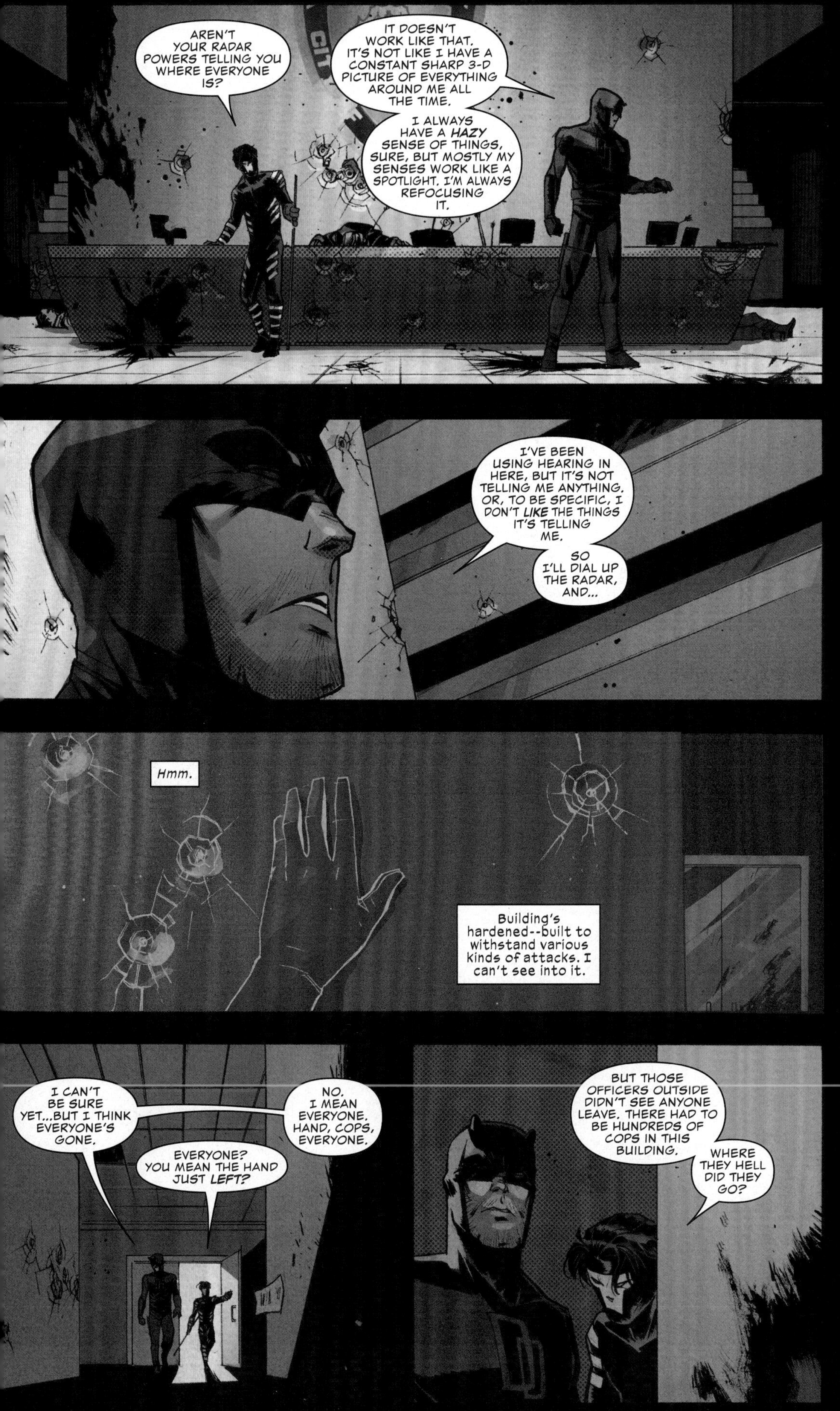
AREN'T YOUR RADAR POWERS TELLING YOU WHERE EVERYONE IS?
IT DOESN'T WORK LIKE THAT. IT'S NOT LIKE I HAVE A CONSTANT SHARP 3-D PICTURE OF EVERYTHING AROUND ME ALL THE TIME.
I ALWAYS HAVE A HAZY SENSE OF THINGS, SURE, BUT MOSTLY MY SENSES WORK LIKE A SPOTLIGHT. I'M ALWAYS REFOCUSING IT.
I'VE BEEN USING HEARING IN HERE, BUT IT'S NOT TELLING ME ANYTHING. OR, TO BE SPECIFIC, I DON'T LIKE THE THINGS IT'S TELLING ME.
SO I'LL DIAL UP THE RADAR, AND...
Hmm.
Building's hardened--built to withstand various kinds of attacks. I can't see into it.
I CAN'T BE SURE YET...BUT I THINK EVERYONE'S GONE.
EVERYONE? YOU MEAN THE HAND JUST LEFT?
NO. I MEAN EVERYONE. HAND, COPS, EVERYONE.
BUT THOSE OFFICERS OUTSIDE DIDN'T SEE ANYONE LEAVE. THERE HAD TO BE HUNDREDS OF COPS IN THIS BUILDING.
WHERE THEY HELL DID THEY GO?

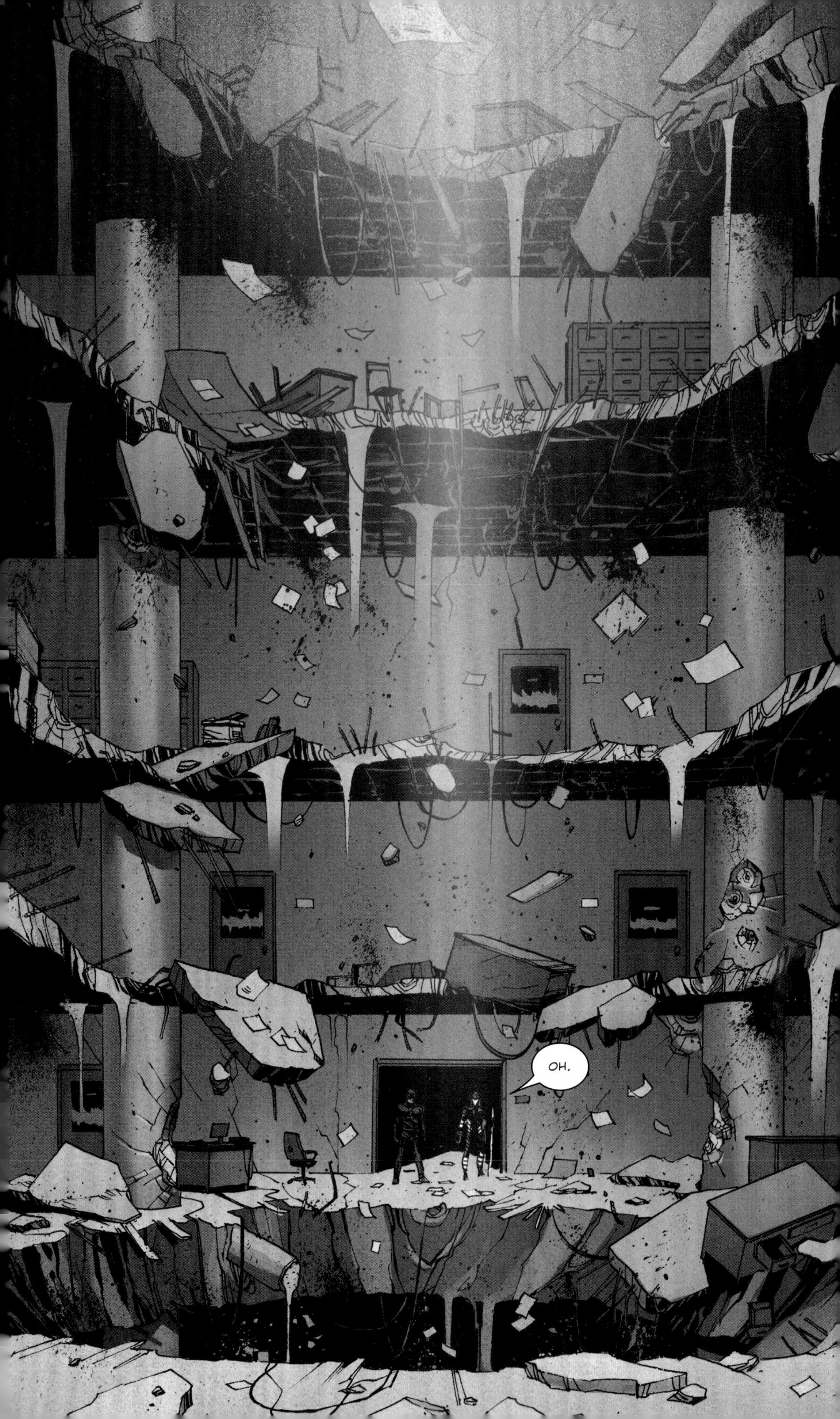
OH.

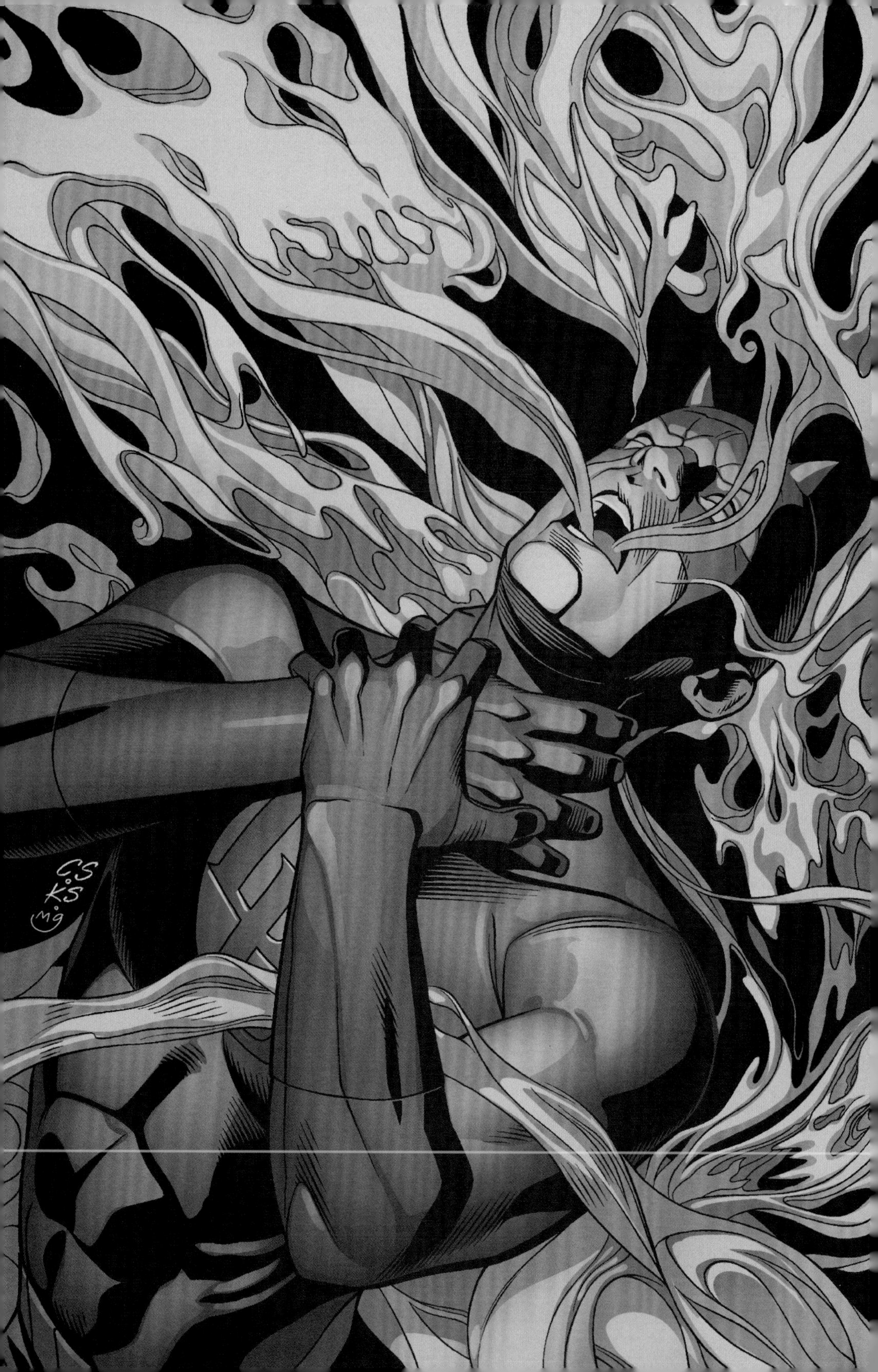

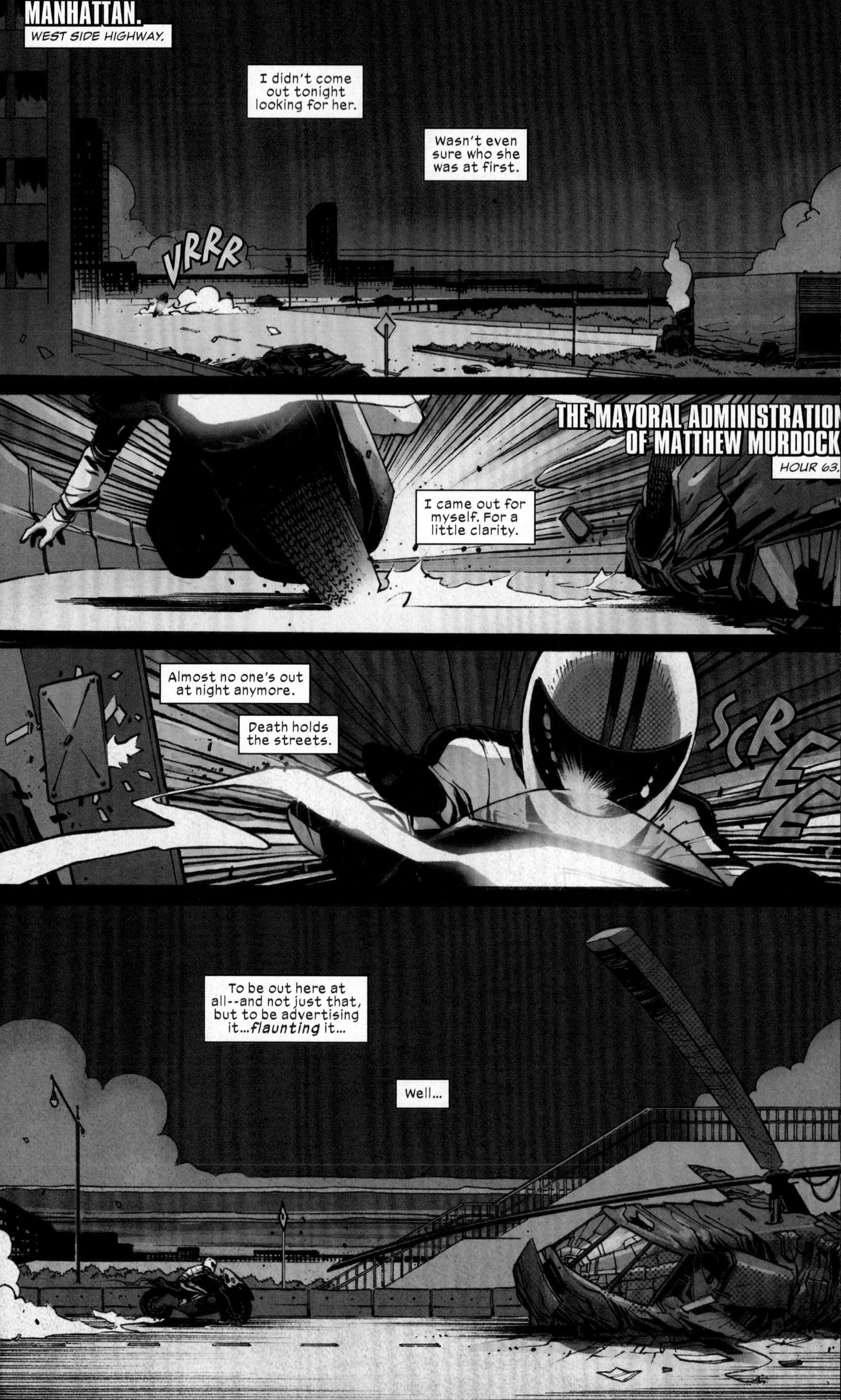
MANHATTAN.
WEST SIDE HIGHWAY.
I didn't come out tonight looking for her.
Wasn't even sure who she was at first.
VRRR
THE MAYORAL ADMINISTRATION OF MATTHEW MURDOCK
HOUR 63.
I came out for myself. For a little clarity.
Almost no one's out at night anymore.
Death holds the streets.
SCREE
To be out here at all--and not just that, but to be advertising it...*flaunting* it...
Well...

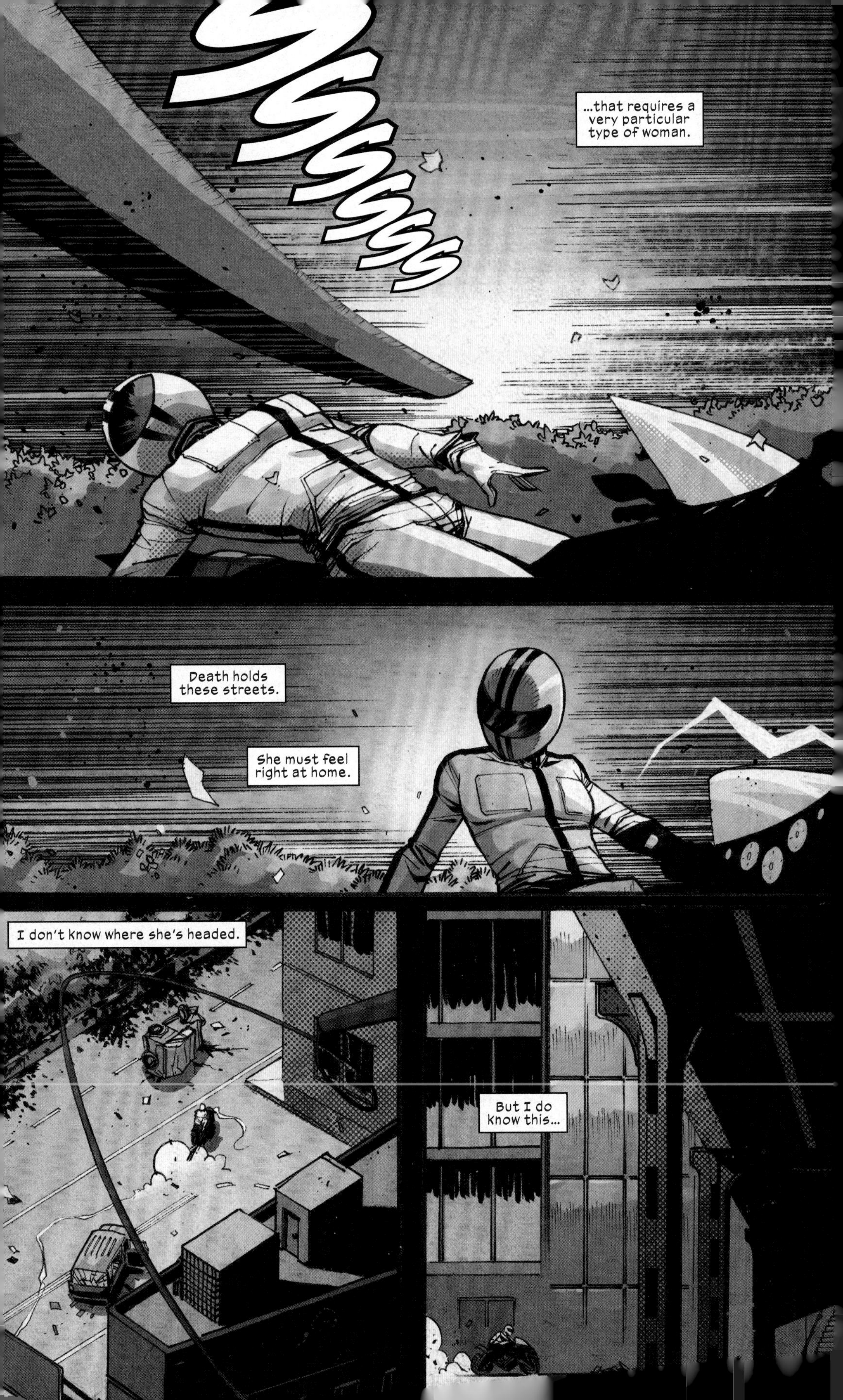

SSSSSSS
...that requires a very particular type of woman.
Death holds these streets.
She must feel right at home.
I don't know where she's headed.
But I do know this...

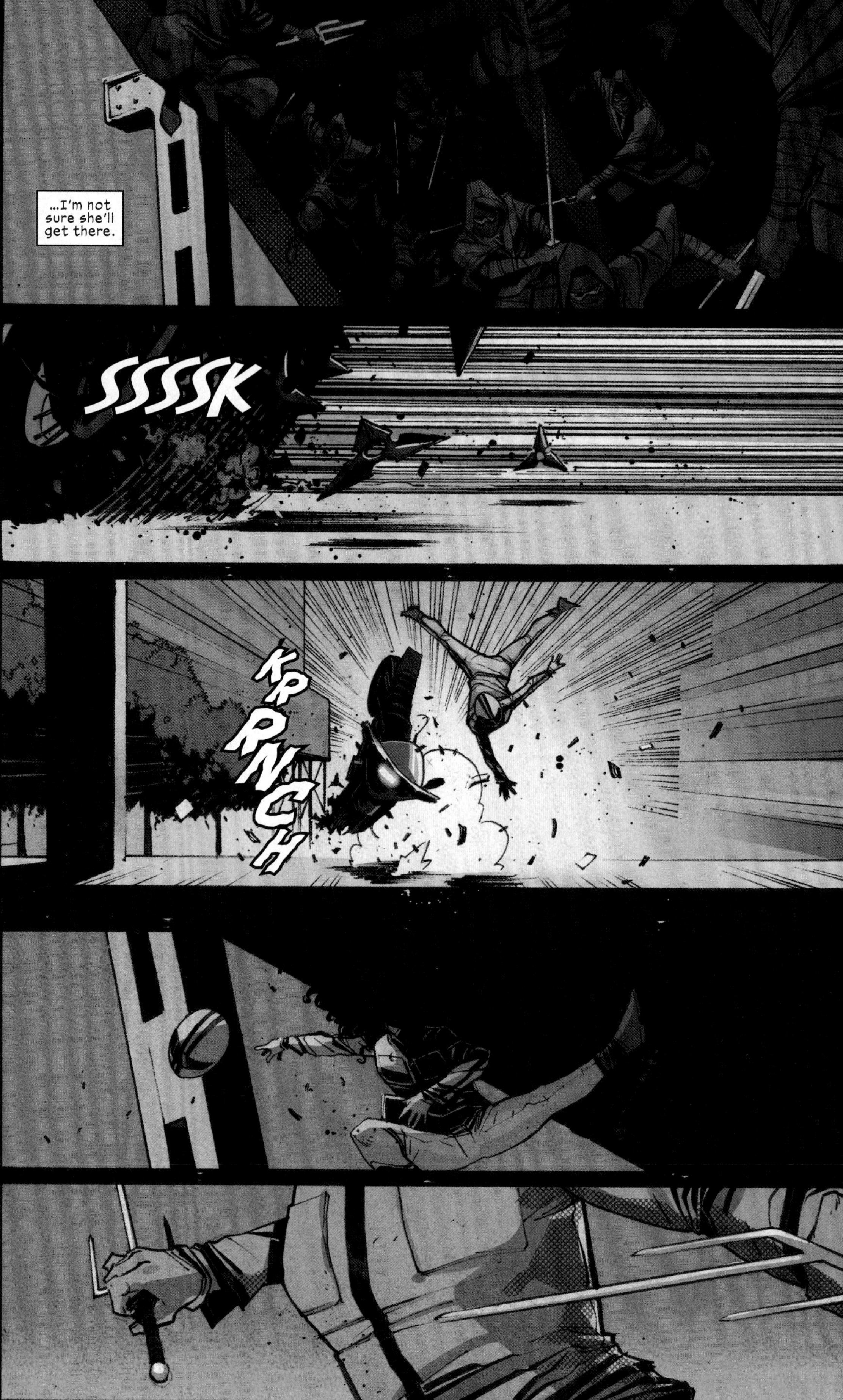

...I'm not sure she'll get there.
SSSSK
KRRNCH

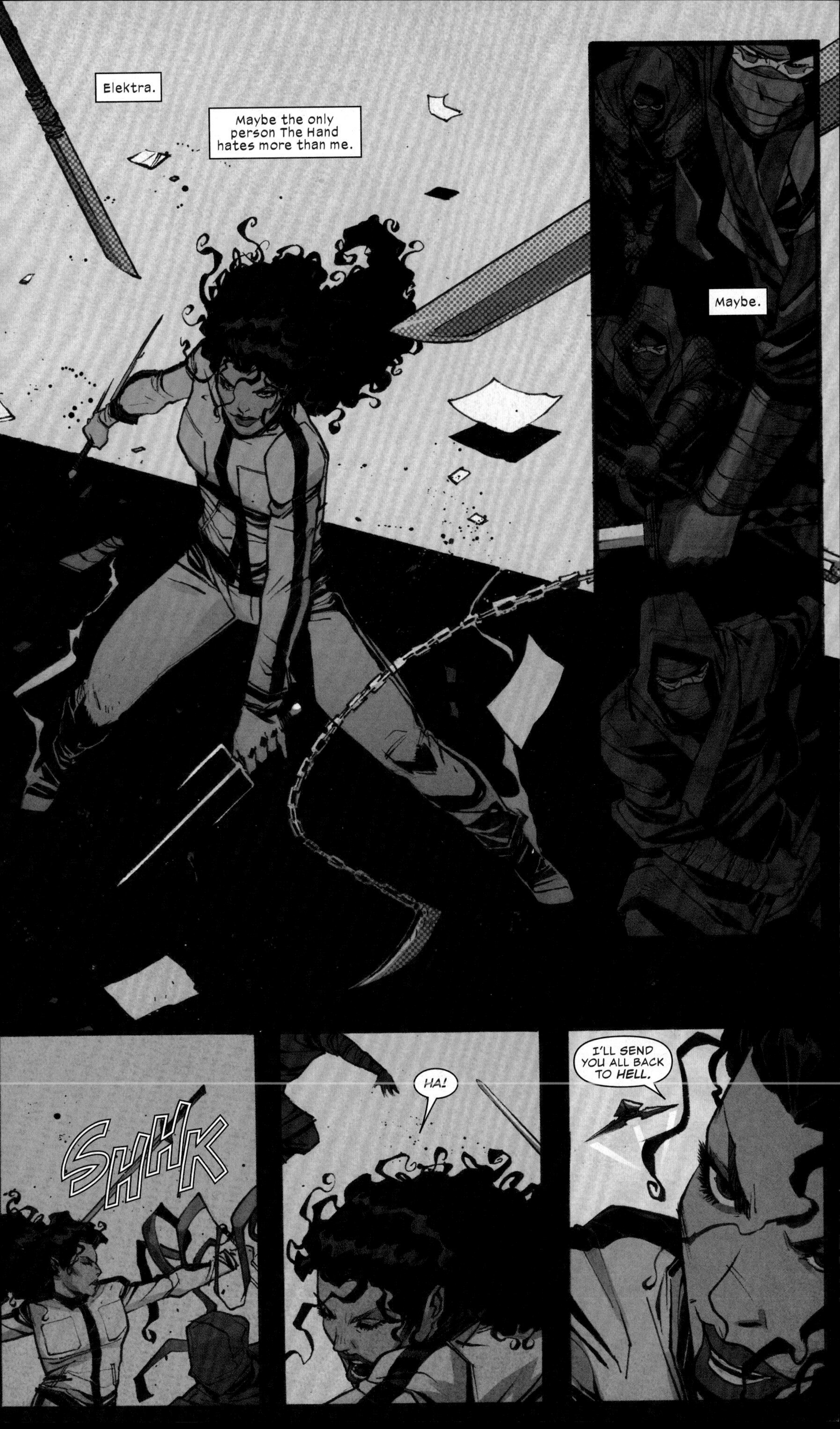
Elektra.
Maybe the only person The Hand hates more than me.
Maybe.
SHHK
HA!
I'LL SEND YOU ALL BACK TO HELL.

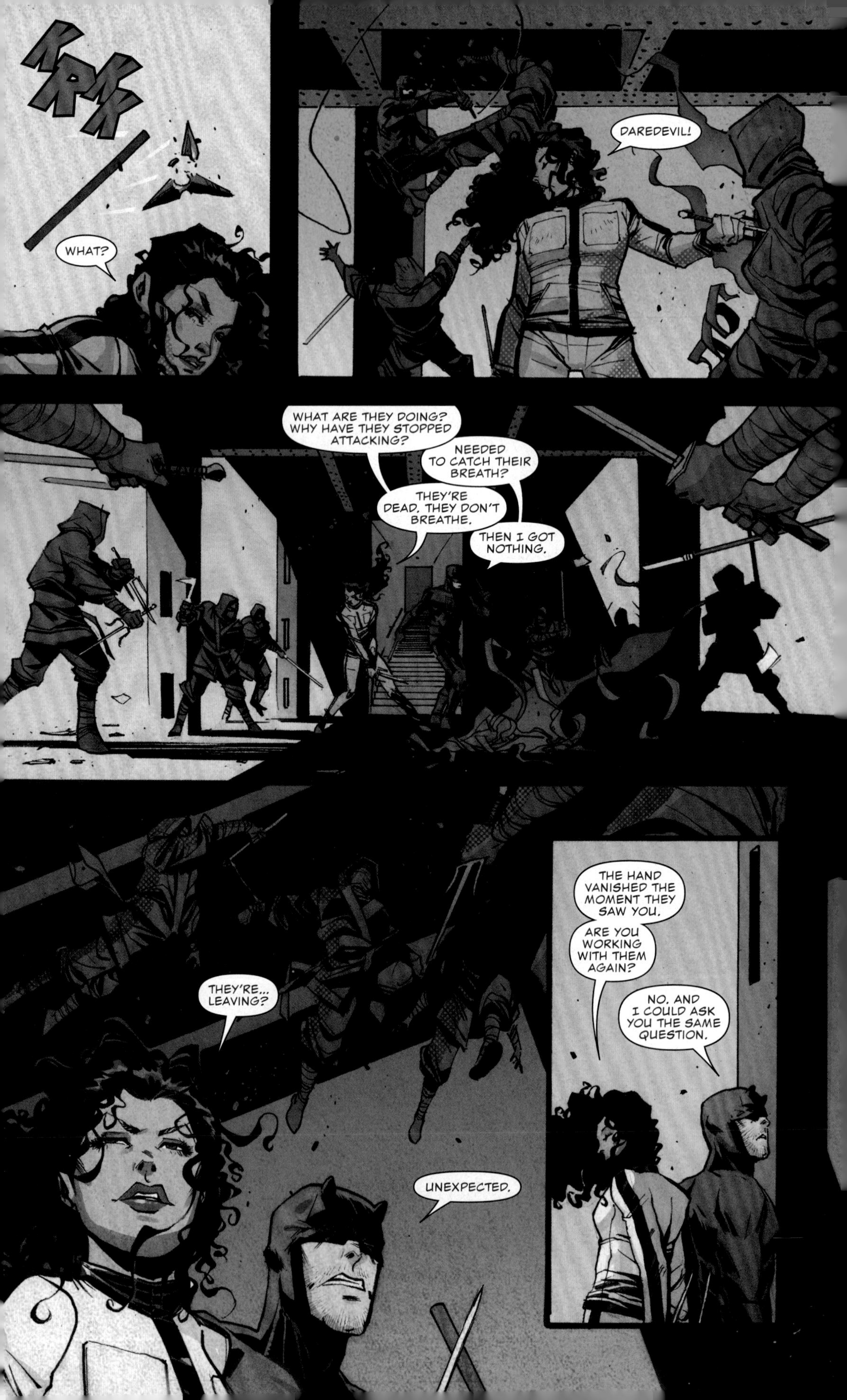
KRAK
WHAT?
DAREDEVIL!
WHAT ARE THEY DOING? WHY HAVE THEY STOPPED ATTACKING?
NEEDED TO CATCH THEIR BREATH?
THEY'RE DEAD. THEY DON'T BREATHE.
THEN I GOT NOTHING.
THEY'RE... LEAVING?
UNEXPECTED.
THE HAND VANISHED THE MOMENT THEY SAW YOU.
ARE YOU WORKING WITH THEM AGAIN?
NO. AND I COULD ASK YOU THE SAME QUESTION.

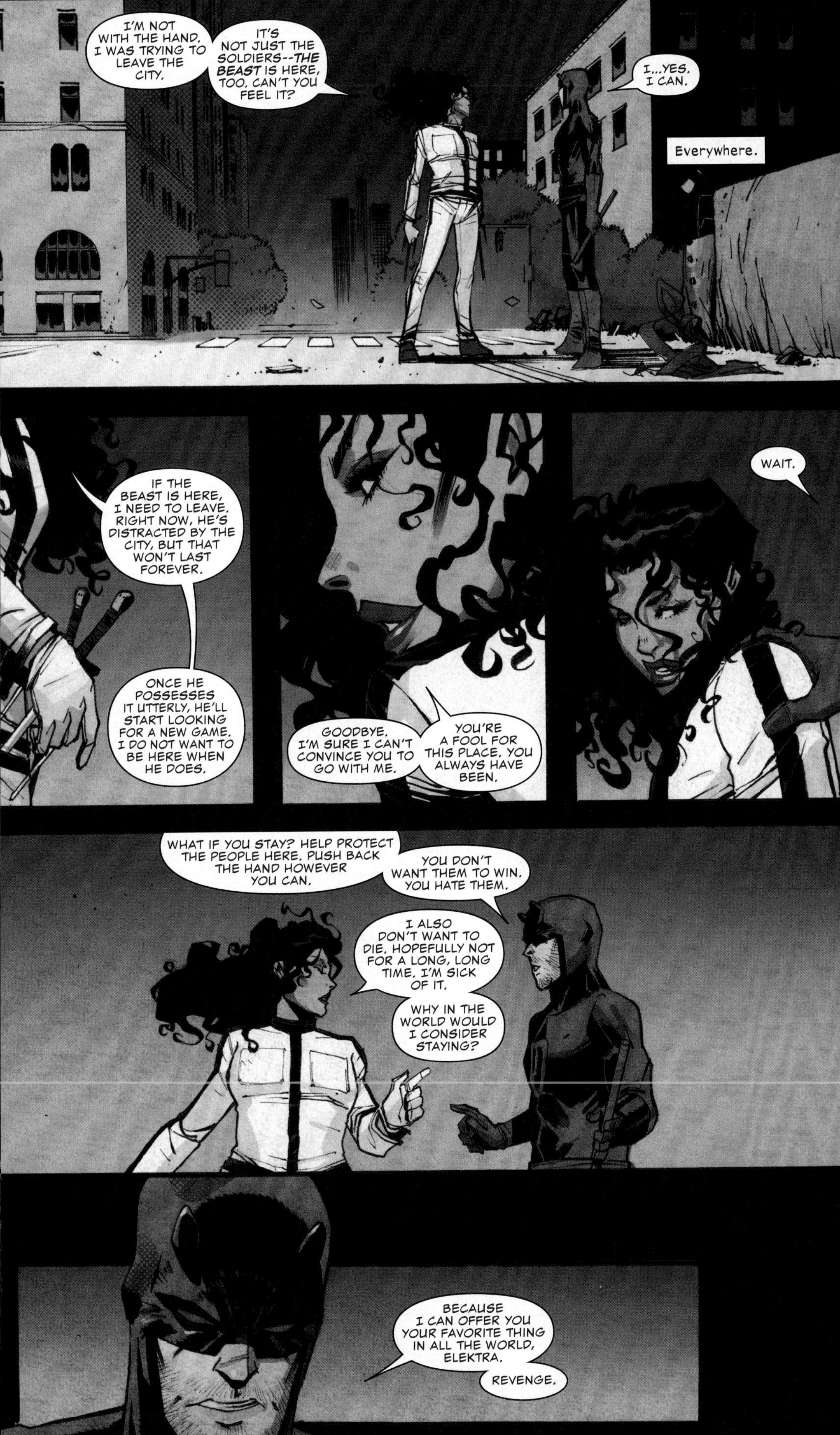
I'M NOT WITH THE HAND. I WAS TRYING TO LEAVE THE CITY.
IT'S NOT JUST THE SOLDIERS--THE BEAST IS HERE, TOO. CAN'T YOU FEEL IT?
I...YES. I CAN.
Everywhere.
IF THE BEAST IS HERE, I NEED TO LEAVE. RIGHT NOW, HE'S DISTRACTED BY THE CITY, BUT THAT WON'T LAST FOREVER.
ONCE HE POSSESSES IT UTTERLY, HE'LL START LOOKING FOR A NEW GAME. I DO NOT WANT TO BE HERE WHEN HE DOES.
GOODBYE. I'M SURE I CAN'T CONVINCE YOU TO GO WITH ME.
YOU'RE A FOOL FOR THIS PLACE. YOU ALWAYS HAVE BEEN.
WAIT.
WHAT IF YOU STAY? HELP PROTECT THE PEOPLE HERE. PUSH BACK THE HAND HOWEVER YOU CAN.
YOU DON'T WANT THEM TO WIN. YOU HATE THEM.
I ALSO DON'T WANT TO DIE. HOPEFULLY NOT FOR A LONG, LONG TIME. I'M SICK OF IT.
WHY IN THE WORLD WOULD I CONSIDER STAYING?
BECAUSE I CAN OFFER YOU YOUR FAVORITE THING IN ALL THE WORLD, ELEKTRA.
REVENGE.

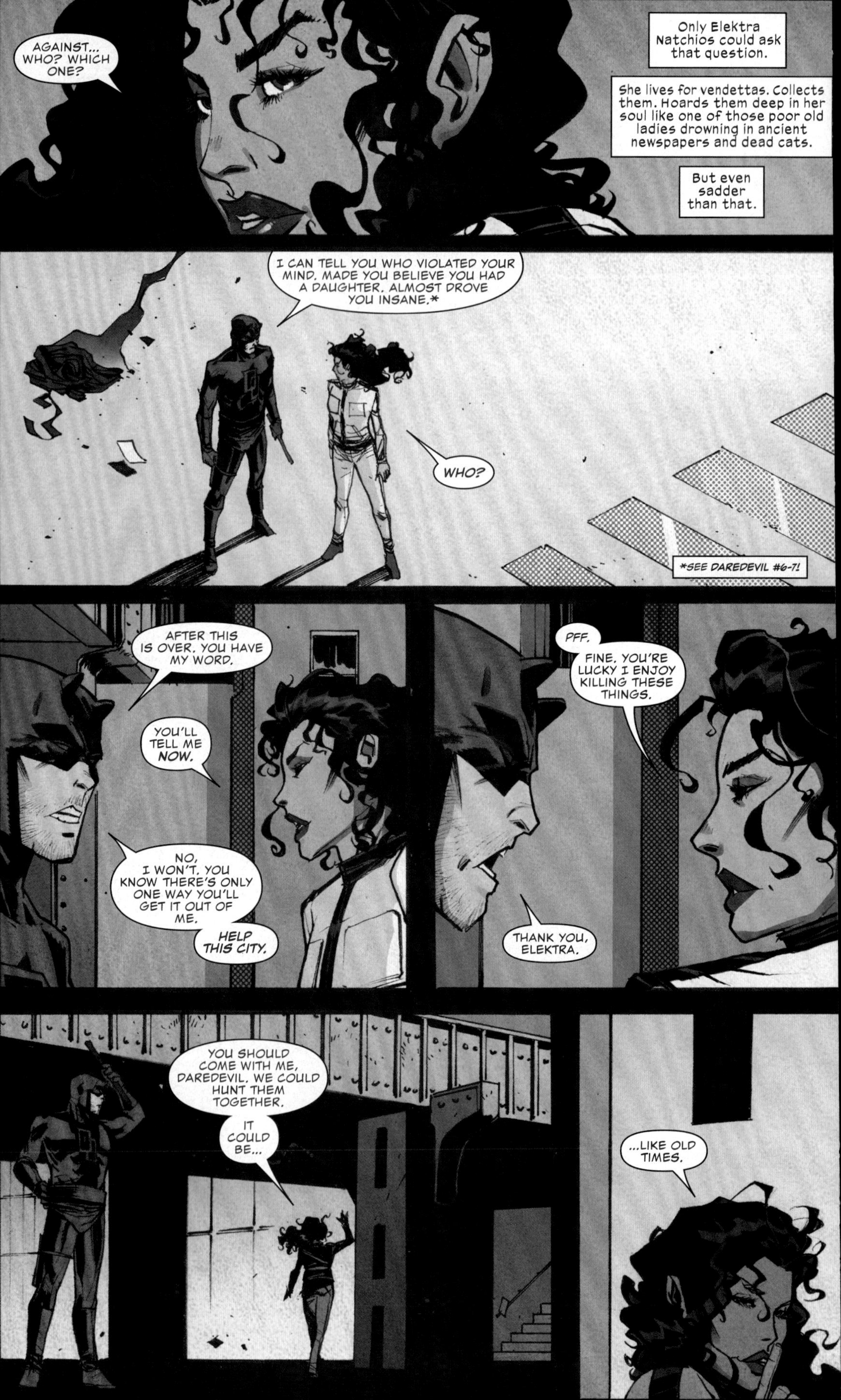
AGAINST... WHO? WHICH ONE?
Only Elektra Natchios could ask that question.
She lives for vendettas. Collects them. Hoards them deep in her soul like one of those poor old ladies drowning in ancient newspapers and dead cats.
But even sadder than that.
I CAN TELL YOU WHO VIOLATED YOUR MIND. MADE YOU BELIEVE YOU HAD A DAUGHTER. ALMOST DROVE YOU INSANE.*
WHO?
*SEE DAREDEVIL #6-7!
AFTER THIS IS OVER. YOU HAVE MY WORD.
YOU'LL TELL ME NOW.
NO, I WON'T. YOU KNOW THERE'S ONLY ONE WAY YOU'LL GET IT OUT OF ME.
HELP THIS CITY.
PFF.
FINE. YOU'RE LUCKY I ENJOY KILLING THESE THINGS.
THANK YOU, ELEKTRA.
YOU SHOULD COME WITH ME, DAREDEVIL. WE COULD HUNT THEM TOGETHER.
IT COULD BE...
...LIKE OLD TIMES.

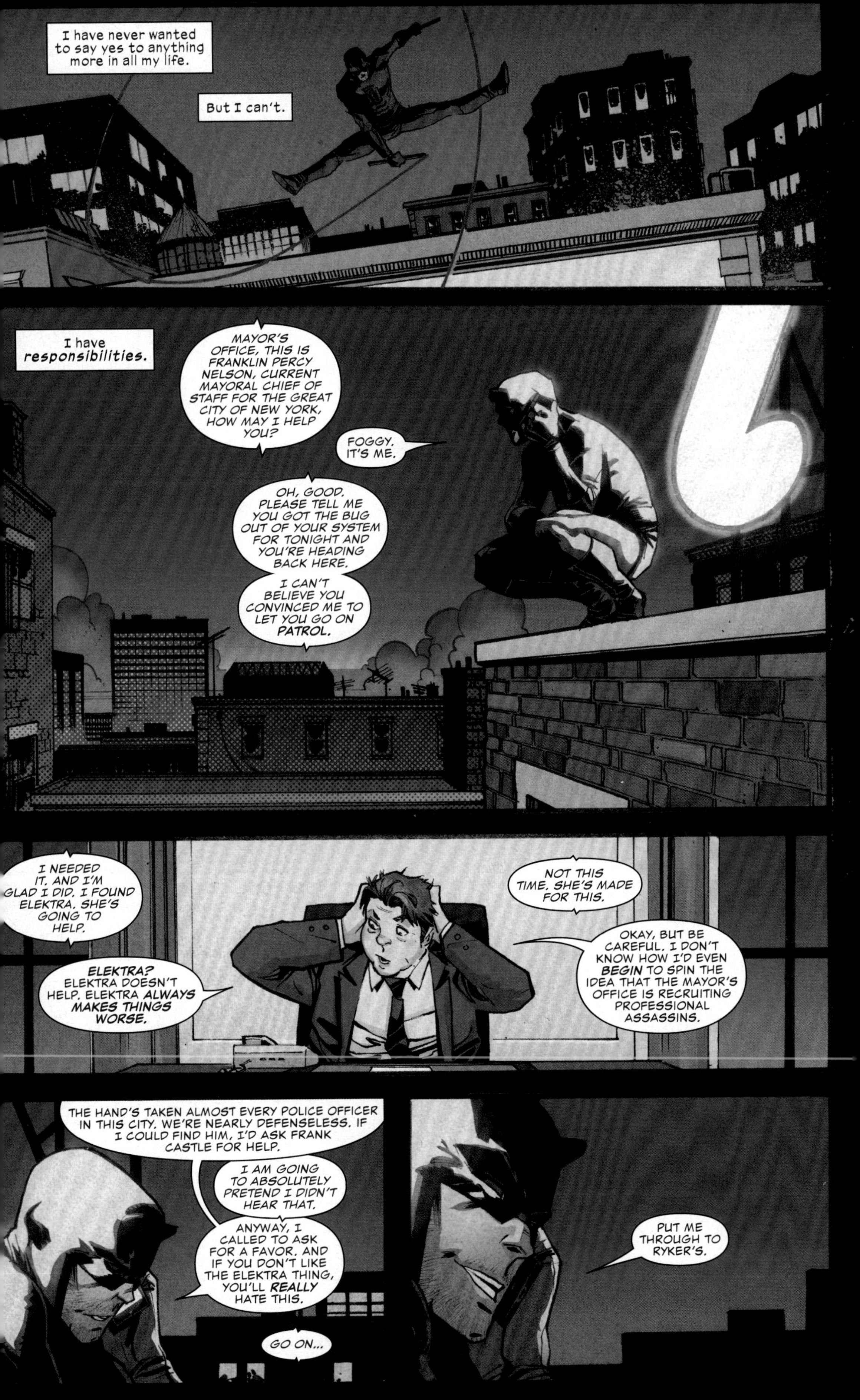

I have never wanted to say yes to anything more in all my life.
But I can't.
I have responsibilities.
MAYOR'S OFFICE, THIS IS FRANKLIN PERCY NELSON, CURRENT MAYORAL CHIEF OF STAFF FOR THE GREAT CITY OF NEW YORK, HOW MAY I HELP YOU?
FOGGY. IT'S ME.
OH, GOOD. PLEASE TELL ME YOU GOT THE BUG OUT OF YOUR SYSTEM FOR TONIGHT AND YOU'RE HEADING BACK HERE.
I CAN'T BELIEVE YOU CONVINCED ME TO LET YOU GO ON PATROL.
I NEEDED IT. AND I'M GLAD I DID. I FOUND ELEKTRA. SHE'S GOING TO HELP.
ELEKTRA? ELEKTRA DOESN'T HELP. ELEKTRA ALWAYS MAKES THINGS WORSE.
NOT THIS TIME. SHE'S MADE FOR THIS.
OKAY, BUT BE CAREFUL. I DON'T KNOW HOW I'D EVEN BEGIN TO SPIN THE IDEA THAT THE MAYOR'S OFFICE IS RECRUITING PROFESSIONAL ASSASSINS.
THE HAND'S TAKEN ALMOST EVERY POLICE OFFICER IN THIS CITY. WE'RE NEARLY DEFENSELESS. IF I COULD FIND HIM, I'D ASK FRANK CASTLE FOR HELP.
I AM GOING TO ABSOLUTELY PRETEND I DIDN'T HEAR THAT.
ANYWAY, I CALLED TO ASK FOR A FAVOR. AND IF YOU DON'T LIKE THE ELEKTRA THING, YOU'LL REALLY HATE THIS.
GO ON...
PUT ME THROUGH TO RYKER'S.

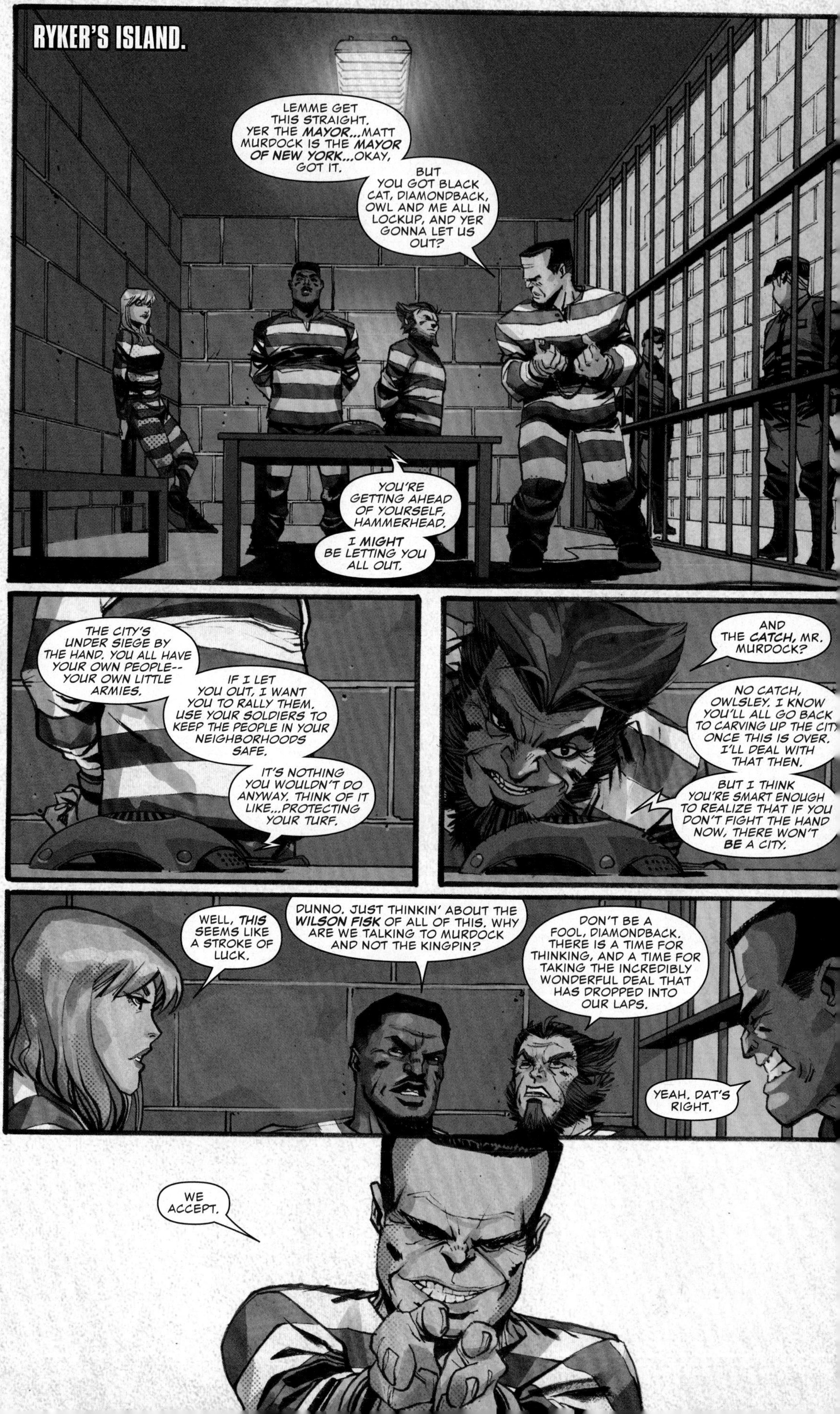
RYKER'S ISLAND.
LEMME GET THIS STRAIGHT. YER THE MAYOR... MATT MURDOCK IS THE MAYOR OF NEW YORK... OKAY, GOT IT.
BUT YOU GOT BLACK CAT, DIAMONDBACK, OWL AND ME ALL IN LOCKUP, AND YER GONNA LET US OUT?
YOU'RE GETTING AHEAD OF YOURSELF, HAMMERHEAD.
I MIGHT BE LETTING YOU ALL OUT.
THE CITY'S UNDER SIEGE BY THE HAND. YOU ALL HAVE YOUR OWN PEOPLE-- YOUR OWN LITTLE ARMIES.
IF I LET YOU OUT, I WANT YOU TO RALLY THEM. USE YOUR SOLDIERS TO KEEP THE PEOPLE IN YOUR NEIGHBORHOODS SAFE.
IT'S NOTHING YOU WOULDN'T DO ANYWAY. THINK OF IT LIKE... PROTECTING YOUR TURF.
AND THE CATCH, MR. MURDOCK?
NO CATCH, OWLSLEY. I KNOW YOU'LL ALL GO BACK TO CARVING UP THE CITY ONCE THIS IS OVER. I'LL DEAL WITH THAT THEN.
BUT I THINK YOU'RE SMART ENOUGH TO REALIZE THAT IF YOU DON'T FIGHT THE HAND NOW, THERE WON'T BE A CITY.
WELL, THIS SEEMS LIKE A STROKE OF LUCK.
DUNNO. JUST THINKIN' ABOUT THE WILSON FISK OF ALL OF THIS. WHY ARE WE TALKING TO MURDOCK AND NOT THE KINGPIN?
DON'T BE A FOOL, DIAMONDBACK. THERE IS A TIME FOR THINKING, AND A TIME FOR TAKING THE INCREDIBLY WONDERFUL DEAL THAT HAS DROPPED INTO OUR LAPS.
YEAH, DAT'S RIGHT.
WE ACCEPT.

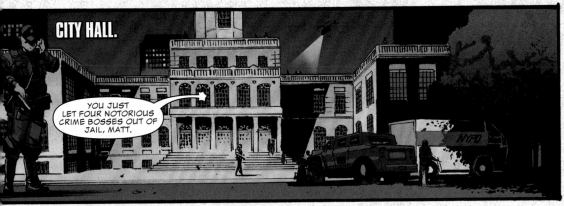

CITY HALL.

YOU JUST LET FOUR NOTORIOUS CRIME BOSSES OUT OF JAIL, MATT.

IT'S TOO BAD THE WHOLE CITY'S COMPLETELY LOCKED DOWN. I'D ACTUALLY BE FASCINATED TO SEE WHERE YOU'D LAND IN THE POLLS.

NINE PERCENT APPROVAL RATING? NAH, TOO HIGH. SIX PERCENT, TOPS.

THE OWL AND THE OTHERS AREN'T CRIME BOSSES, FOGGY, NOT RIGHT NOW.

RIGHT NOW, WE'RE AT WAR.

AND THEY'RE GENERALS.

BESIDES, I'M NOT PLANNING TO RUN FOR RE-ELECTION.

ELECTION.

WHATEVER.

SO YOU'RE SAYING IT'LL BE FISK'S PROBLEM DOWN THE ROAD. HOW IS GOOD OLD WILSON, BY THE WAY?

EH. I'VE BEEN A LITTLE BUSY, FOGGY.

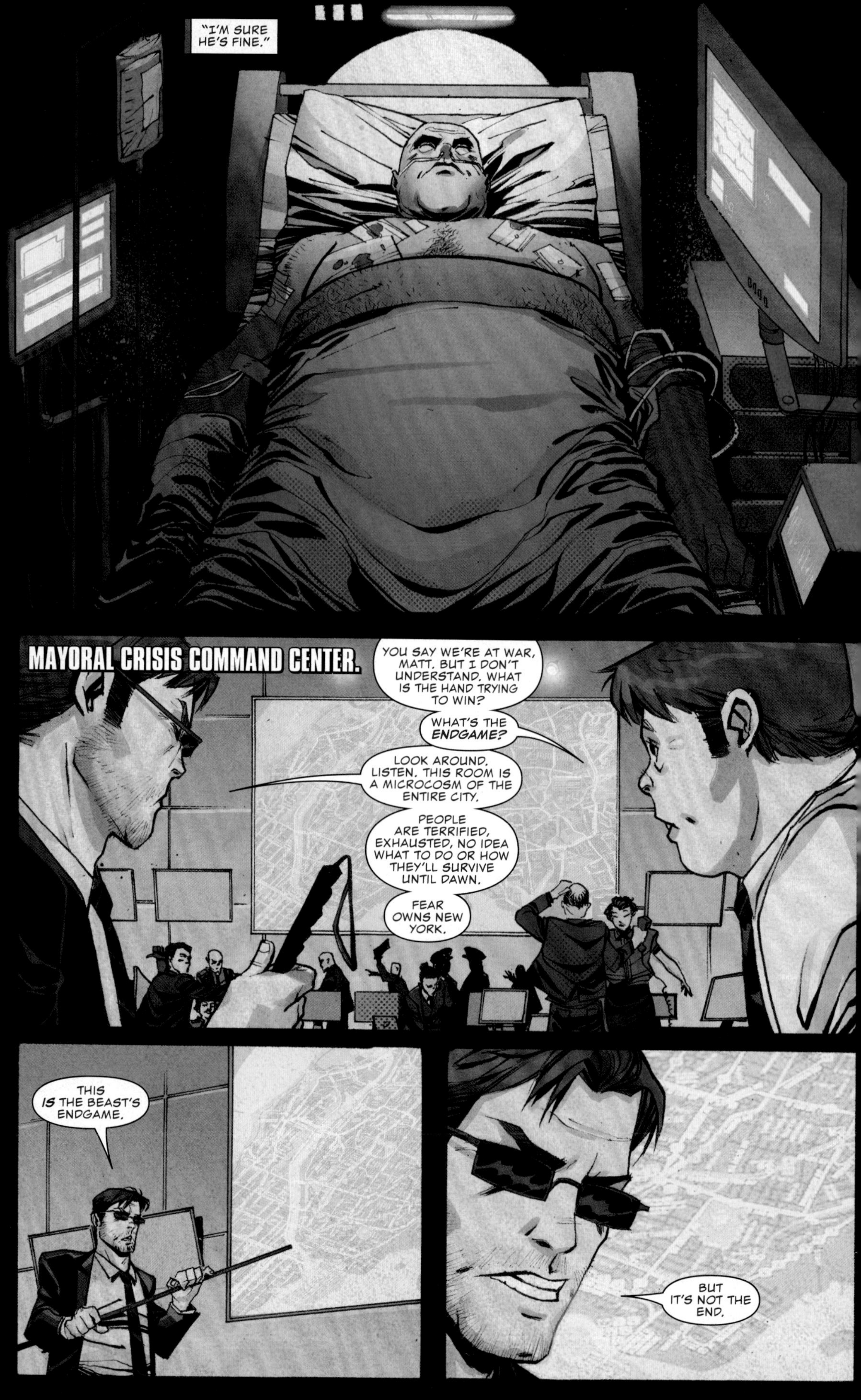
"I'M SURE HE'S FINE."
MAYORAL CRISIS COMMAND CENTER.
YOU SAY WE'RE AT WAR, MATT. BUT I DON'T UNDERSTAND. WHAT IS THE HAND TRYING TO WIN?
WHAT'S THE ENDGAME?
LOOK AROUND. LISTEN. THIS ROOM IS A MICROCOSM OF THE ENTIRE CITY.
PEOPLE ARE TERRIFIED, EXHAUSTED, NO IDEA WHAT TO DO OR HOW THEY'LL SURVIVE UNTIL DAWN.
FEAR OWNS NEW YORK.
THIS IS THE BEAST'S ENDGAME.
BUT IT'S NOT THE END.

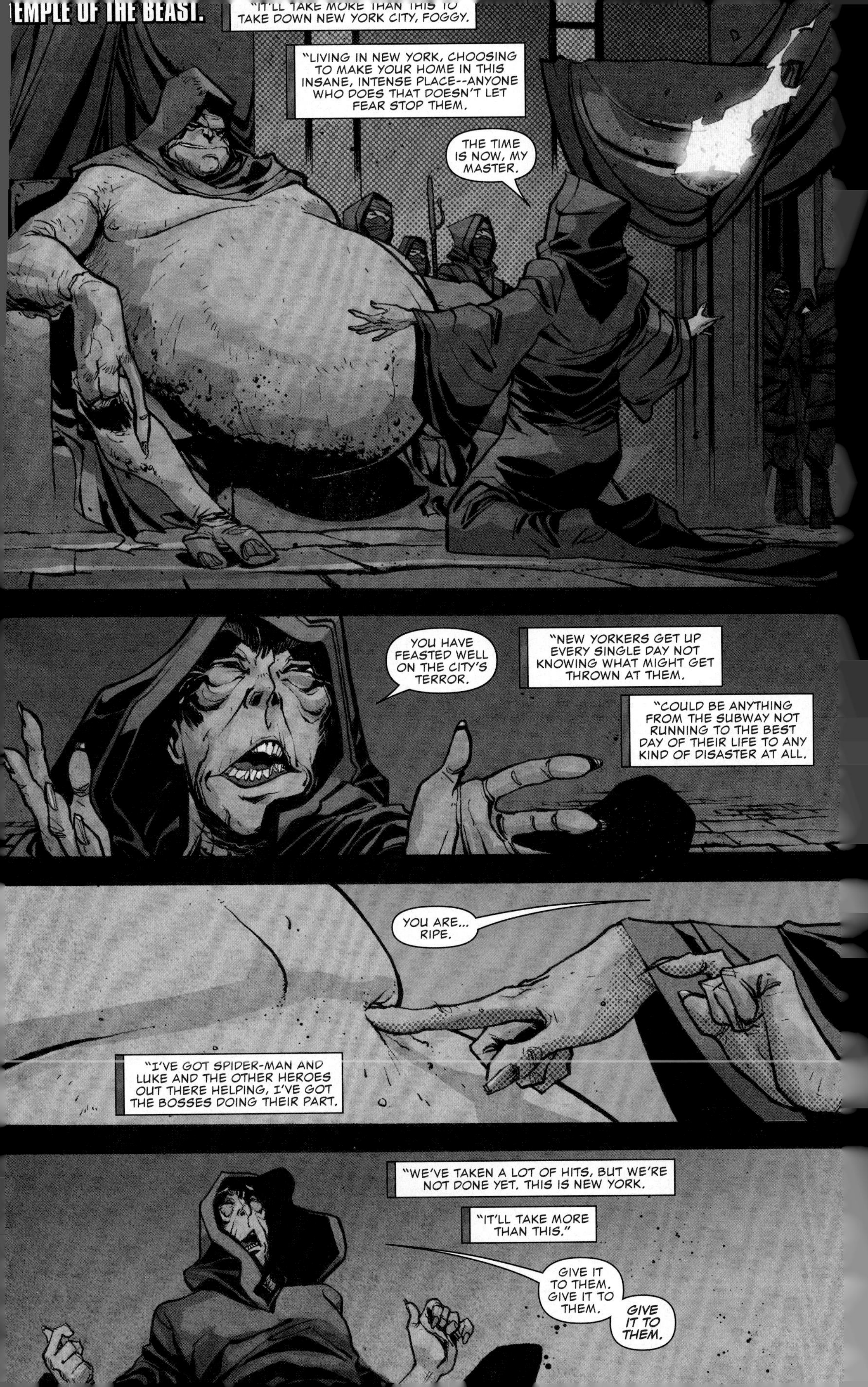
TEMPLE OF THE BEAST.
"IT'LL TAKE MORE THAN THIS TO TAKE DOWN NEW YORK CITY, FOGGY.
"LIVING IN NEW YORK, CHOOSING TO MAKE YOUR HOME IN THIS INSANE, INTENSE PLACE--ANYONE WHO DOES THAT DOESN'T LET FEAR STOP THEM.
THE TIME IS NOW, MY MASTER.
YOU HAVE FEASTED WELL ON THE CITY'S TERROR.
"NEW YORKERS GET UP EVERY SINGLE DAY NOT KNOWING WHAT MIGHT GET THROWN AT THEM.
"COULD BE ANYTHING FROM THE SUBWAY NOT RUNNING TO THE BEST DAY OF THEIR LIFE TO ANY KIND OF DISASTER AT ALL.
YOU ARE... RIPE.
"I'VE GOT SPIDER-MAN AND LUKE AND THE OTHER HEROES OUT THERE HELPING, I'VE GOT THE BOSSES DOING THEIR PART.
"WE'VE TAKEN A LOT OF HITS, BUT WE'RE NOT DONE YET. THIS IS NEW YORK.
"IT'LL TAKE MORE THAN THIS."
GIVE IT TO THEM. GIVE IT TO THEM.
GIVE IT TO THEM.

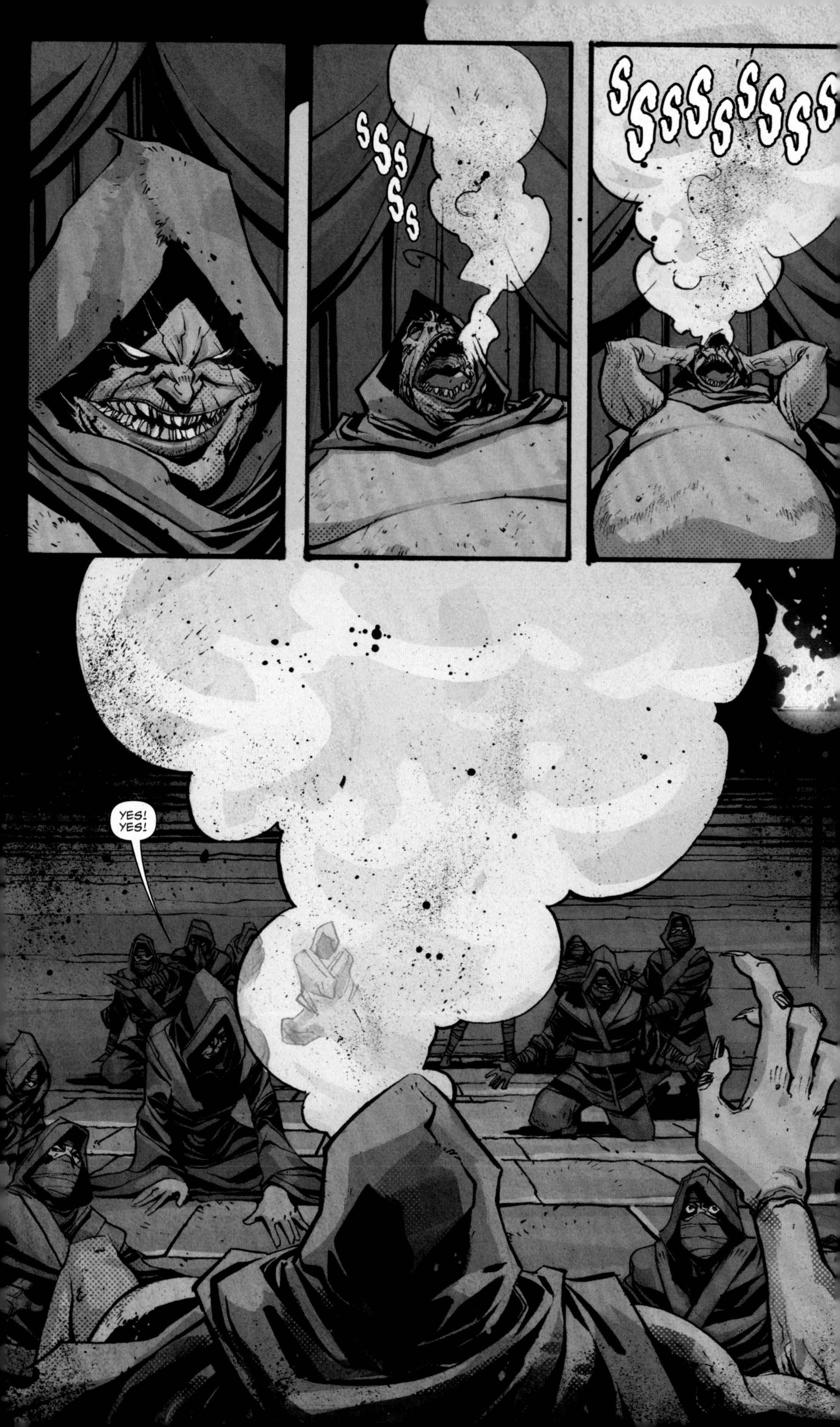
SSSSS
SSSSSSSSSSS
YES! YES!

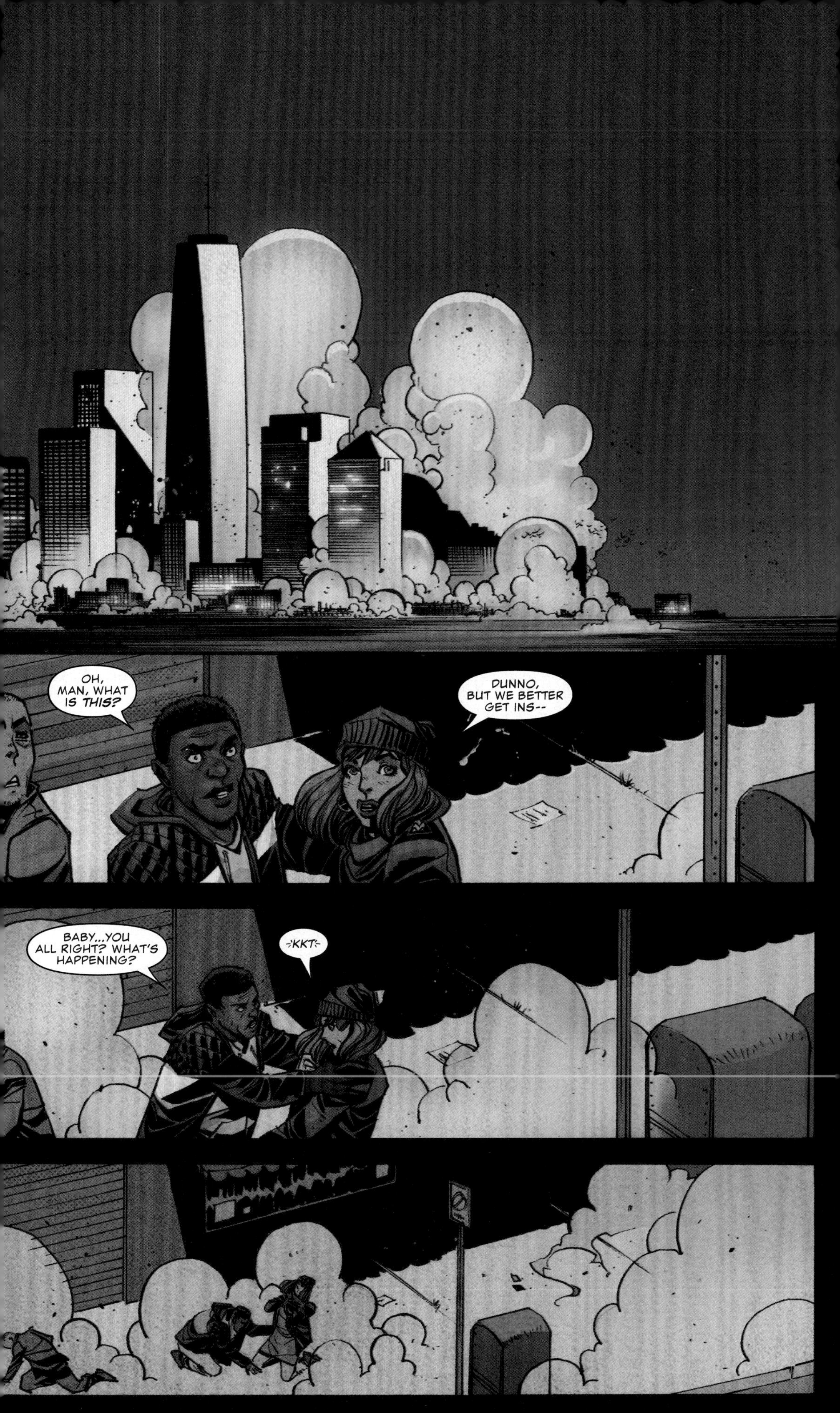
OH, MAN, WHAT IS THIS?
DUNNO, BUT WE BETTER GET INS--
BABY...YOU ALL RIGHT? WHAT'S HAPPENING?
KKT

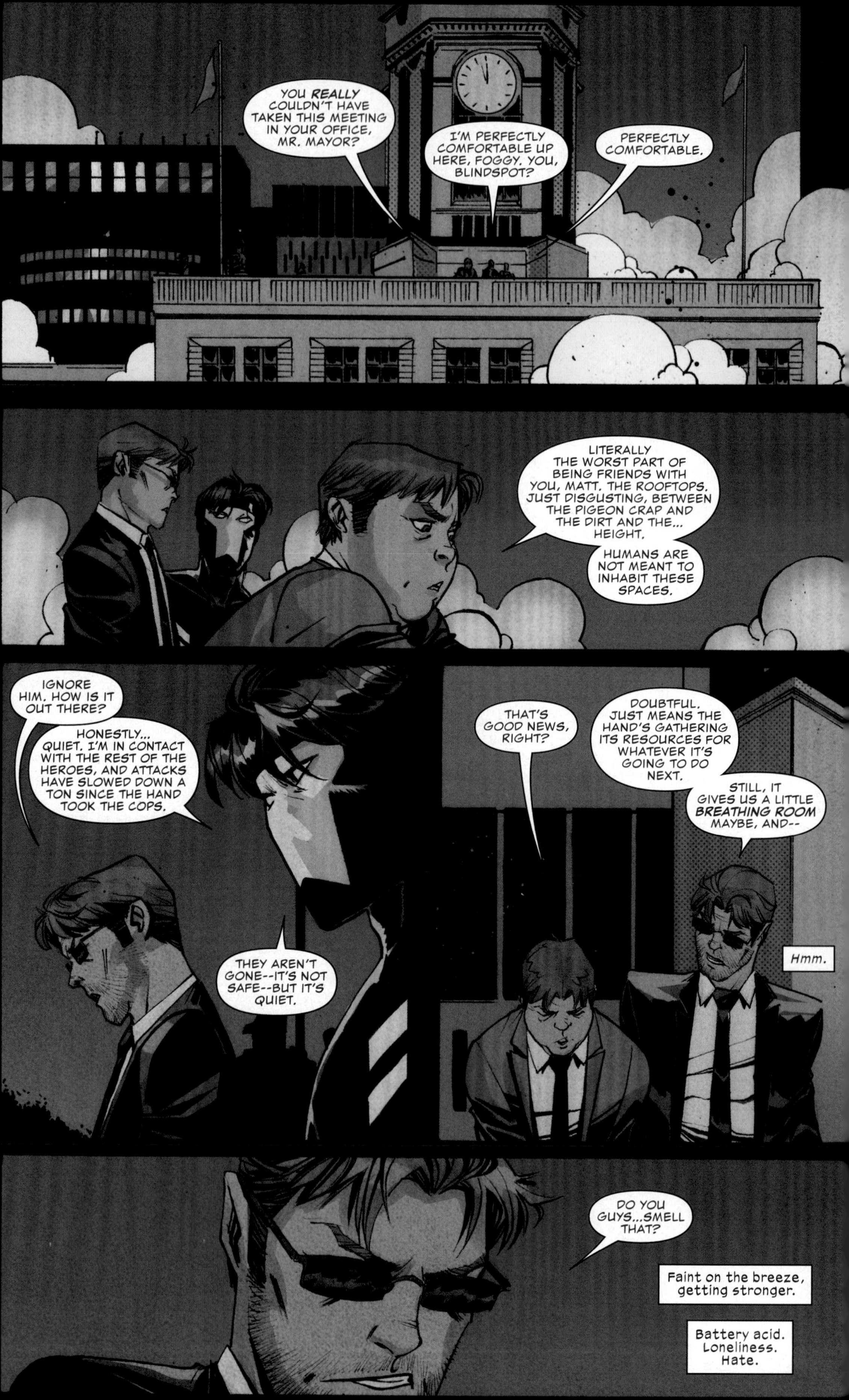
YOU REALLY COULDN'T HAVE TAKEN THIS MEETING IN YOUR OFFICE, MR. MAYOR?
I'M PERFECTLY COMFORTABLE UP HERE, FOGGY. YOU, BLINDSPOT?
PERFECTLY COMFORTABLE.
LITERALLY THE WORST PART OF BEING FRIENDS WITH YOU, MATT. THE ROOFTOPS. JUST DISGUSTING, BETWEEN THE PIGEON CRAP AND THE DIRT AND THE... HEIGHT.
HUMANS ARE NOT MEANT TO INHABIT THESE SPACES.
IGNORE HIM. HOW IS IT OUT THERE?
HONESTLY... QUIET. I'M IN CONTACT WITH THE REST OF THE HEROES, AND ATTACKS HAVE SLOWED DOWN A TON SINCE THE HAND TOOK THE COPS.
THEY AREN'T GONE--IT'S NOT SAFE--BUT IT'S QUIET.
THAT'S GOOD NEWS, RIGHT?
DOUBTFUL. JUST MEANS THE HAND'S GATHERING ITS RESOURCES FOR WHATEVER IT'S GOING TO DO NEXT.
STILL, IT GIVES US A LITTLE BREATHING ROOM MAYBE, AND--
Hmm.
DO YOU GUYS...SMELL THAT?
Faint on the breeze, getting stronger.
Battery acid. Loneliness. Hate.

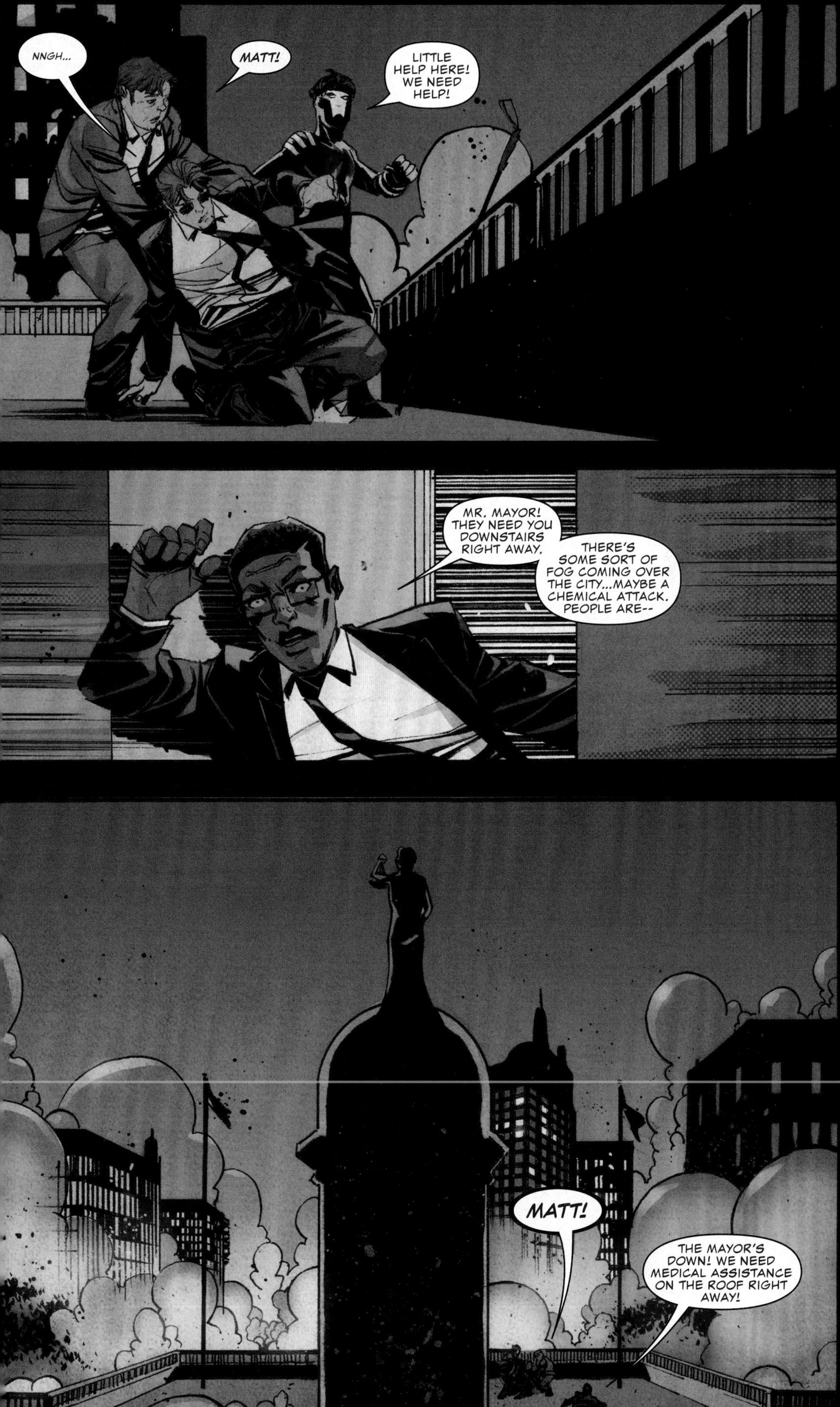
NNGH...
MATT!
LITTLE HELP HERE! WE NEED HELP!
MR. MAYOR! THEY NEED YOU DOWNSTAIRS RIGHT AWAY.
THERE'S SOME SORT OF FOG COMING OVER THE CITY...MAYBE A CHEMICAL ATTACK. PEOPLE ARE--
MATT!
THE MAYOR'S DOWN! WE NEED MEDICAL ASSISTANCE ON THE ROOF RIGHT AWAY!

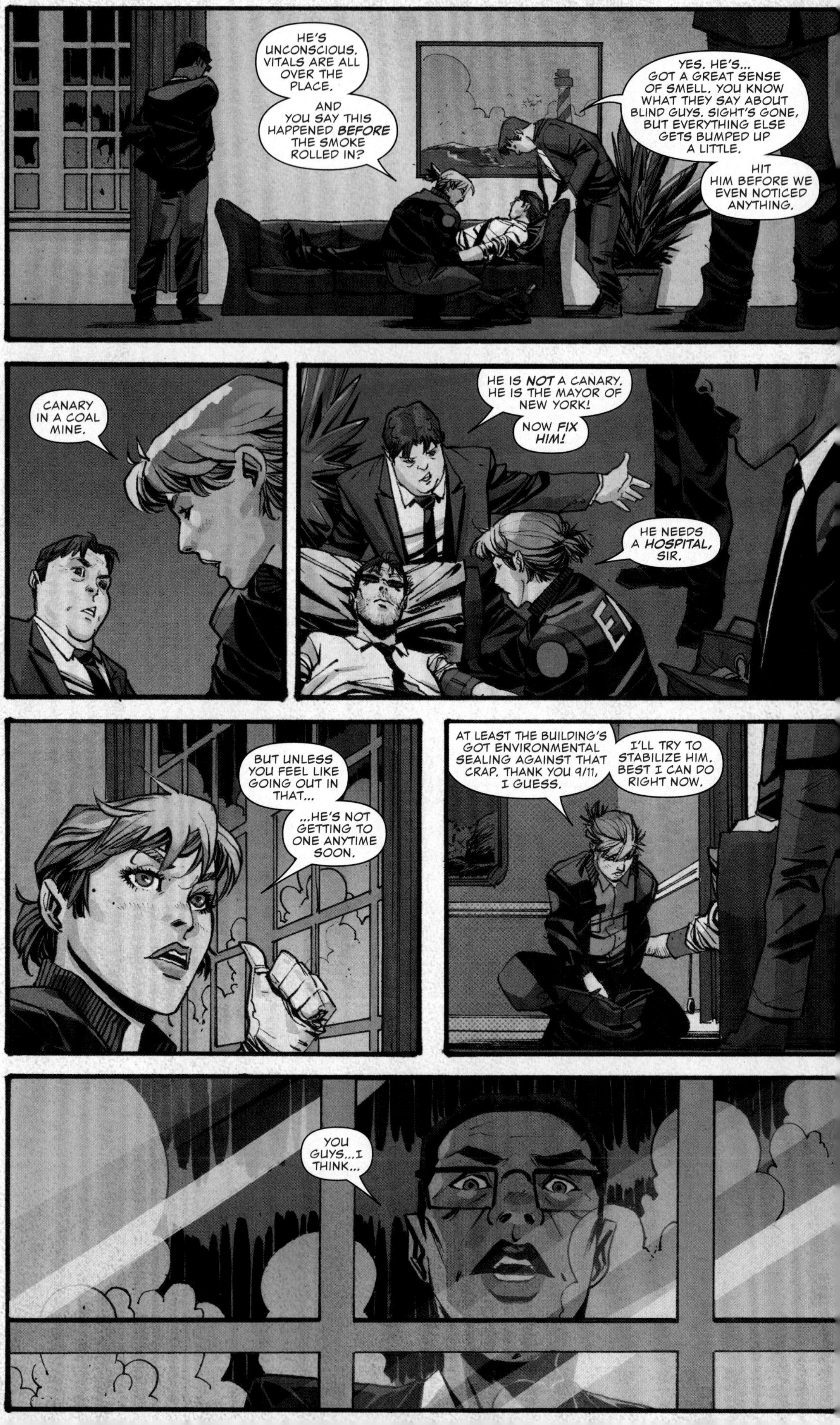
HE'S UNCONSCIOUS. VITALS ARE ALL OVER THE PLACE.
AND YOU SAY THIS HAPPENED BEFORE THE SMOKE ROLLED IN?
YES. HE'S... GOT A GREAT SENSE OF SMELL. YOU KNOW WHAT THEY SAY ABOUT BLIND GUYS. SIGHT'S GONE, BUT EVERYTHING ELSE GETS BUMPED UP A LITTLE.
HIT HIM BEFORE WE EVEN NOTICED ANYTHING.
CANARY IN A COAL MINE.
HE IS NOT A CANARY. HE IS THE MAYOR OF NEW YORK!
NOW FIX HIM!
HE NEEDS A HOSPITAL, SIR.
BUT UNLESS YOU FEEL LIKE GOING OUT IN THAT...
...HE'S NOT GETTING TO ONE ANYTIME SOON.
AT LEAST THE BUILDING'S GOT ENVIRONMENTAL SEALING AGAINST THAT CRAP. THANK YOU 9/11, I GUESS.
I'LL TRY TO STABILIZE HIM. BEST I CAN DO RIGHT NOW.
YOU GUYS...I THINK...

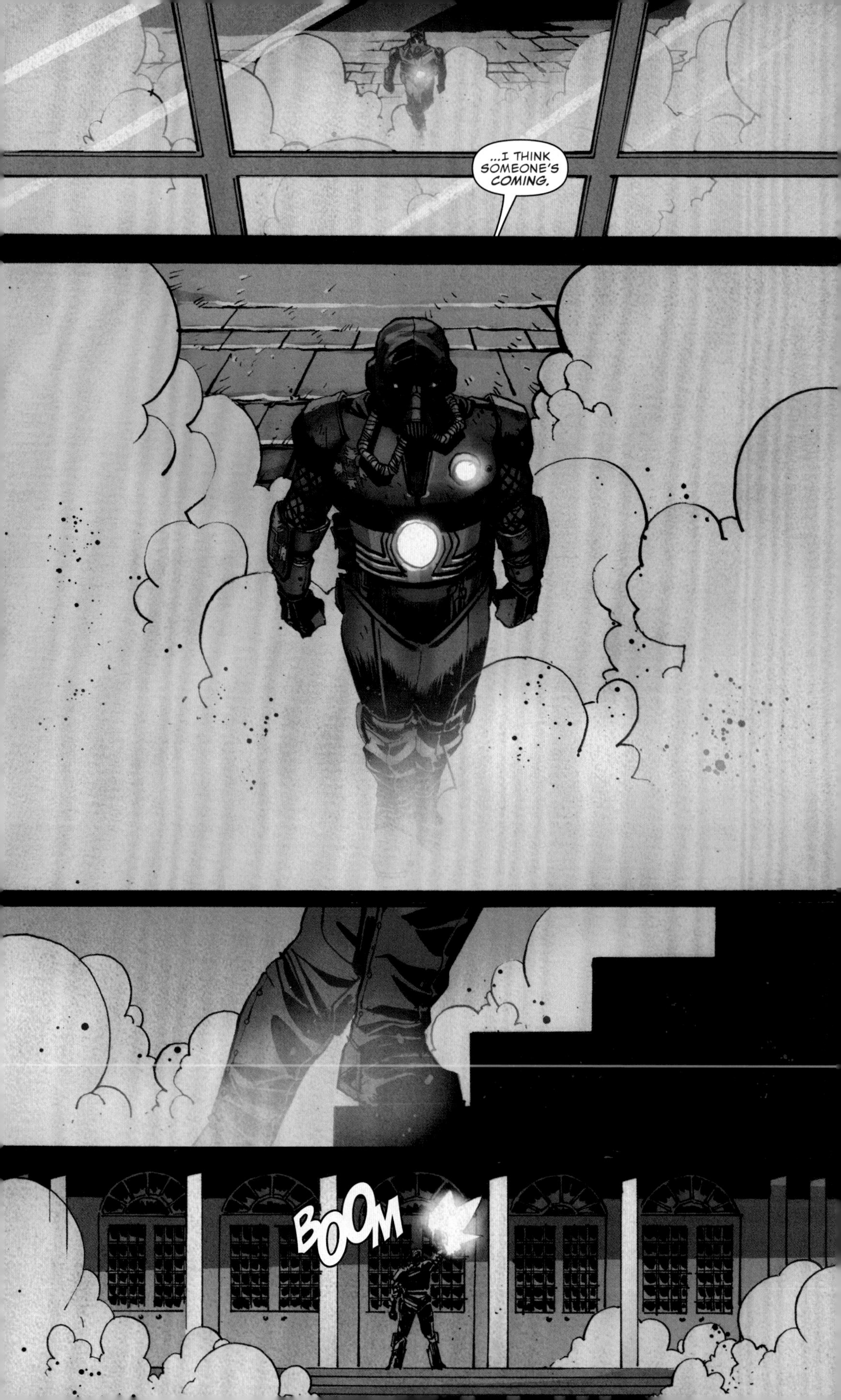
...I THINK SOMEONE'S COMING.
BOOM

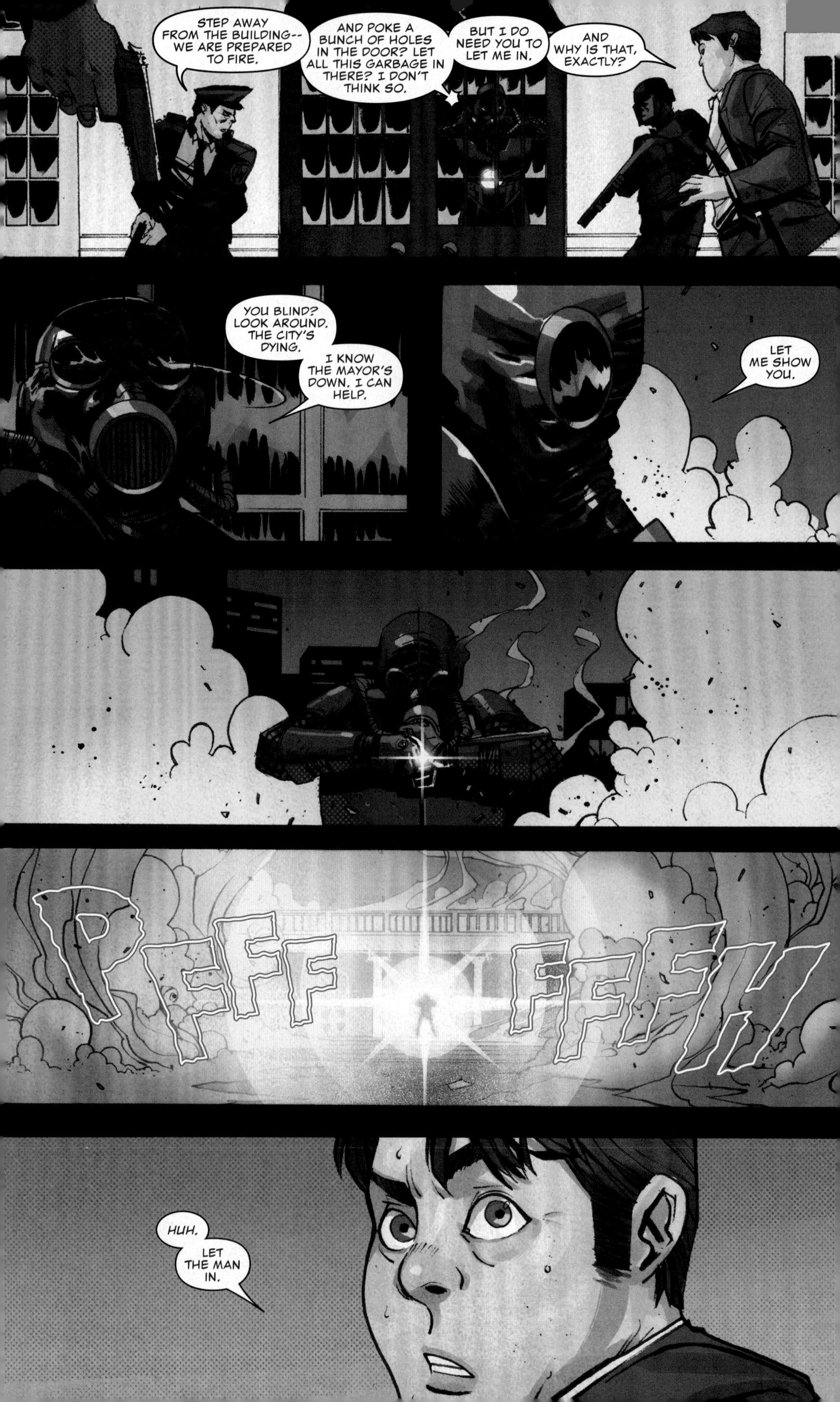

STEP AWAY FROM THE BUILDING-- WE ARE PREPARED TO FIRE.
AND POKE A BUNCH OF HOLES IN THE DOOR? LET ALL THIS GARBAGE IN THERE? I DON'T THINK SO.
BUT I DO NEED YOU TO LET ME IN.
AND WHY IS THAT, EXACTLY?
YOU BLIND? LOOK AROUND. THE CITY'S DYING.
I KNOW THE MAYOR'S DOWN. I CAN HELP.
LET ME SHOW YOU.
PFFF FFFFH
HUH.
LET THE MAN IN.

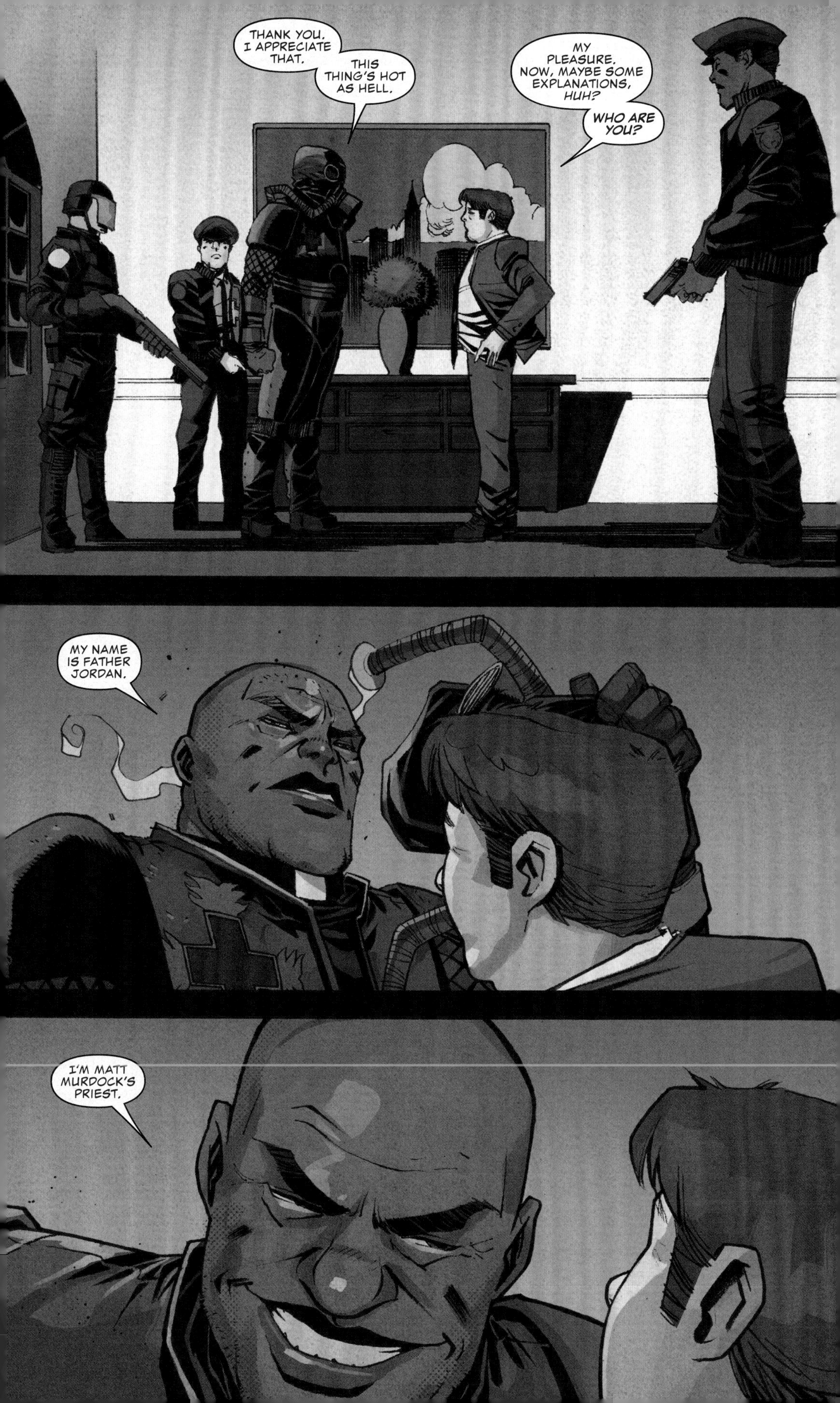
THANK YOU. I APPRECIATE THAT.
THIS THING'S HOT AS HELL.
MY PLEASURE. NOW, MAYBE SOME EXPLANATIONS, HUH?
WHO ARE YOU?
MY NAME IS FATHER JORDAN.
I'M MATT MURDOCK'S PRIEST.

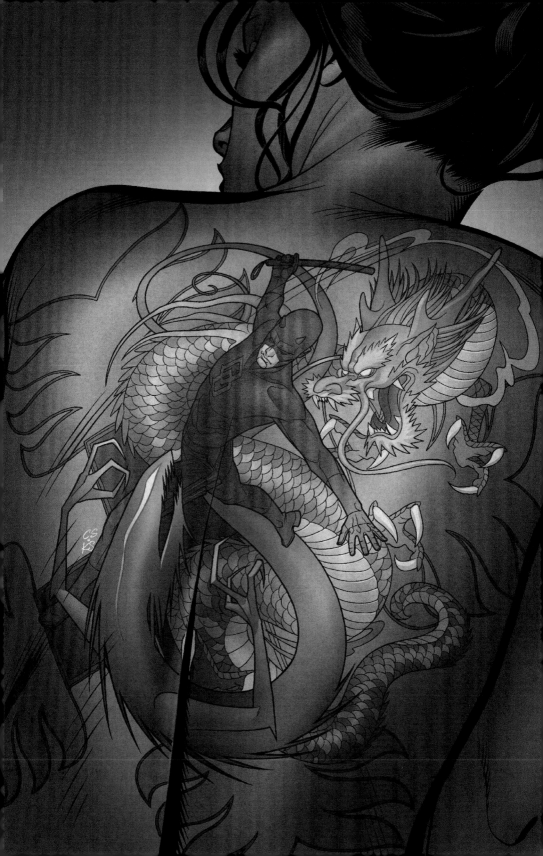

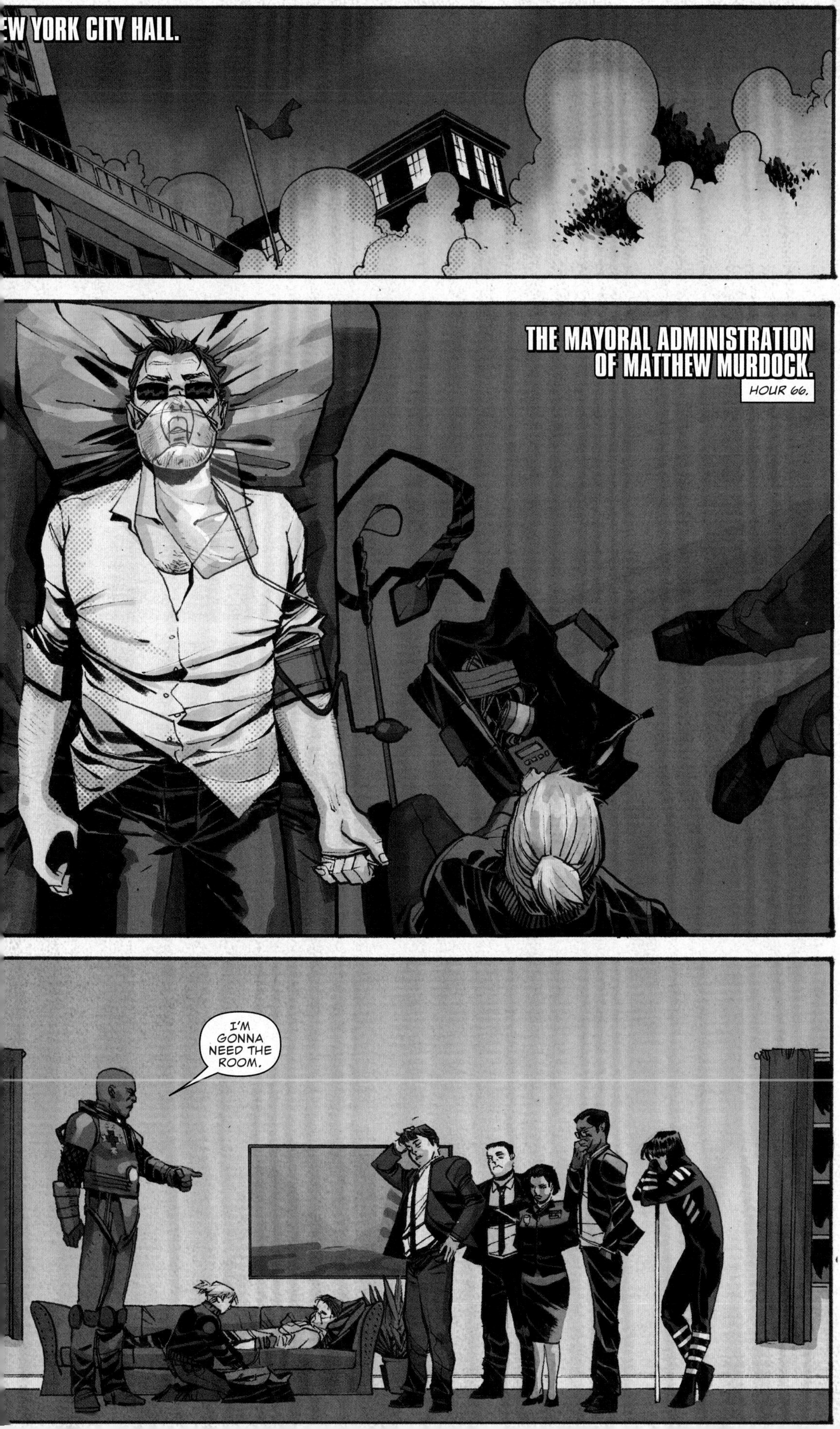
EW YORK CITY HALL.
THE MAYORAL ADMINISTRATION OF MATTHEW MURDOCK.
HOUR 66.
I'M GONNA NEED THE ROOM.

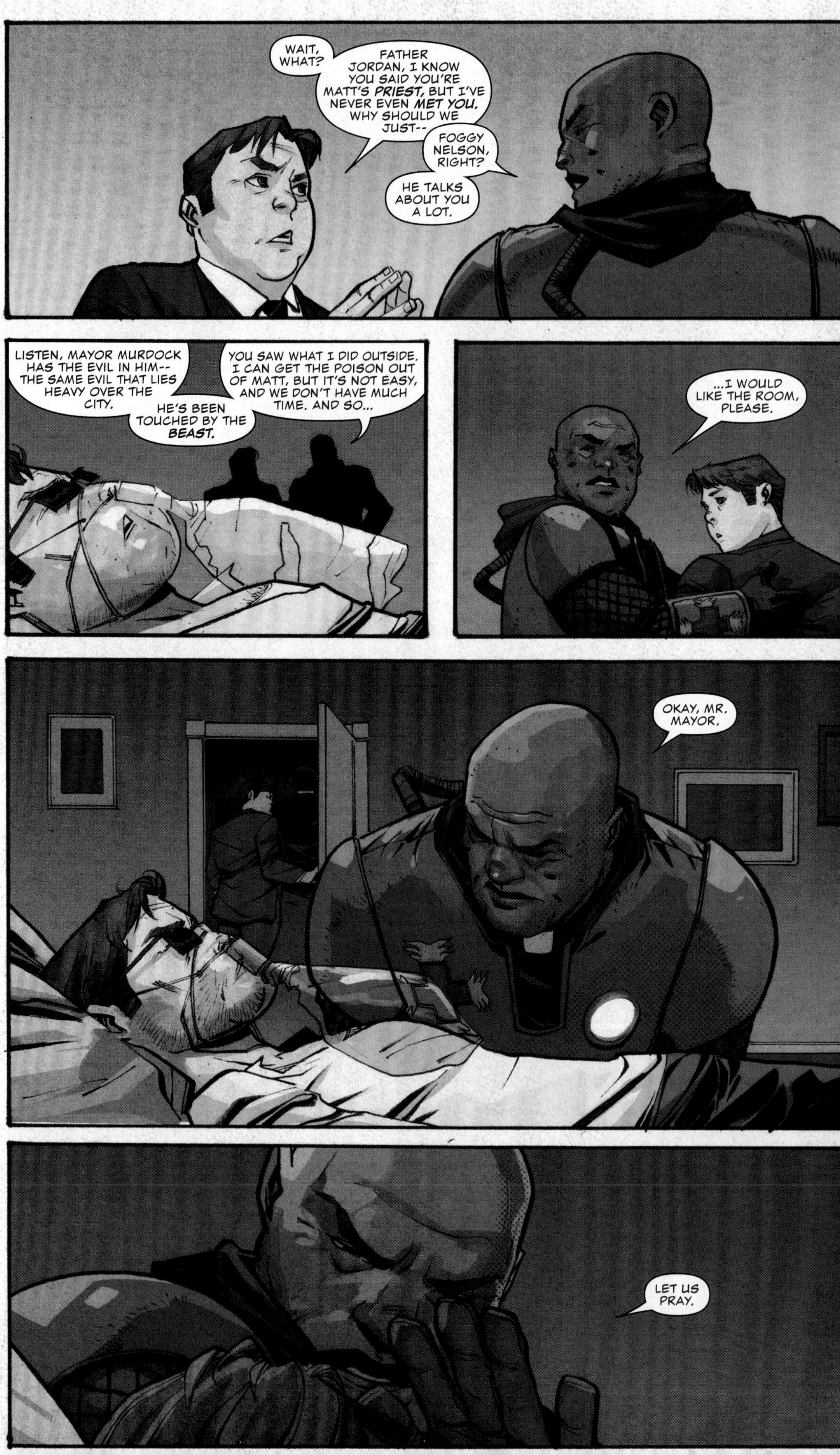
WAIT, WHAT?
FATHER JORDAN, I KNOW YOU SAID YOU'RE MATT'S PRIEST, BUT I'VE NEVER EVEN MET YOU. WHY SHOULD WE JUST--
FOGGY NELSON, RIGHT?
HE TALKS ABOUT YOU A LOT.
LISTEN, MAYOR MURDOCK HAS THE EVIL IN HIM-- THE SAME EVIL THAT LIES HEAVY OVER THE CITY.
HE'S BEEN TOUCHED BY THE BEAST.
YOU SAW WHAT I DID OUTSIDE. I CAN GET THE POISON OUT OF MATT, BUT IT'S NOT EASY, AND WE DON'T HAVE MUCH TIME. AND SO...
...I WOULD LIKE THE ROOM, PLEASE.
OKAY, MR. MAYOR.
LET US PRAY.

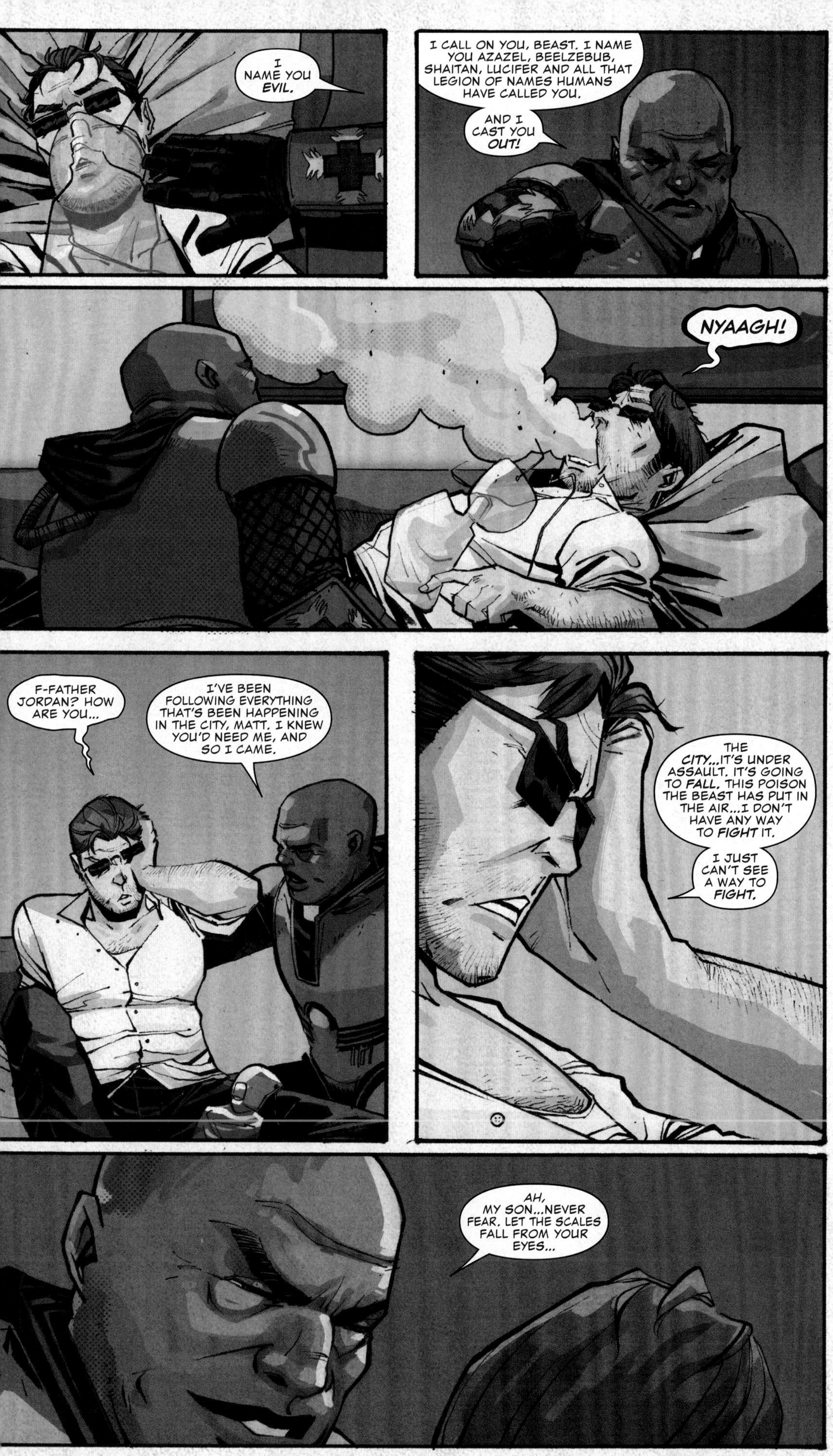

I NAME YOU EVIL.
I CALL ON YOU, BEAST. I NAME YOU AZAZEL, BEELZEBUB, SHAITAN, LUCIFER AND ALL THAT LEGION OF NAMES HUMANS HAVE CALLED YOU.
AND I CAST YOU OUT!
NYAAGH!
F-FATHER JORDAN? HOW ARE YOU...
I'VE BEEN FOLLOWING EVERYTHING THAT'S BEEN HAPPENING IN THE CITY, MATT. I KNEW YOU'D NEED ME, AND SO I CAME.
THE CITY...IT'S UNDER ASSAULT. IT'S GOING TO FALL. THIS POISON THE BEAST HAS PUT IN THE AIR...I DON'T HAVE ANY WAY TO FIGHT IT.
I JUST CAN'T SEE A WAY TO FIGHT.
AH, MY SON...NEVER FEAR. LET THE SCALES FALL FROM YOUR EYES...

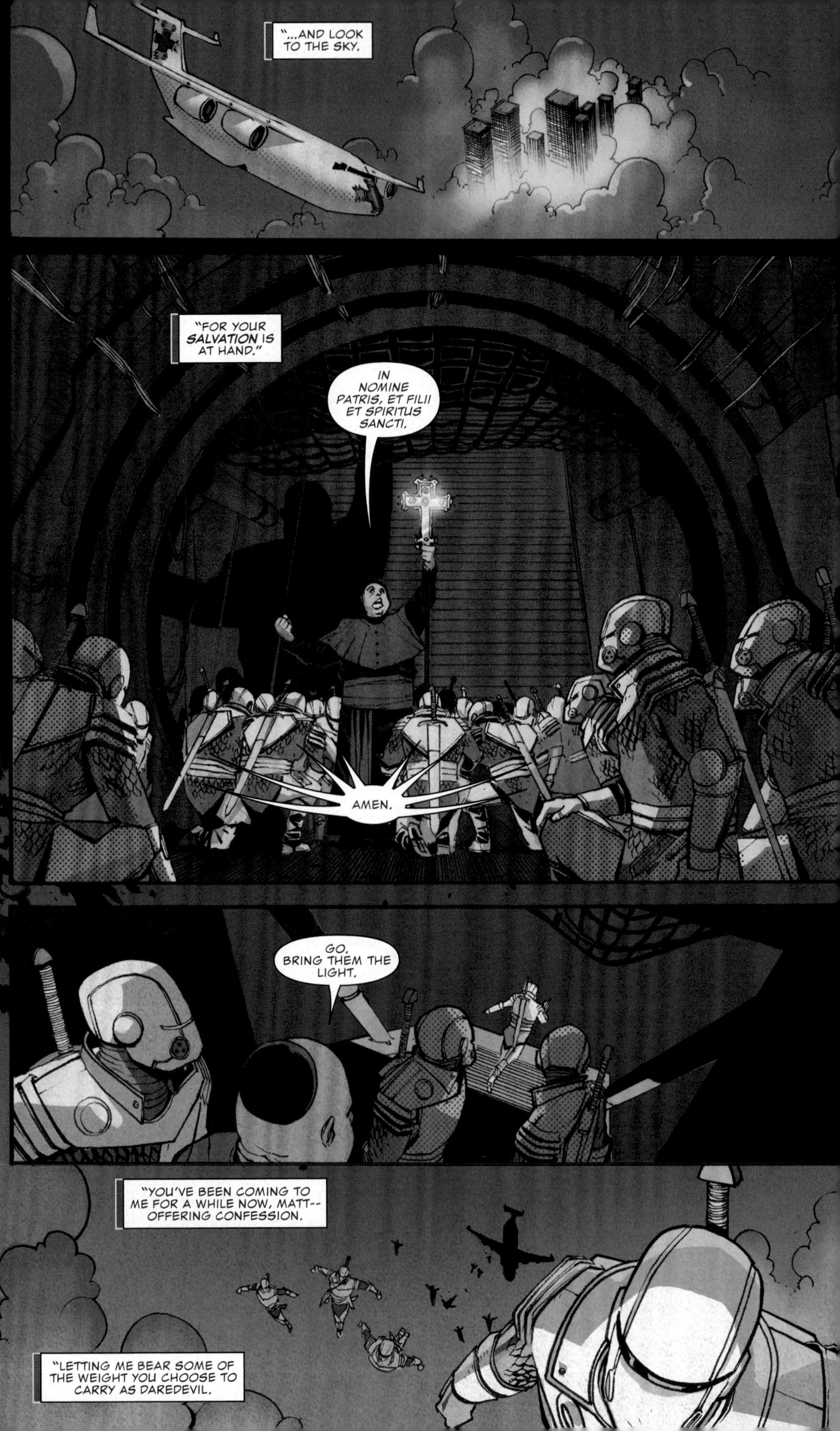
"...AND LOOK TO THE SKY.
"FOR YOUR SALVATION IS AT HAND."
IN NOMINE PATRIS, ET FILII ET SPIRITUS SANCTI.
AMEN.
GO. BRING THEM THE LIGHT.
"YOU'VE BEEN COMING TO ME FOR A WHILE NOW, MATT--OFFERING CONFESSION.
"LETTING ME BEAR SOME OF THE WEIGHT YOU CHOOSE TO CARRY AS DAREDEVIL.

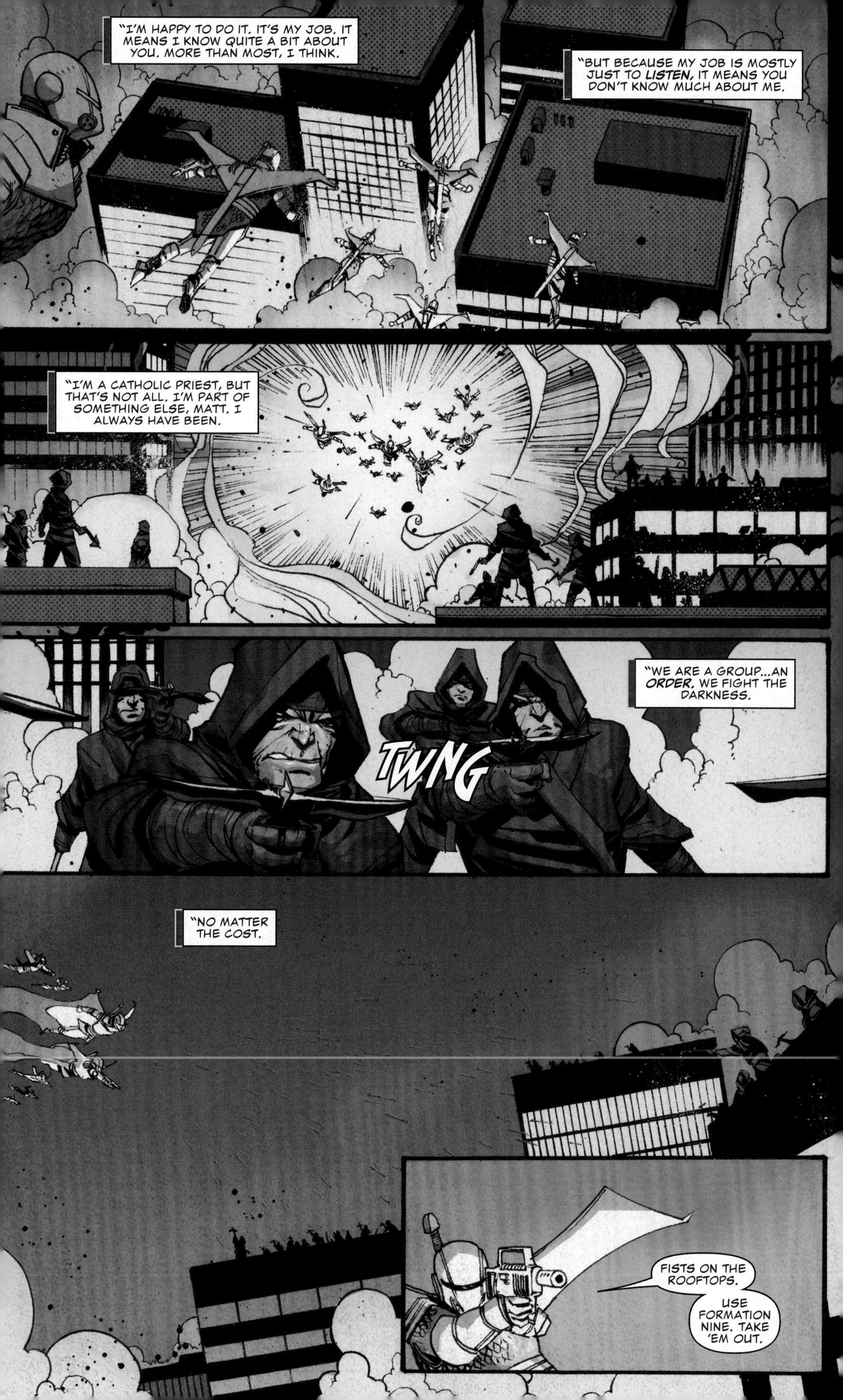
"I'M HAPPY TO DO IT. IT'S MY JOB. IT MEANS I KNOW QUITE A BIT ABOUT YOU. MORE THAN MOST, I THINK.
"BUT BECAUSE MY JOB IS MOSTLY JUST TO LISTEN, IT MEANS YOU DON'T KNOW MUCH ABOUT ME.
"I'M A CATHOLIC PRIEST, BUT THAT'S NOT ALL. I'M PART OF SOMETHING ELSE, MATT. I ALWAYS HAVE BEEN.
"WE ARE A GROUP...AN ORDER. WE FIGHT THE DARKNESS.
TWNG
"NO MATTER THE COST.
FISTS ON THE ROOFTOPS.
USE FORMATION NINE. TAKE 'EM OUT.

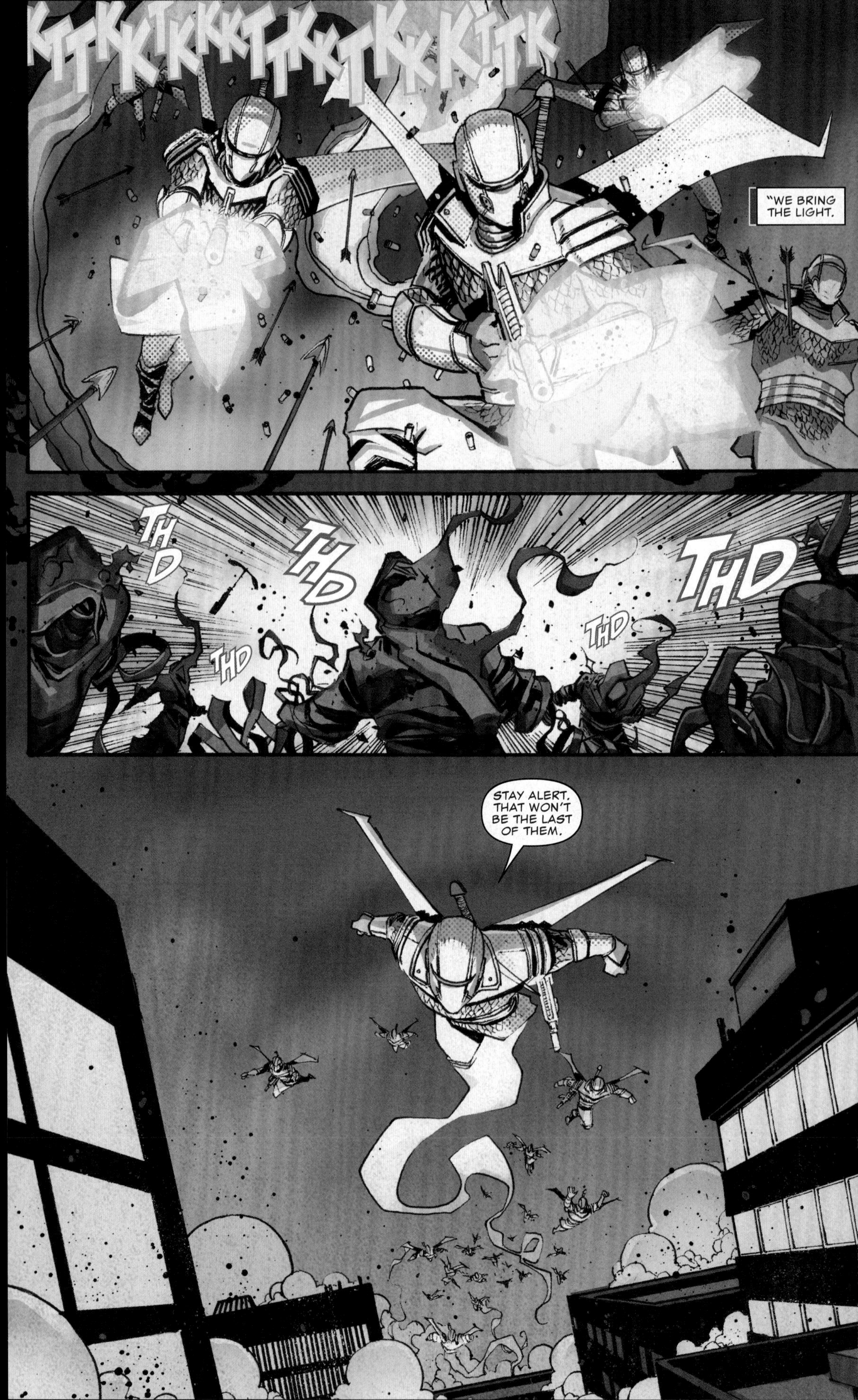
KTTKKTKKKTTKKTKKTTK
"WE BRING THE LIGHT.
THD
THD
THD
THD
THD
STAY ALERT. THAT WON'T BE THE LAST OF THEM.

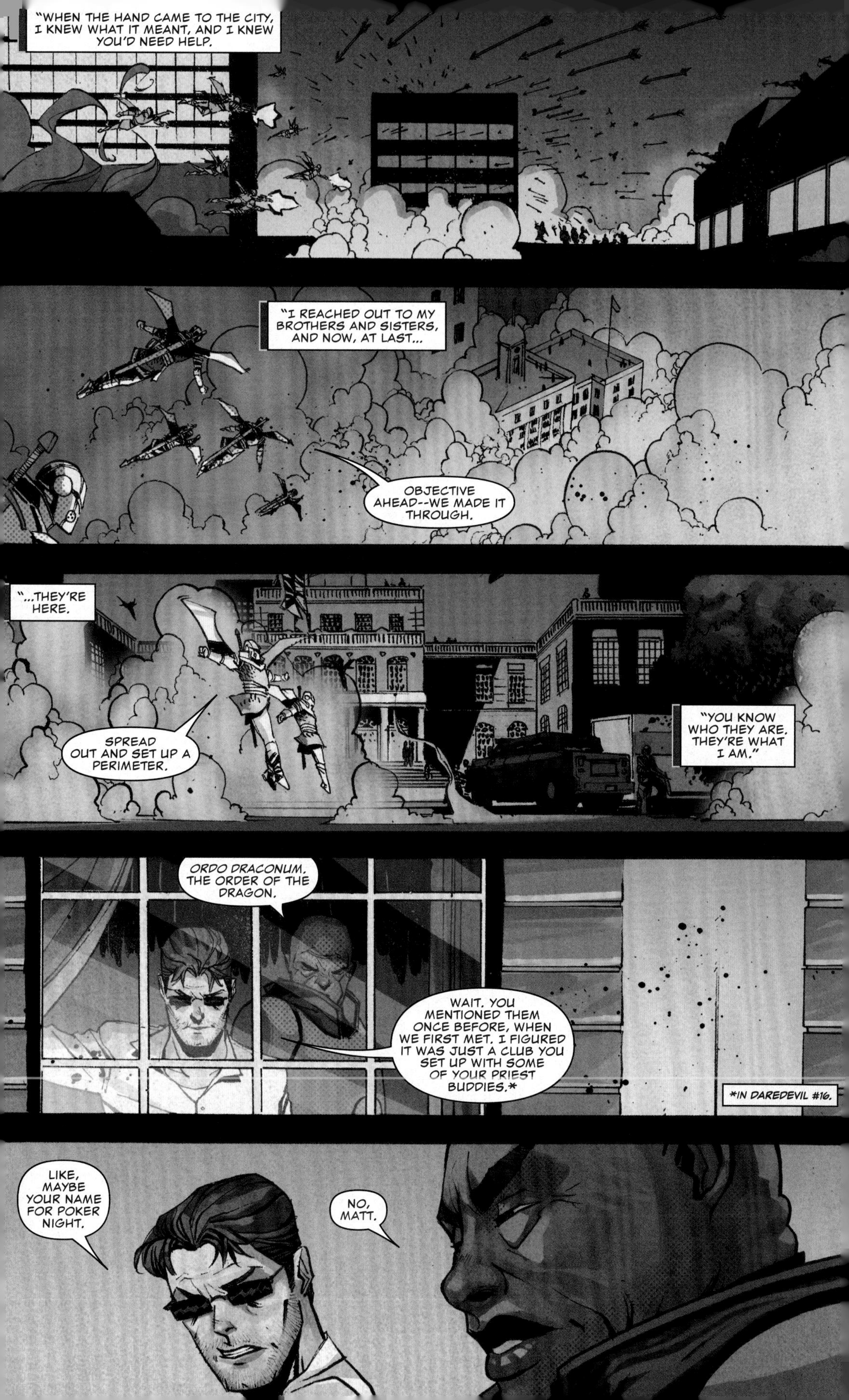
"WHEN THE HAND CAME TO THE CITY, I KNEW WHAT IT MEANT, AND I KNEW YOU'D NEED HELP.
"I REACHED OUT TO MY BROTHERS AND SISTERS, AND NOW, AT LAST...
OBJECTIVE AHEAD--WE MADE IT THROUGH.
"...THEY'RE HERE.
SPREAD OUT AND SET UP A PERIMETER.
"YOU KNOW WHO THEY ARE. THEY'RE WHAT I AM."
ORDO DRACONUM. THE ORDER OF THE DRAGON.
WAIT. YOU MENTIONED THEM ONCE BEFORE, WHEN WE FIRST MET. I FIGURED IT WAS JUST A CLUB YOU SET UP WITH SOME OF YOUR PRIEST BUDDIES.*
*IN DAREDEVIL #16.
LIKE, MAYBE YOUR NAME FOR POKER NIGHT.
NO, MATT.

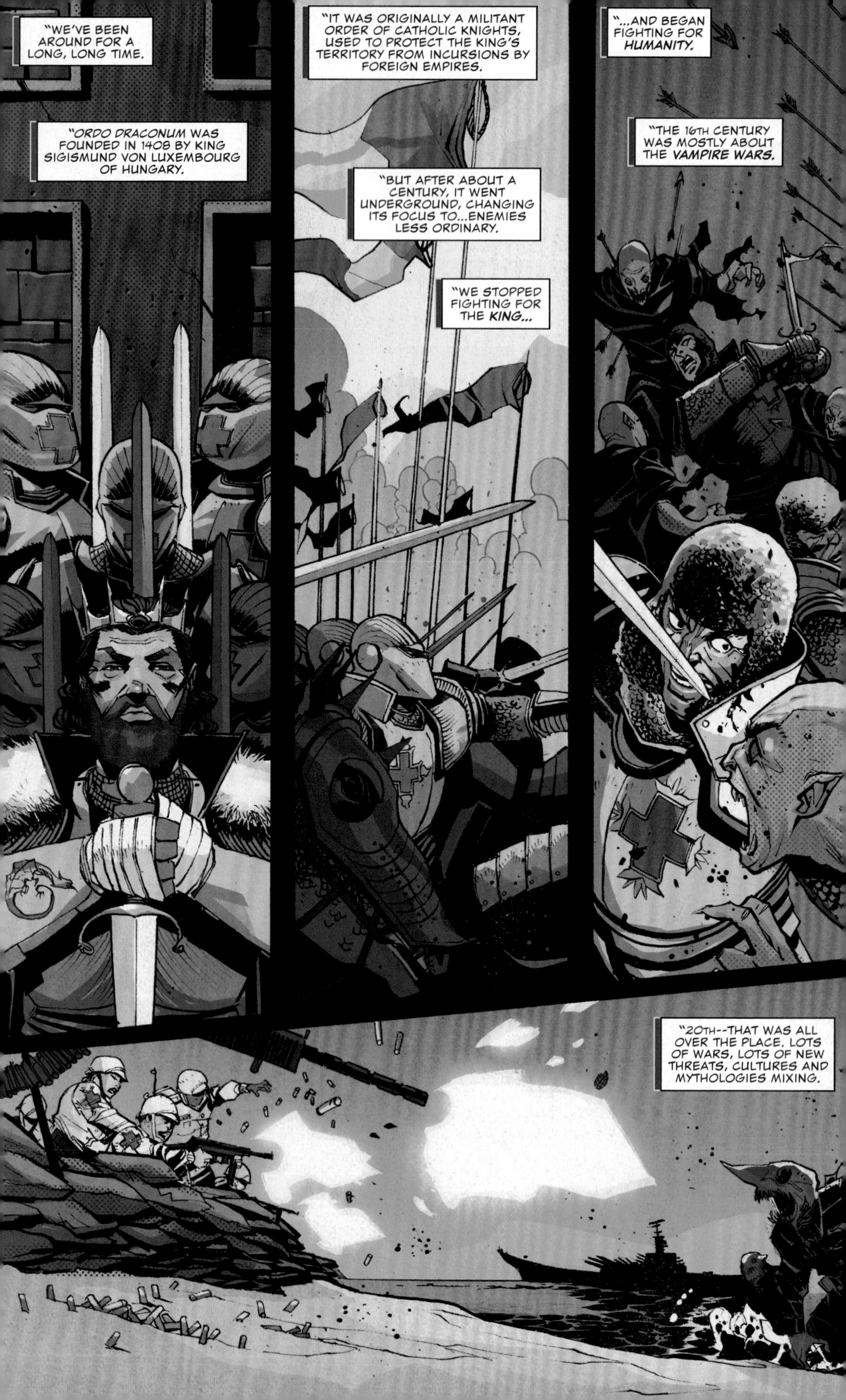
"WE'VE BEEN AROUND FOR A LONG, LONG TIME.
"ORDO DRACONUM WAS FOUNDED IN 1408 BY KING SIGISMUND VON LUXEMBOURG OF HUNGARY.
"IT WAS ORIGINALLY A MILITANT ORDER OF CATHOLIC KNIGHTS, USED TO PROTECT THE KING'S TERRITORY FROM INCURSIONS BY FOREIGN EMPIRES.
"BUT AFTER ABOUT A CENTURY, IT WENT UNDERGROUND, CHANGING ITS FOCUS TO...ENEMIES LESS ORDINARY.
"WE STOPPED FIGHTING FOR THE KING...
"...AND BEGAN FIGHTING FOR HUMANITY.
"THE 16TH CENTURY WAS MOSTLY ABOUT THE VAMPIRE WARS.
"20TH--THAT WAS ALL OVER THE PLACE. LOTS OF WARS, LOTS OF NEW THREATS, CULTURES AND MYTHOLOGIES MIXING.

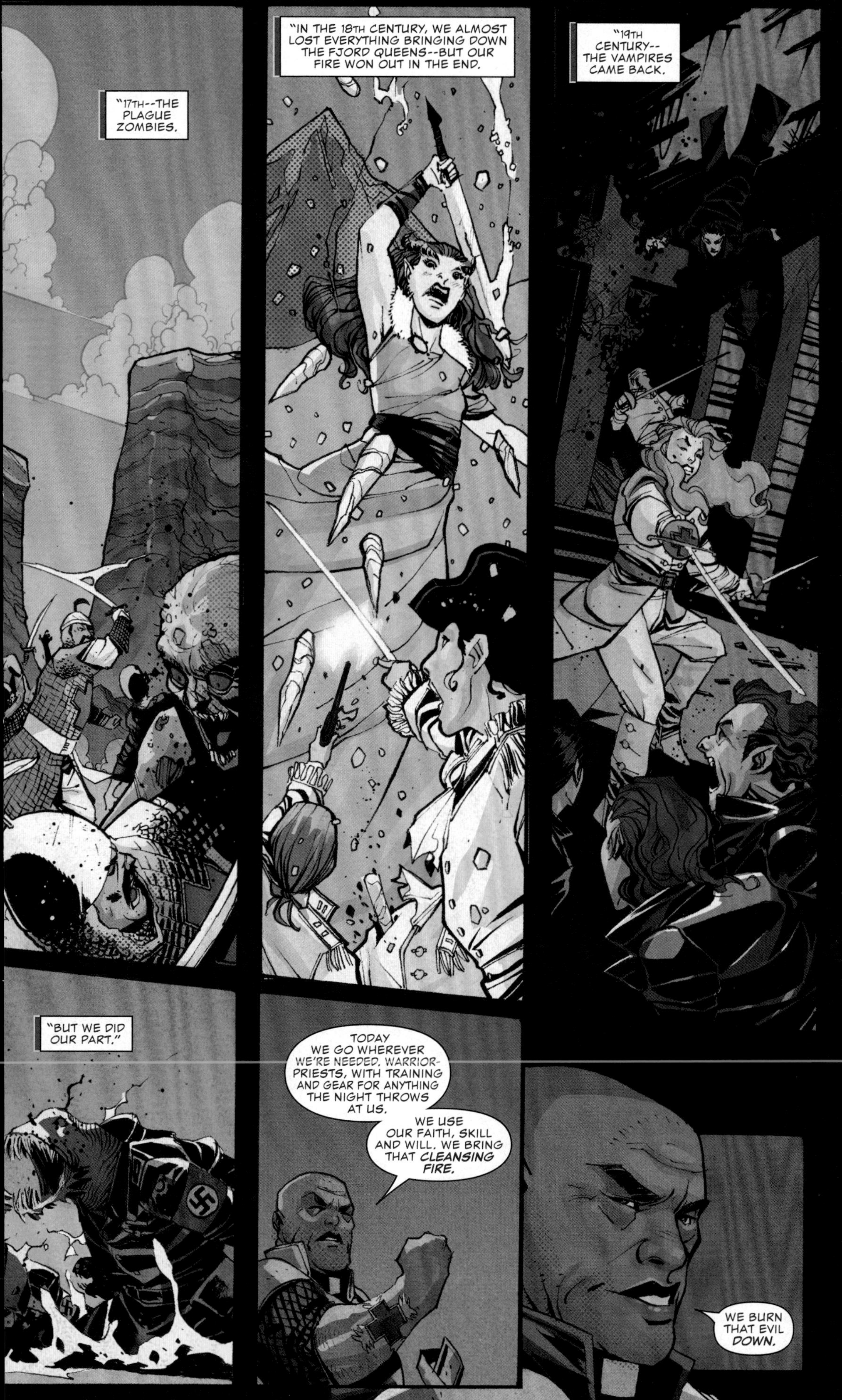
"17TH--THE PLAGUE ZOMBIES.
"IN THE 18TH CENTURY, WE ALMOST LOST EVERYTHING BRINGING DOWN THE FJORD QUEENS--BUT OUR FIRE WON OUT IN THE END.
"19TH CENTURY-- THE VAMPIRES CAME BACK.
"BUT WE DID OUR PART."
TODAY WE GO WHEREVER WE'RE NEEDED, WARRIOR-PRIESTS, WITH TRAINING AND GEAR FOR ANYTHING THE NIGHT THROWS AT US.
WE USE OUR FAITH, SKILL AND WILL. WE BRING THAT *CLEANSING FIRE.*
WE BURN THAT EVIL *DOWN.*

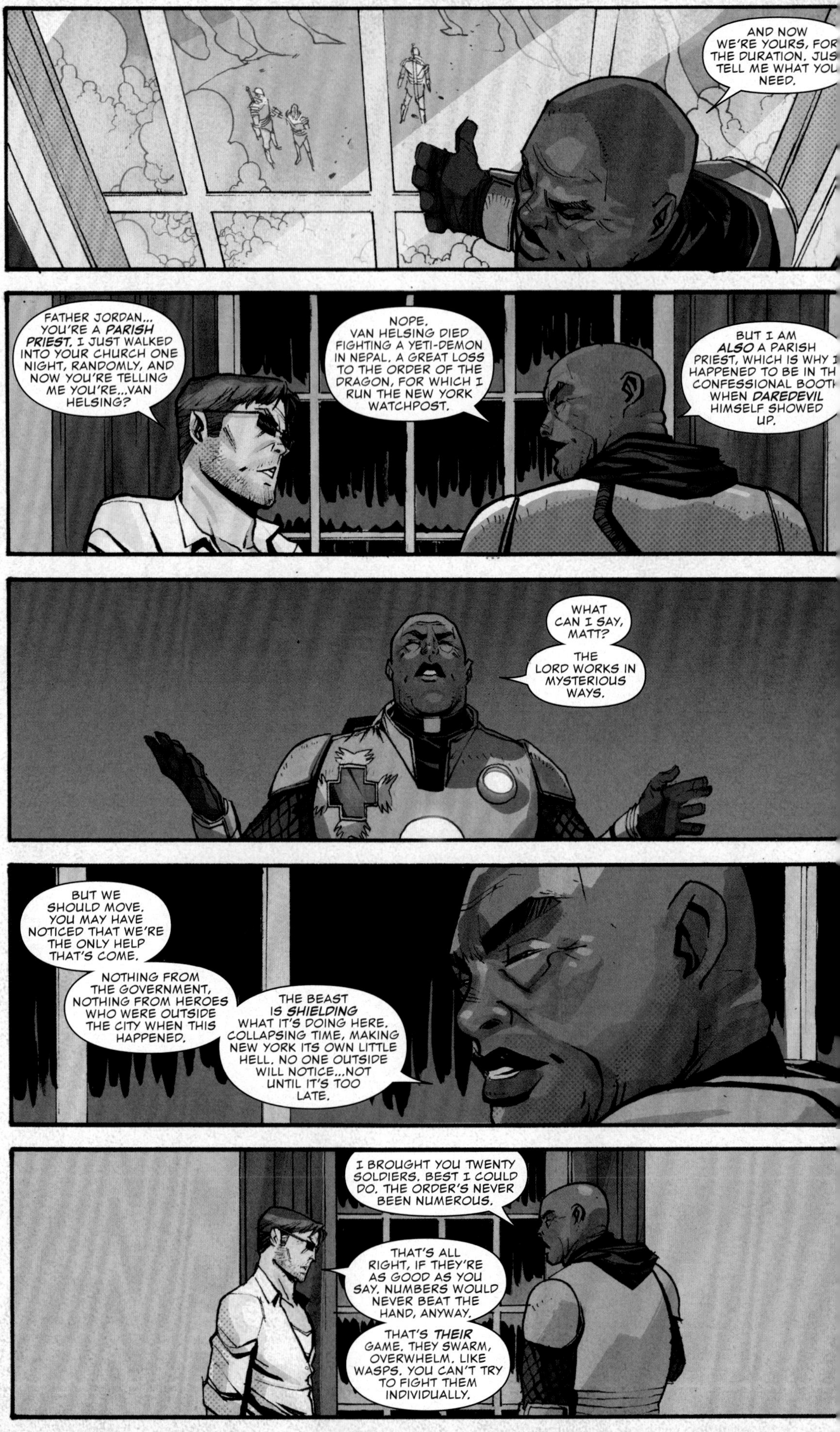

AND NOW WE'RE YOURS, FOR THE DURATION. JUS TELL ME WHAT YOU NEED.
FATHER JORDAN... YOU'RE A PARISH PRIEST. I JUST WALKED INTO YOUR CHURCH ONE NIGHT, RANDOMLY, AND NOW YOU'RE TELLING ME YOU'RE...VAN HELSING?
NOPE. VAN HELSING DIED FIGHTING A YETI-DEMON IN NEPAL. A GREAT LOSS TO THE ORDER OF THE DRAGON, FOR WHICH I RUN THE NEW YORK WATCHPOST.
BUT I AM ALSO A PARISH PRIEST, WHICH IS WHY I HAPPENED TO BE IN TH CONFESSIONAL BOOTH WHEN DAREDEVIL HIMSELF SHOWED UP.
WHAT CAN I SAY, MATT?
THE LORD WORKS IN MYSTERIOUS WAYS.
BUT WE SHOULD MOVE. YOU MAY HAVE NOTICED THAT WE'RE THE ONLY HELP THAT'S COME.
NOTHING FROM THE GOVERNMENT, NOTHING FROM HEROES WHO WERE OUTSIDE THE CITY WHEN THIS HAPPENED.
THE BEAST IS SHIELDING WHAT IT'S DOING HERE. COLLAPSING TIME, MAKING NEW YORK ITS OWN LITTLE HELL. NO ONE OUTSIDE WILL NOTICE...NOT UNTIL IT'S TOO LATE.
I BROUGHT YOU TWENTY SOLDIERS. BEST I COULD DO. THE ORDER'S NEVER BEEN NUMEROUS.
THAT'S ALL RIGHT, IF THEY'RE AS GOOD AS YOU SAY. NUMBERS WOULD NEVER BEAT THE HAND, ANYWAY.
THAT'S THEIR GAME. THEY SWARM, OVERWHELM. LIKE WASPS. YOU CAN'T TRY TO FIGHT THEM INDIVIDUALLY.

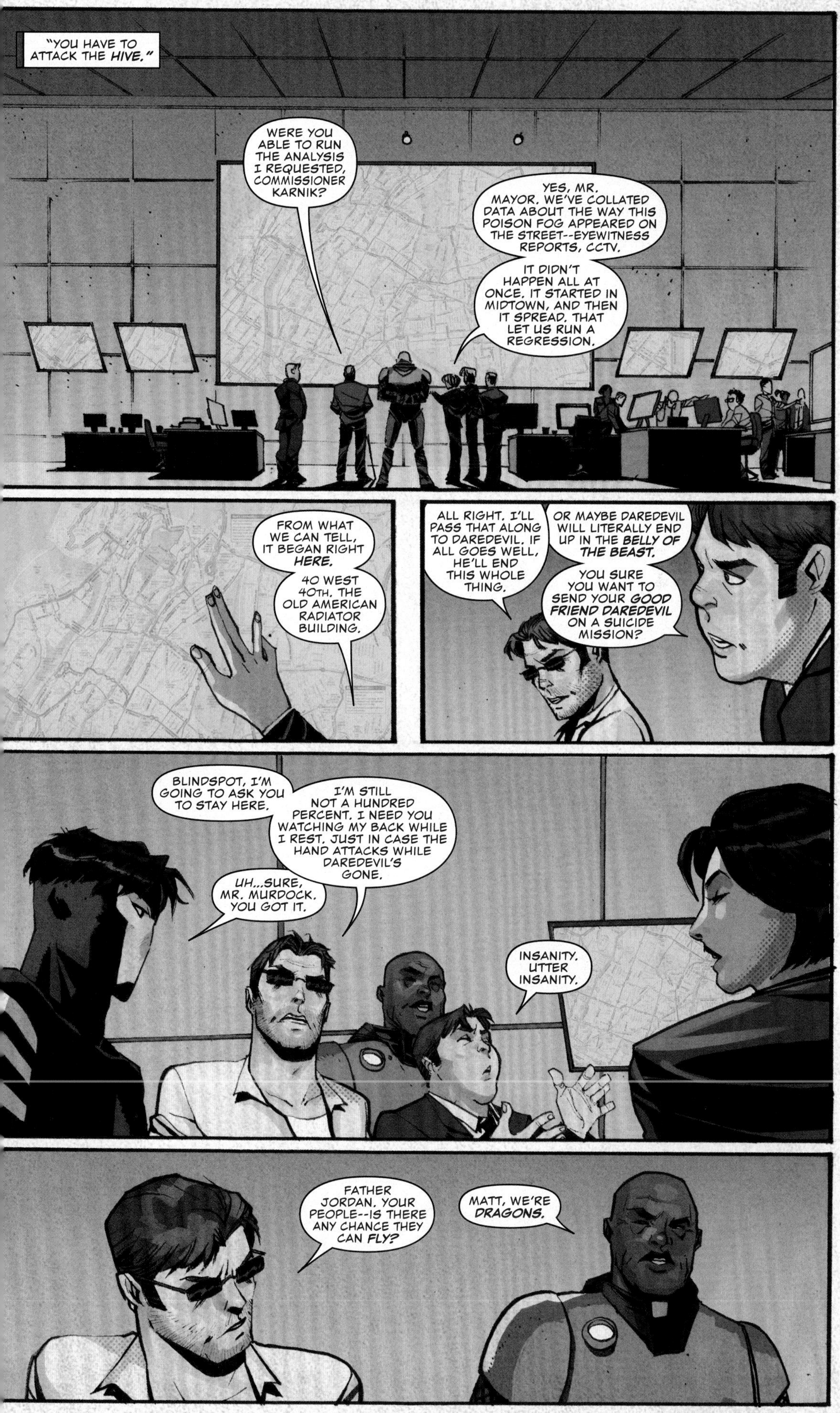
"YOU HAVE TO ATTACK THE HIVE."
WERE YOU ABLE TO RUN THE ANALYSIS I REQUESTED, COMMISSIONER KARNIK?
YES, MR. MAYOR. WE'VE COLLATED DATA ABOUT THE WAY THIS POISON FOG APPEARED ON THE STREET--EYEWITNESS REPORTS, CCTV.
IT DIDN'T HAPPEN ALL AT ONCE. IT STARTED IN MIDTOWN, AND THEN IT SPREAD. THAT LET US RUN A REGRESSION.
FROM WHAT WE CAN TELL, IT BEGAN RIGHT HERE.
40 WEST 40TH. THE OLD AMERICAN RADIATOR BUILDING.
ALL RIGHT. I'LL PASS THAT ALONG TO DAREDEVIL. IF ALL GOES WELL, HE'LL END THIS WHOLE THING.
OR MAYBE DAREDEVIL WILL LITERALLY END UP IN THE BELLY OF THE BEAST.
YOU SURE YOU WANT TO SEND YOUR GOOD FRIEND DAREDEVIL ON A SUICIDE MISSION?
BLINDSPOT, I'M GOING TO ASK YOU TO STAY HERE.
I'M STILL NOT A HUNDRED PERCENT. I NEED YOU WATCHING MY BACK WHILE I REST. JUST IN CASE THE HAND ATTACKS WHILE DAREDEVIL'S GONE.
UH...SURE, MR. MURDOCK. YOU GOT IT.
INSANITY. UTTER INSANITY.
FATHER JORDAN. YOUR PEOPLE--IS THERE ANY CHANCE THEY CAN FLY?
MATT, WE'RE DRAGONS.

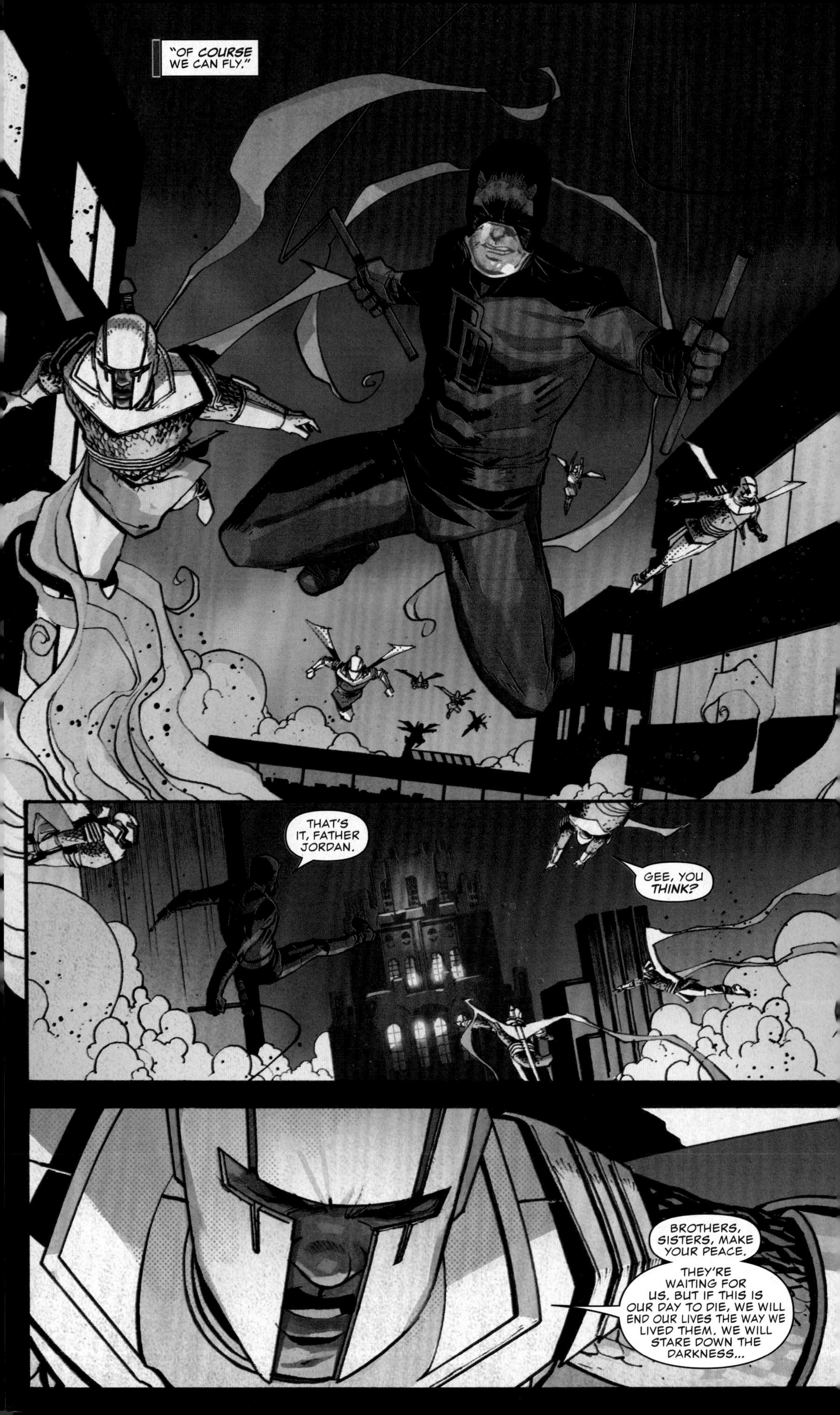
"OF COURSE WE CAN FLY."
THAT'S IT, FATHER JORDAN.
GEE, YOU THINK?
BROTHERS, SISTERS, MAKE YOUR PEACE.
THEY'RE WAITING FOR US. BUT IF THIS IS OUR DAY TO DIE, WE WILL END OUR LIVES THE WAY WE LIVED THEM. WE WILL STARE DOWN THE DARKNESS...

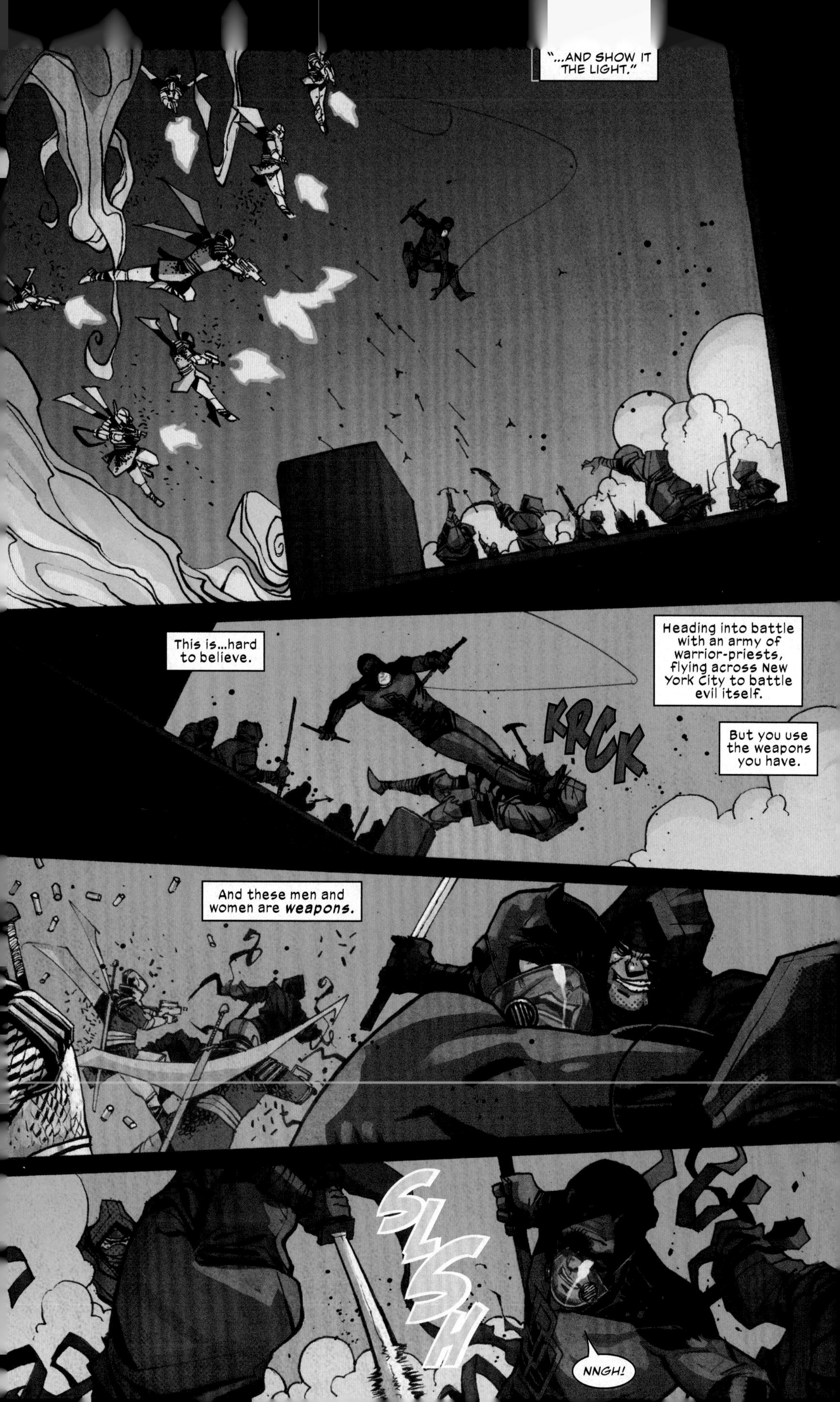

"...AND SHOW IT THE LIGHT."
This is...hard to believe.
Heading into battle with an army of warrior-priests, flying across New York City to battle evil itself.
KRCK
But you use the weapons you have.
And these men and women are *weapons.*
SLSH
NNGH!

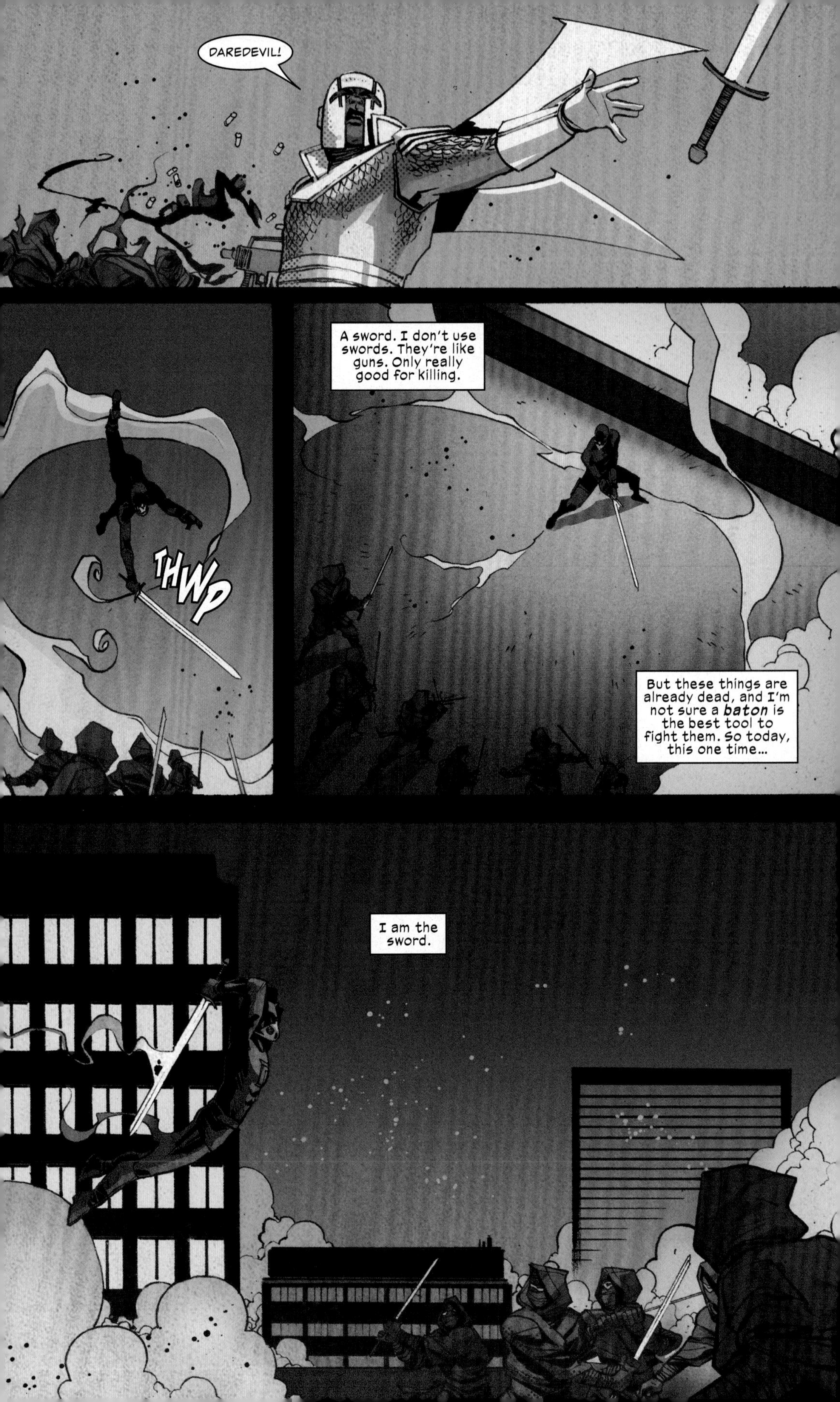
DAREDEVIL!
A sword. I don't use swords. They're like guns. Only really good for killing.
THWP
But these things are already dead, and I'm not sure a *baton* is the best tool to fight them. So today, this one time...
I am the sword.

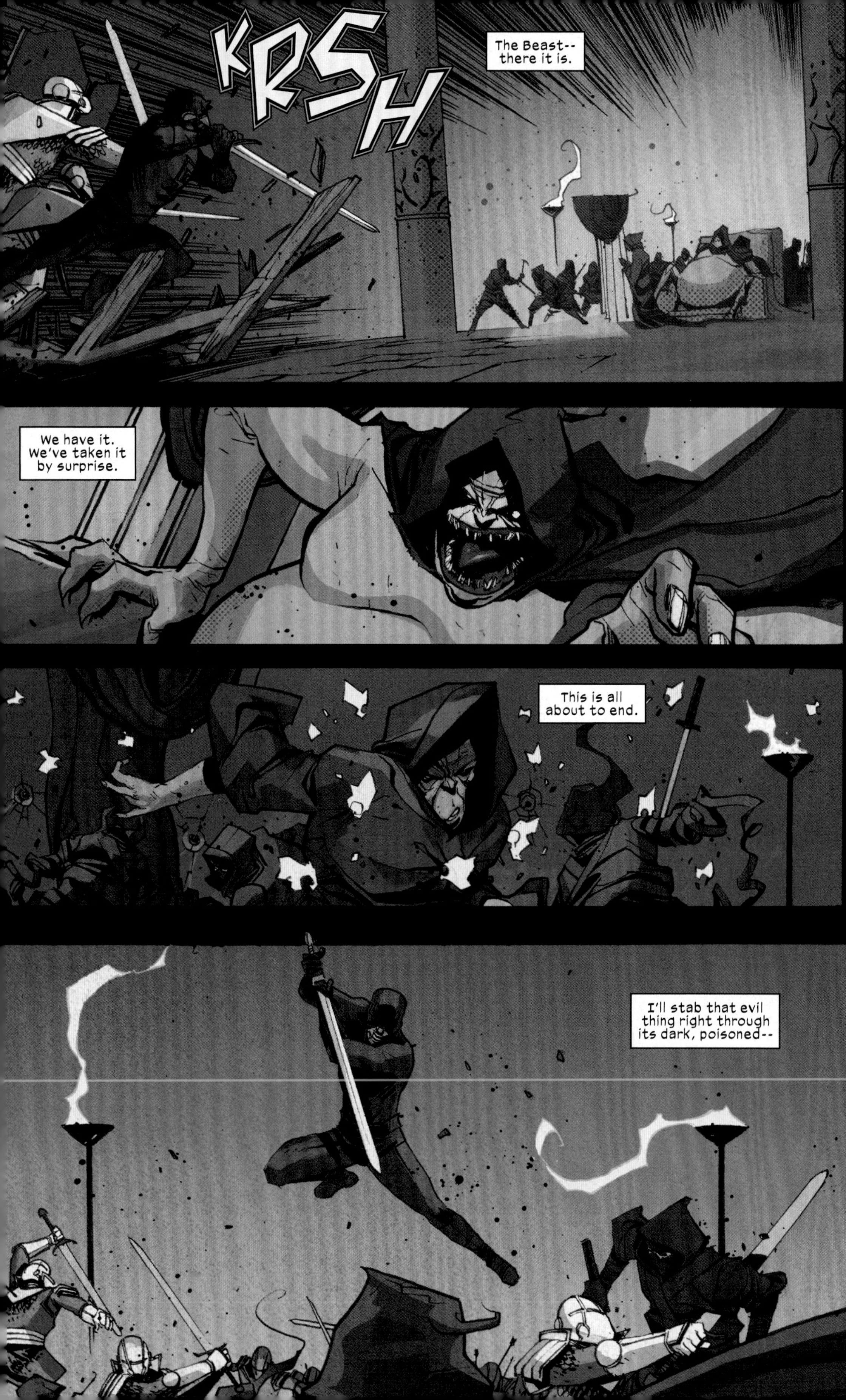
KRSH
The Beast--
there it is.
We have it.
We've taken it
by surprise.
This is all
about to end.
I'll stab that evil
thing right through
its dark, poisoned--

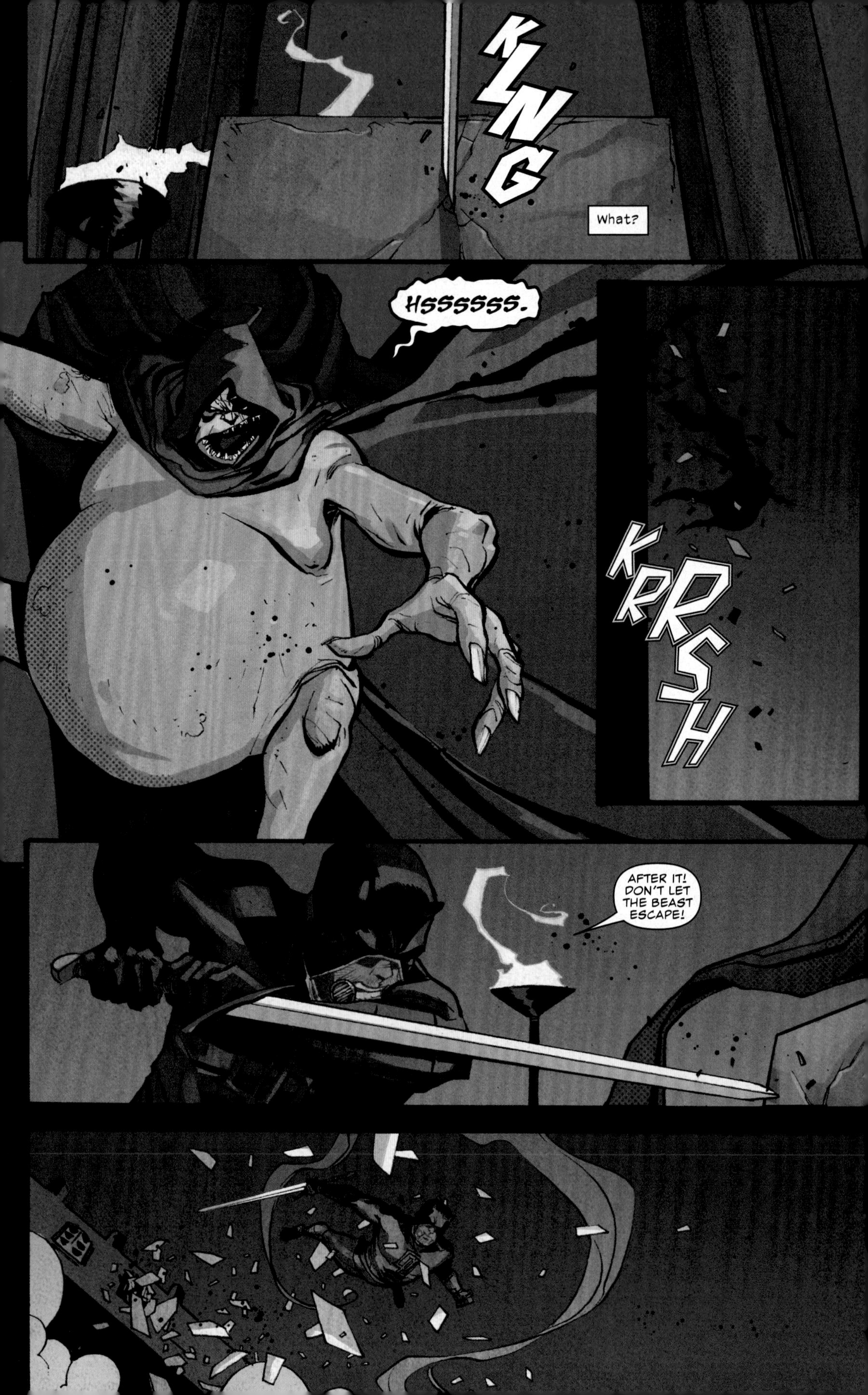
KLING
What?
HSSSSSS.
KRRSH
AFTER IT! DON'T LET THE BEAST ESCAPE!

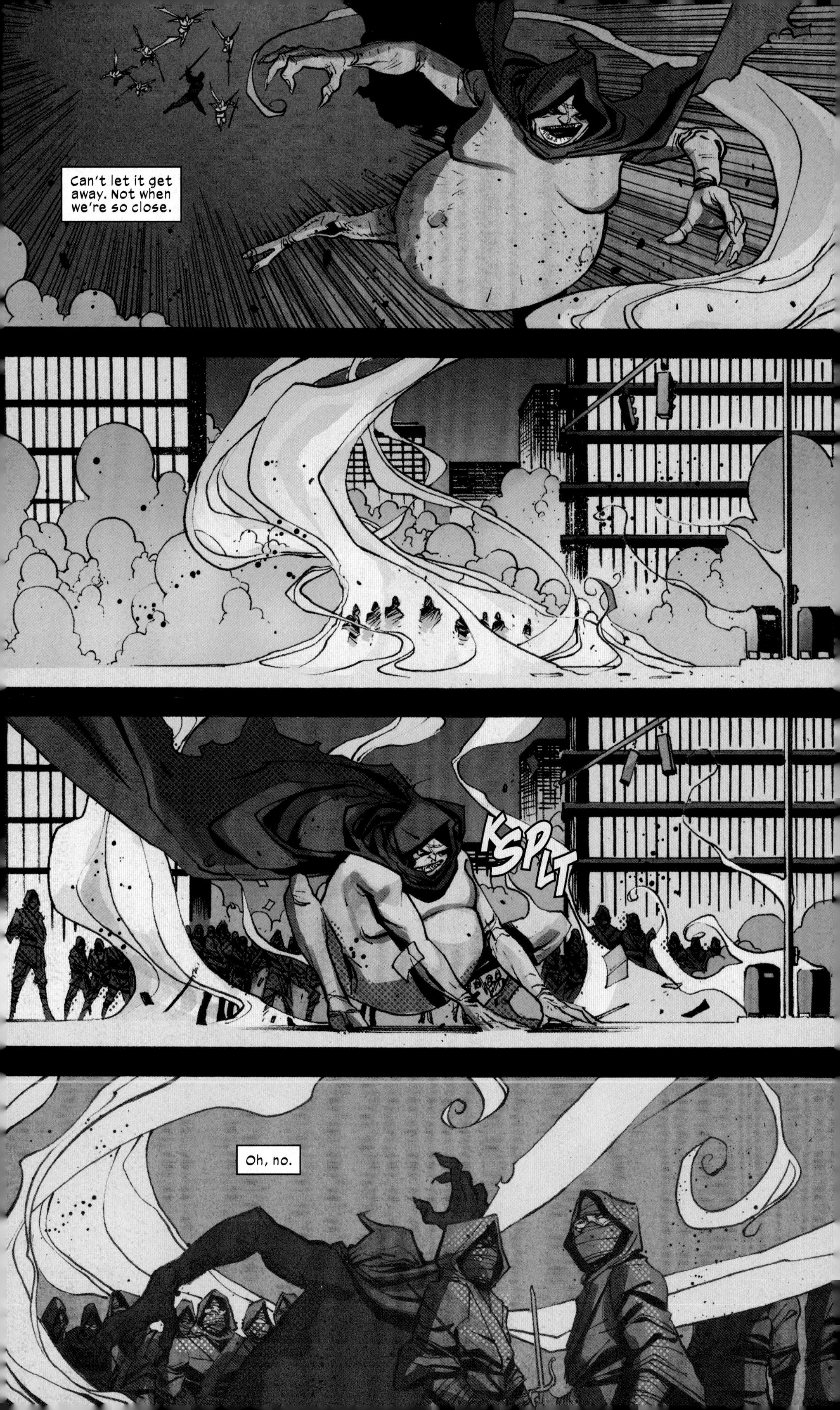
Can't let it get away. Not when we're so close.
KSPLT
Oh, no.

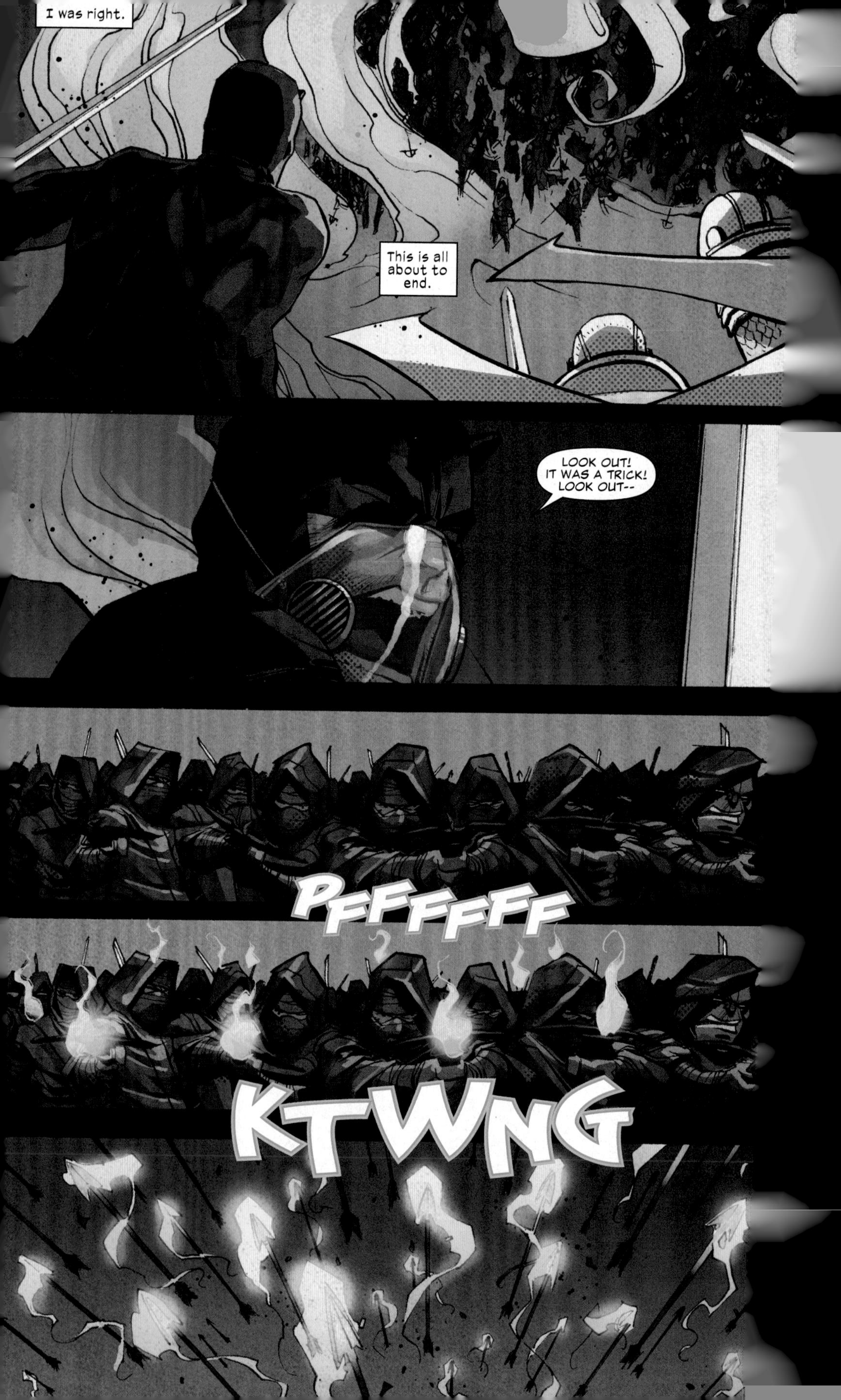
I was right.
This is all about to end.
LOOK OUT! IT WAS A TRICK! LOOK OUT--
PFFFFFFF
KTWNG

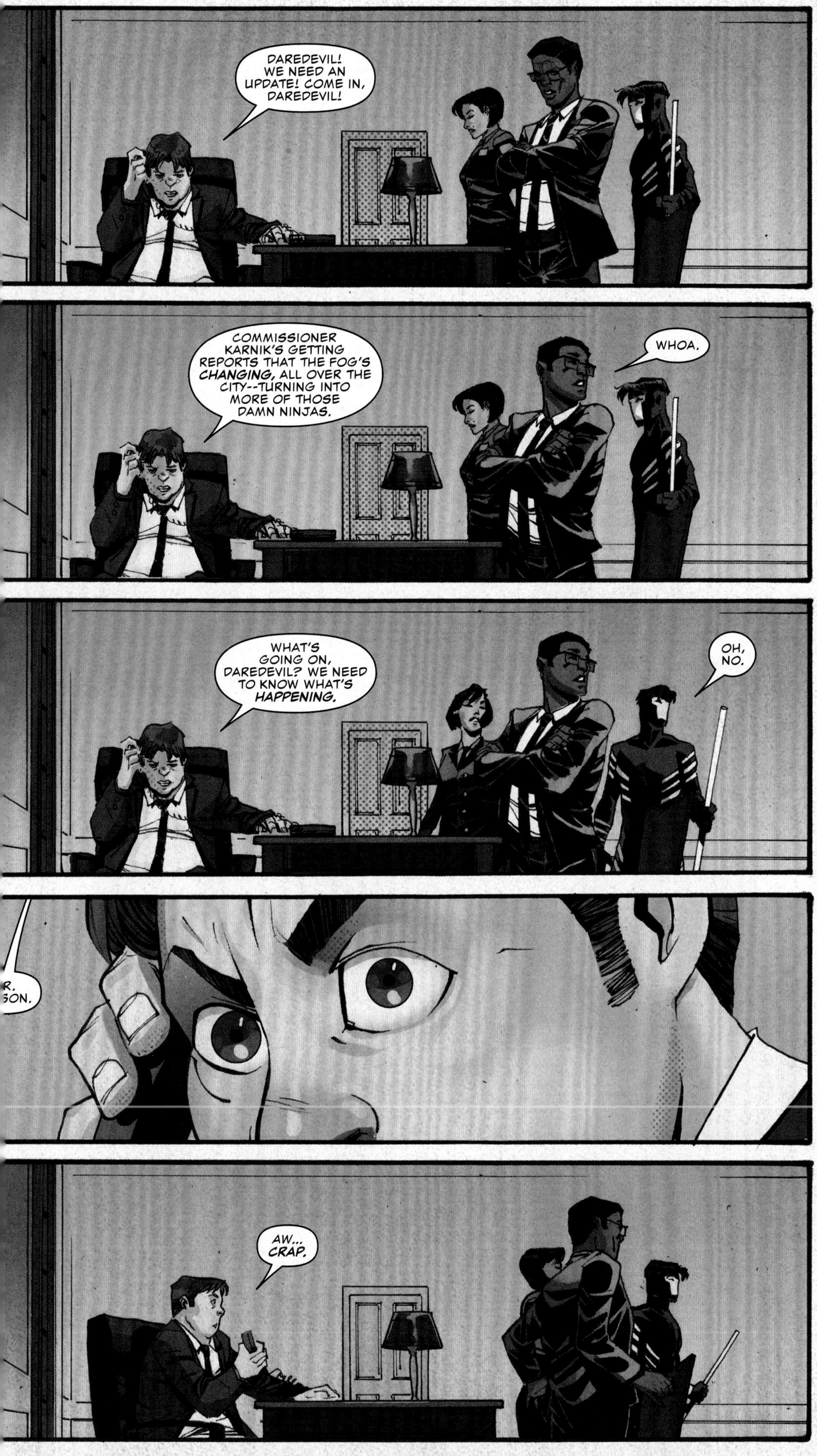
DAREDEVIL! WE NEED AN UPDATE! COME IN, DAREDEVIL!
COMMISSIONER KARNIK'S GETTING REPORTS THAT THE FOG'S *CHANGING*, ALL OVER THE CITY--TURNING INTO MORE OF THOSE DAMN NINJAS.
WHOA.
WHAT'S GOING ON, DAREDEVIL? WE NEED TO KNOW WHAT'S *HAPPENING*.
OH, NO.
AW... *CRAP*.

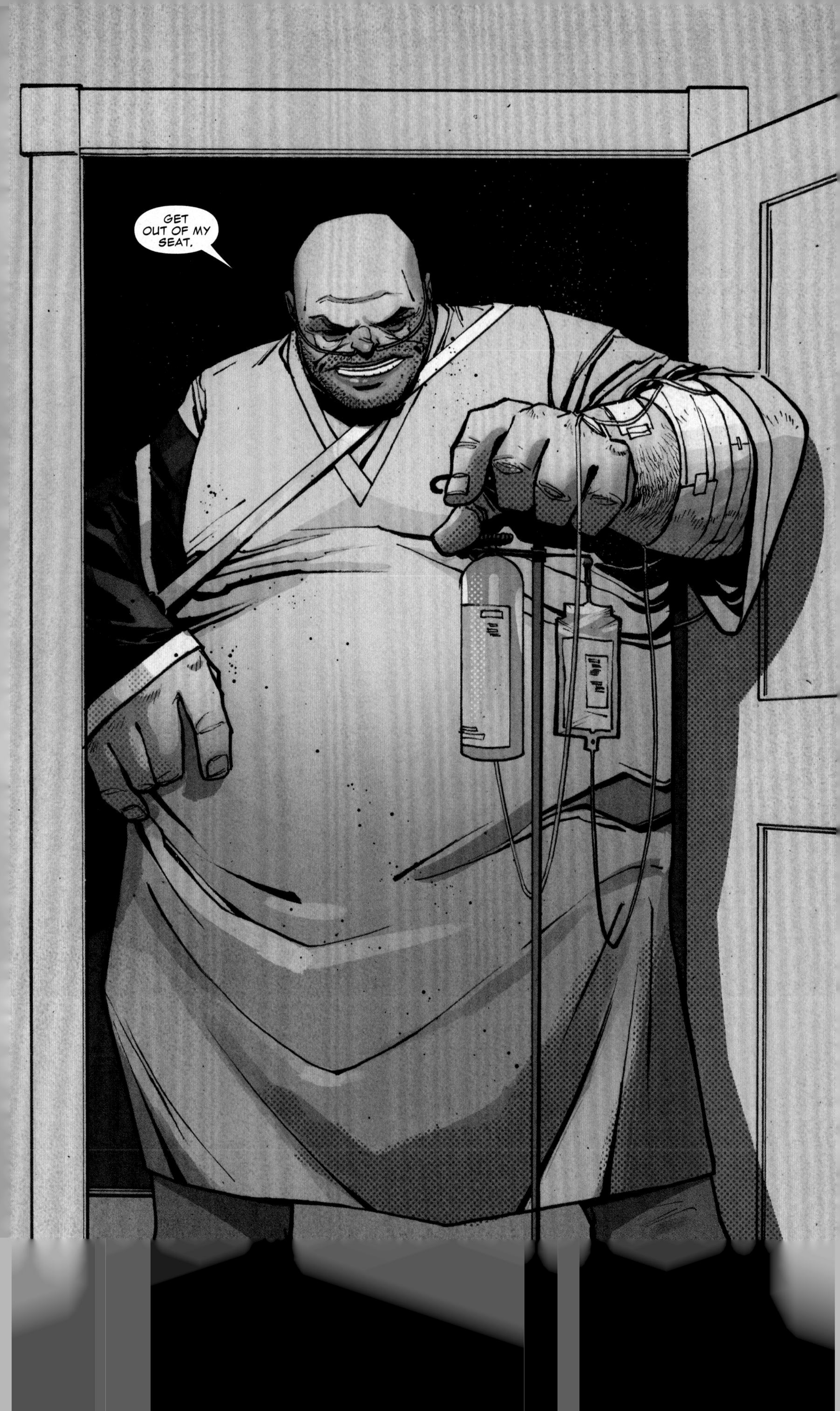
GET OUT OF MY SEAT.

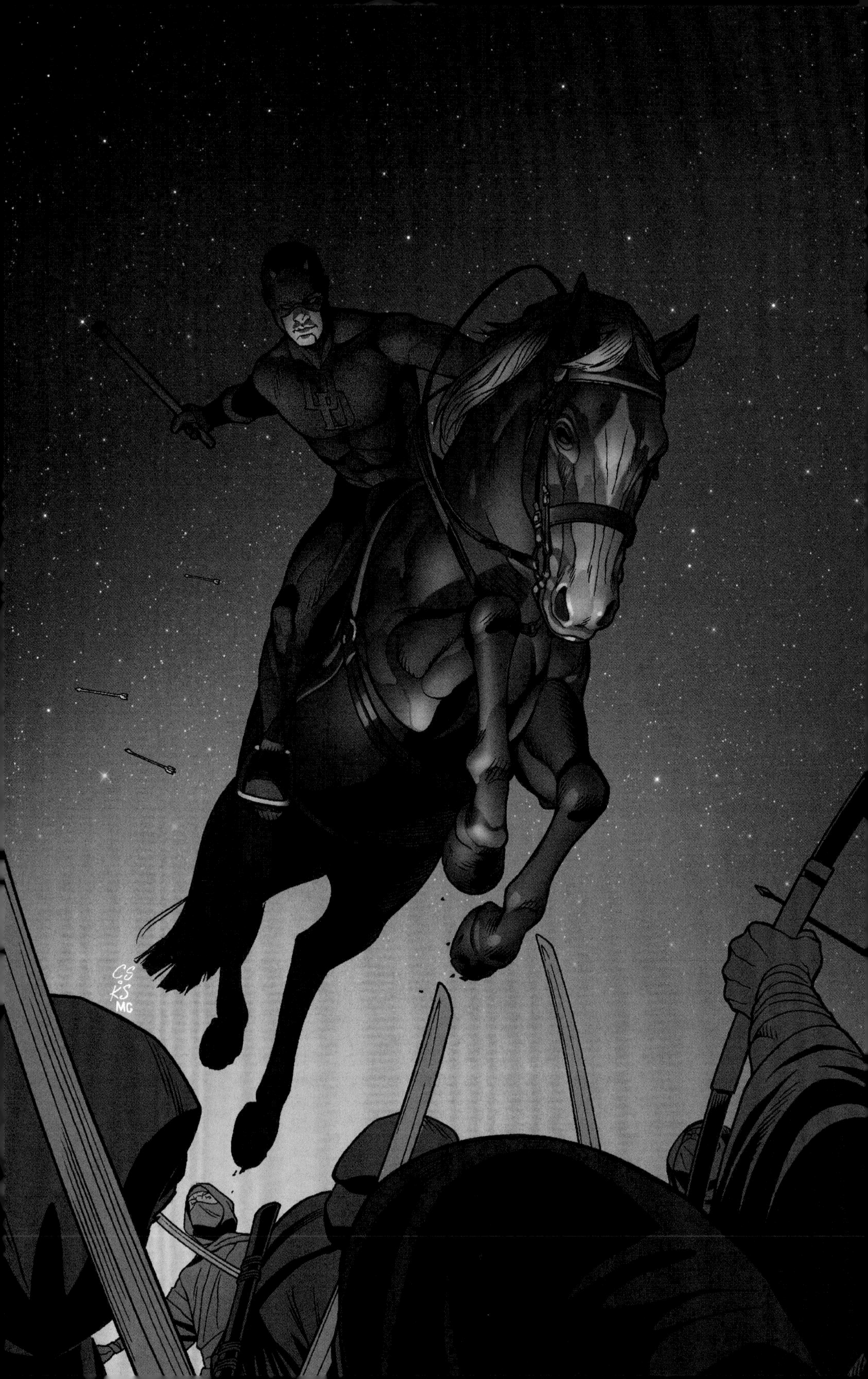
CS
KS
MG

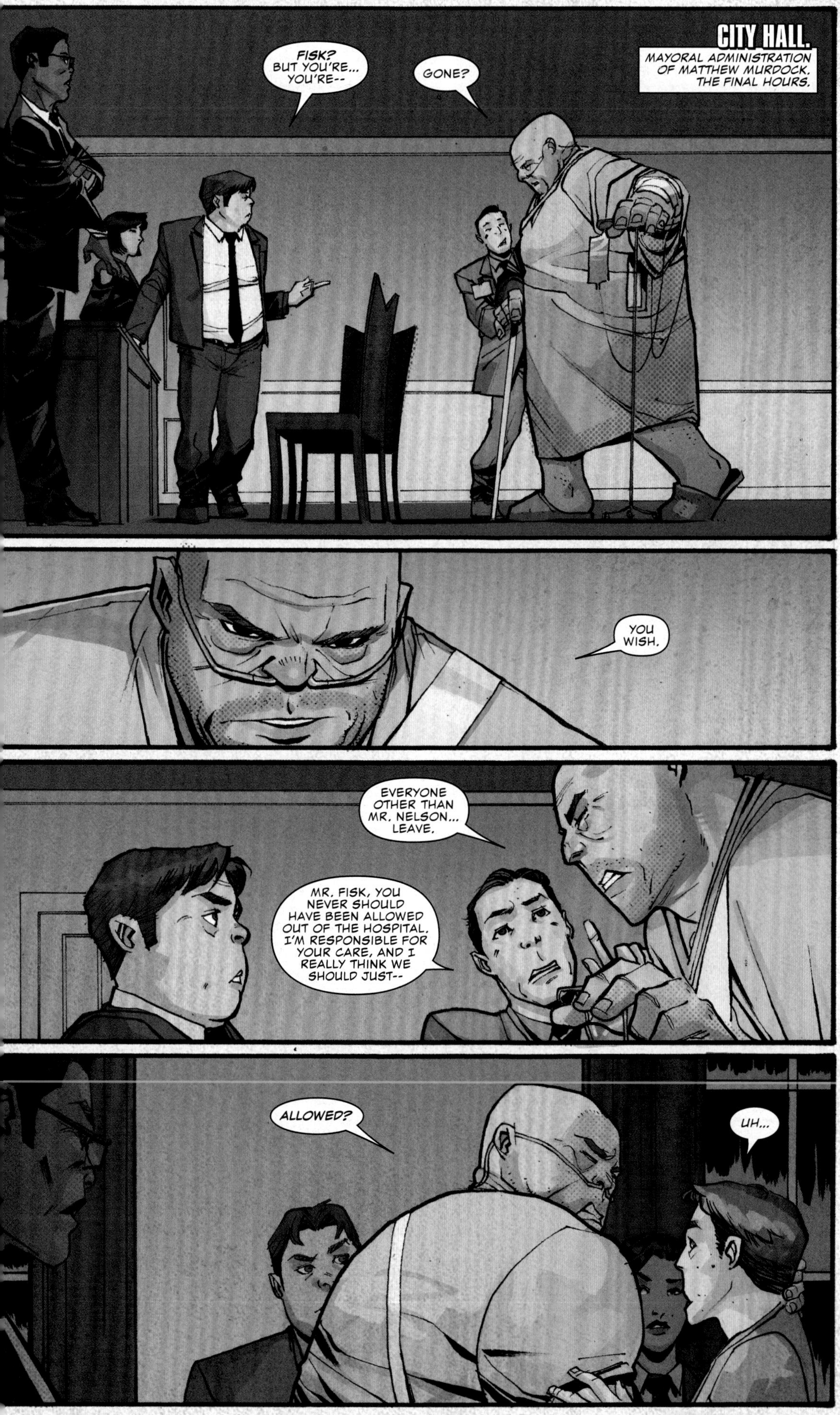
CITY HALL.
MAYORAL ADMINISTRATION OF MATTHEW MURDOCK, THE FINAL HOURS.
FISK? BUT YOU'RE... YOU'RE--
GONE?
YOU WISH.
EVERYONE OTHER THAN MR. NELSON... LEAVE.
MR. FISK, YOU NEVER SHOULD HAVE BEEN ALLOWED OUT OF THE HOSPITAL. I'M RESPONSIBLE FOR YOUR CARE, AND I REALLY THINK WE SHOULD JUST--
ALLOWED?
UH...

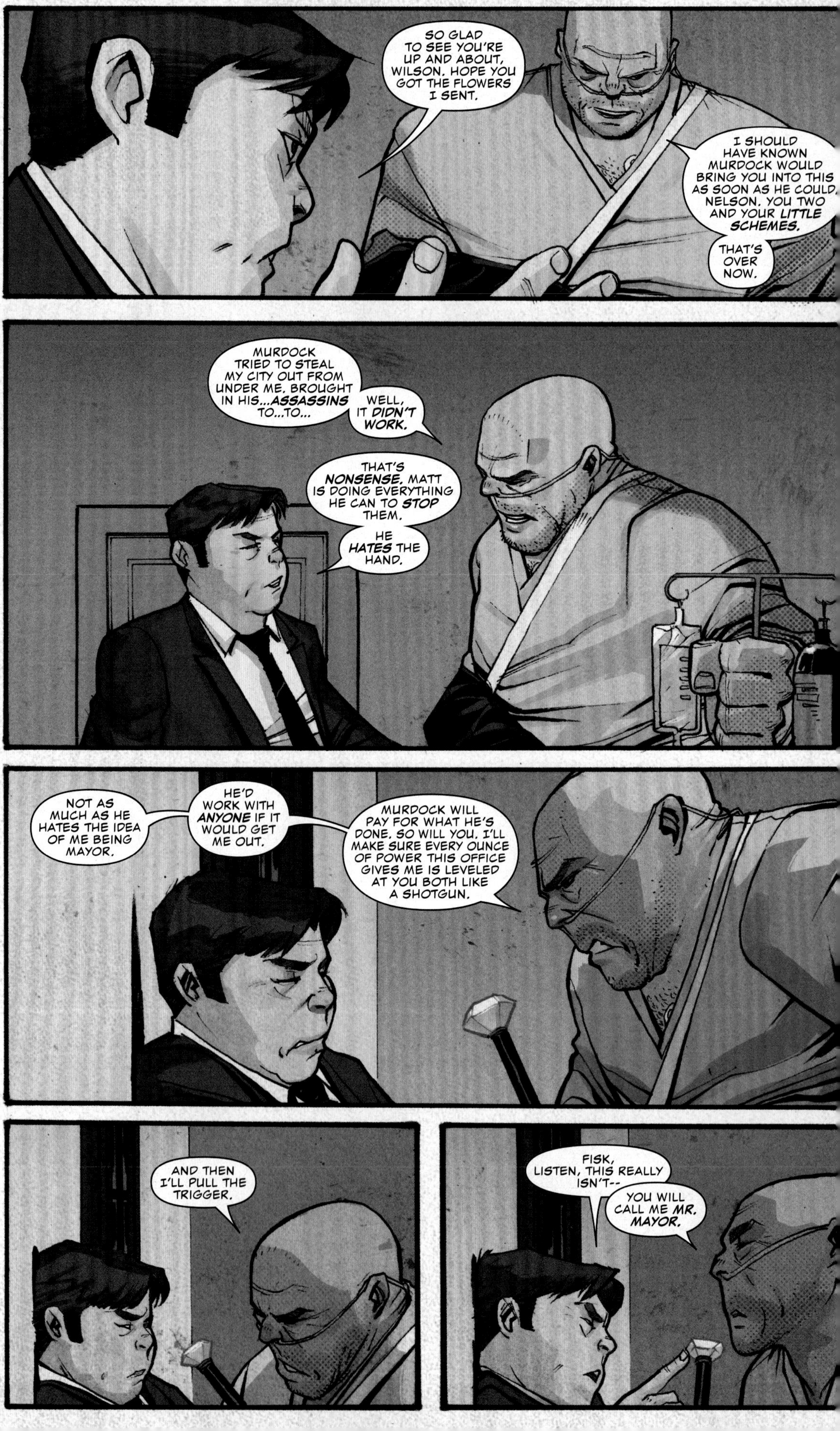
SO GLAD TO SEE YOU'RE UP AND ABOUT, WILSON. HOPE YOU GOT THE FLOWERS I SENT.
I SHOULD HAVE KNOWN MURDOCK WOULD BRING YOU INTO THIS AS SOON AS HE COULD, NELSON. YOU TWO AND YOUR LITTLE SCHEMES.
THAT'S OVER NOW.
MURDOCK TRIED TO STEAL MY CITY OUT FROM UNDER ME. BROUGHT IN HIS...ASSASSINS TO...TO...
WELL, IT DIDN'T WORK.
THAT'S NONSENSE. MATT IS DOING EVERYTHING HE CAN TO STOP THEM.
HE HATES THE HAND.
NOT AS MUCH AS HE HATES THE IDEA OF ME BEING MAYOR.
HE'D WORK WITH ANYONE IF IT WOULD GET ME OUT.
MURDOCK WILL PAY FOR WHAT HE'S DONE. SO WILL YOU. I'LL MAKE SURE EVERY OUNCE OF POWER THIS OFFICE GIVES ME IS LEVELED AT YOU BOTH LIKE A SHOTGUN.
AND THEN I'LL PULL THE TRIGGER.
FISK, LISTEN, THIS REALLY ISN'T--
YOU WILL CALL ME MR. MAYOR.

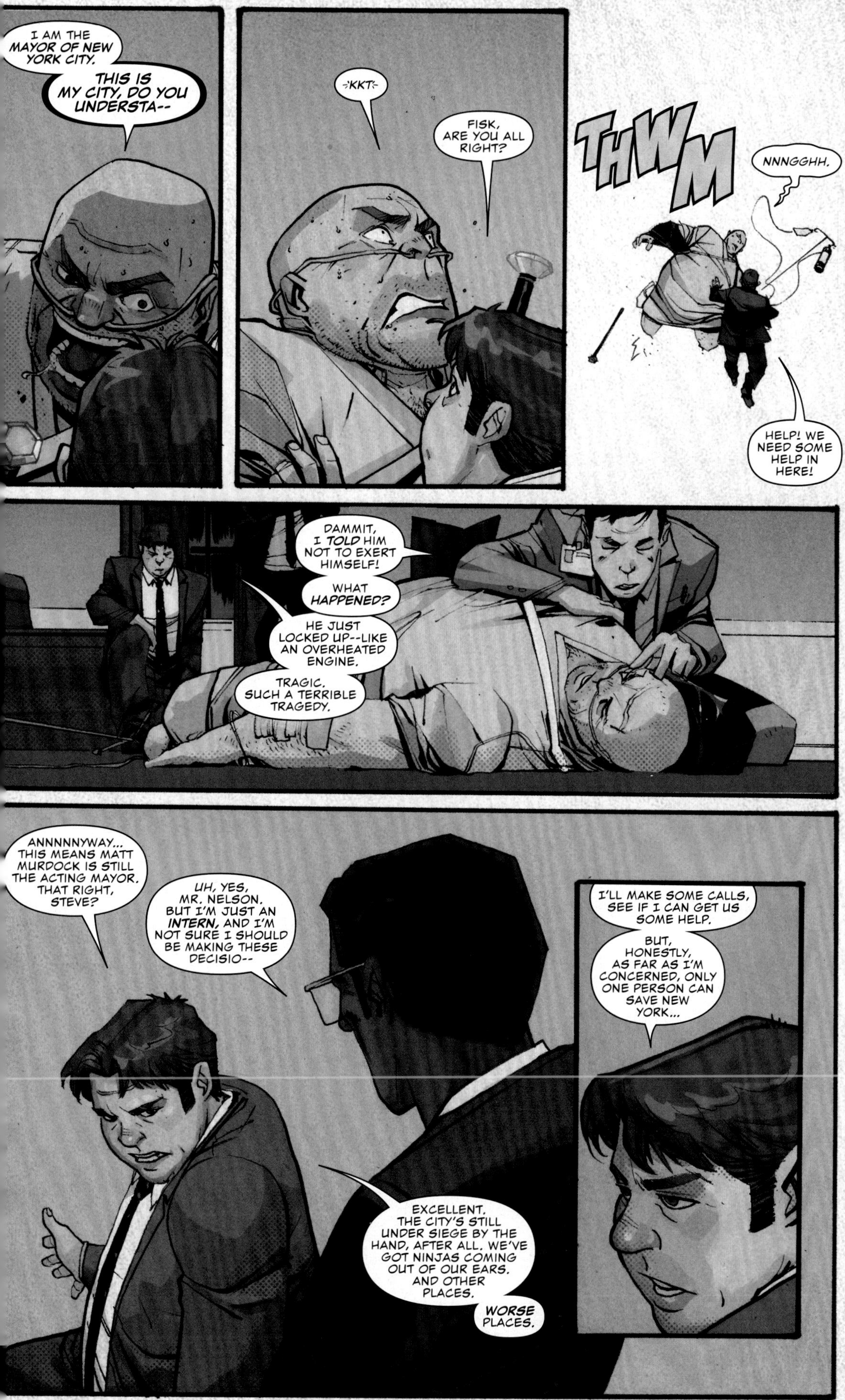
I AM THE MAYOR OF NEW YORK CITY.
THIS IS MY CITY, DO YOU UNDERSTA--
KKT
FISK, ARE YOU ALL RIGHT?
THWM
NNNGGHH.
HELP! WE NEED SOME HELP IN HERE!
DAMMIT, I TOLD HIM NOT TO EXERT HIMSELF!
WHAT HAPPENED?
HE JUST LOCKED UP--LIKE AN OVERHEATED ENGINE.
TRAGIC. SUCH A TERRIBLE TRAGEDY.
ANNNNNYWAY... THIS MEANS MATT MURDOCK IS STILL THE ACTING MAYOR. THAT RIGHT, STEVE?
UH, YES, MR. NELSON. BUT I'M JUST AN INTERN, AND I'M NOT SURE I SHOULD BE MAKING THESE DECISIO--
EXCELLENT. THE CITY'S STILL UNDER SIEGE BY THE HAND, AFTER ALL. WE'VE GOT NINJAS COMING OUT OF OUR EARS.
AND OTHER PLACES.
WORSE PLACES.
I'LL MAKE SOME CALLS, SEE IF I CAN GET US SOME HELP.
BUT, HONESTLY, AS FAR AS I'M CONCERNED, ONLY ONE PERSON CAN SAVE NEW YORK...

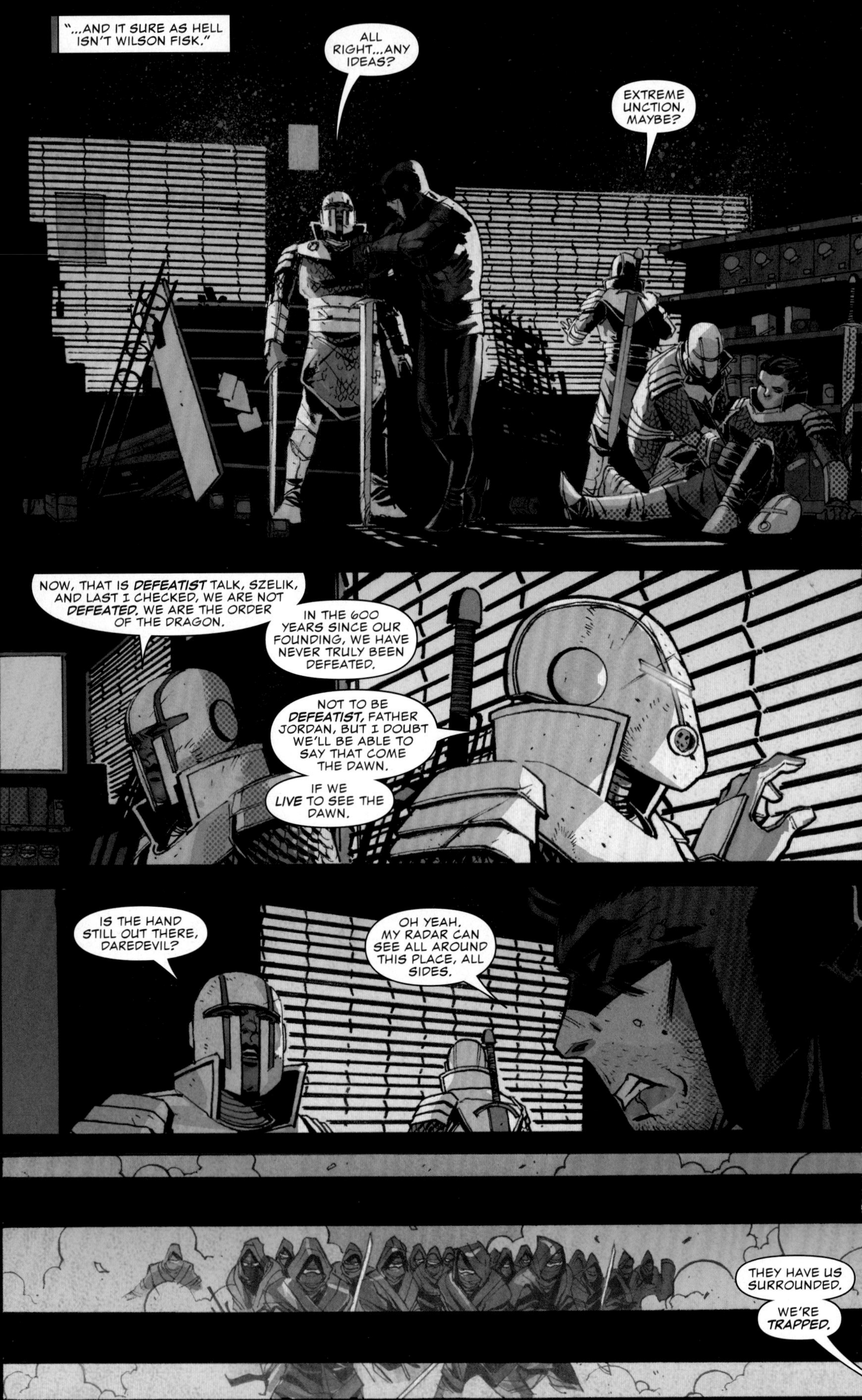
"...AND IT SURE AS HELL ISN'T WILSON FISK."
ALL RIGHT...ANY IDEAS?
EXTREME UNCTION, MAYBE?
NOW, THAT IS DEFEATIST TALK, SZELIK, AND LAST I CHECKED, WE ARE NOT DEFEATED. WE ARE THE ORDER OF THE DRAGON.
IN THE 600 YEARS SINCE OUR FOUNDING, WE HAVE NEVER TRULY BEEN DEFEATED.
NOT TO BE DEFEATIST, FATHER JORDAN, BUT I DOUBT WE'LL BE ABLE TO SAY THAT COME THE DAWN.
IF WE LIVE TO SEE THE DAWN.
IS THE HAND STILL OUT THERE, DAREDEVIL?
OH YEAH. MY RADAR CAN SEE ALL AROUND THIS PLACE, ALL SIDES.
THEY HAVE US SURROUNDED.
WE'RE TRAPPED.

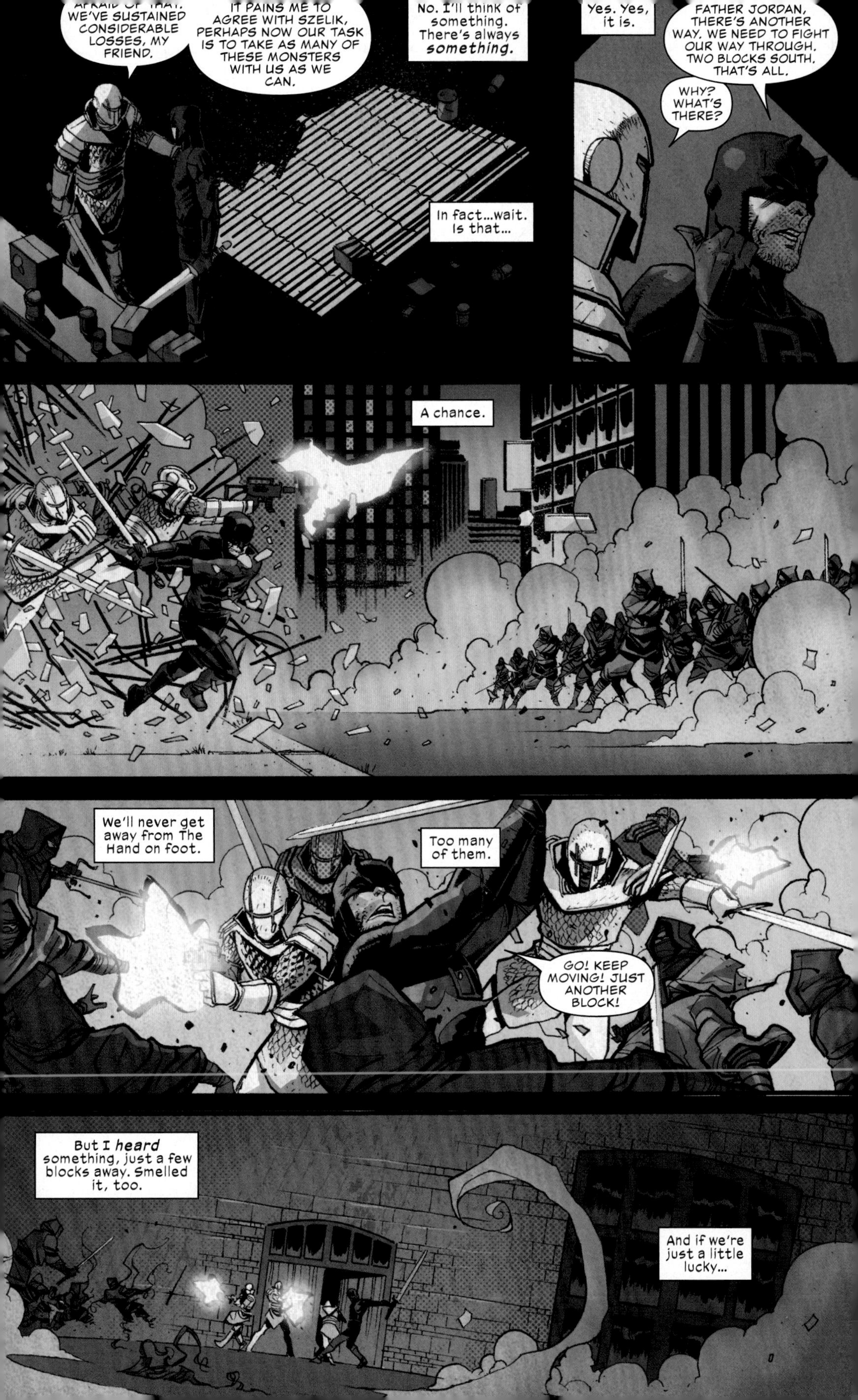

WE'VE SUSTAINED CONSIDERABLE LOSSES, MY FRIEND.
IT PAINS ME TO AGREE WITH SZELIK. PERHAPS NOW OUR TASK IS TO TAKE AS MANY OF THESE MONSTERS WITH US AS WE CAN.
No. I'll think of something. There's always *something.*
In fact...wait. Is that...
Yes. Yes, it is.
FATHER JORDAN, THERE'S ANOTHER WAY. WE NEED TO FIGHT OUR WAY THROUGH. TWO BLOCKS SOUTH. THAT'S ALL.
WHY? WHAT'S THERE?
A chance.
We'll never get away from The Hand on foot.
Too many of them.
GO! KEEP MOVING! JUST ANOTHER BLOCK!
But I *heard* something, just a few blocks away. Smelled it, too.
And if we're just a little lucky...

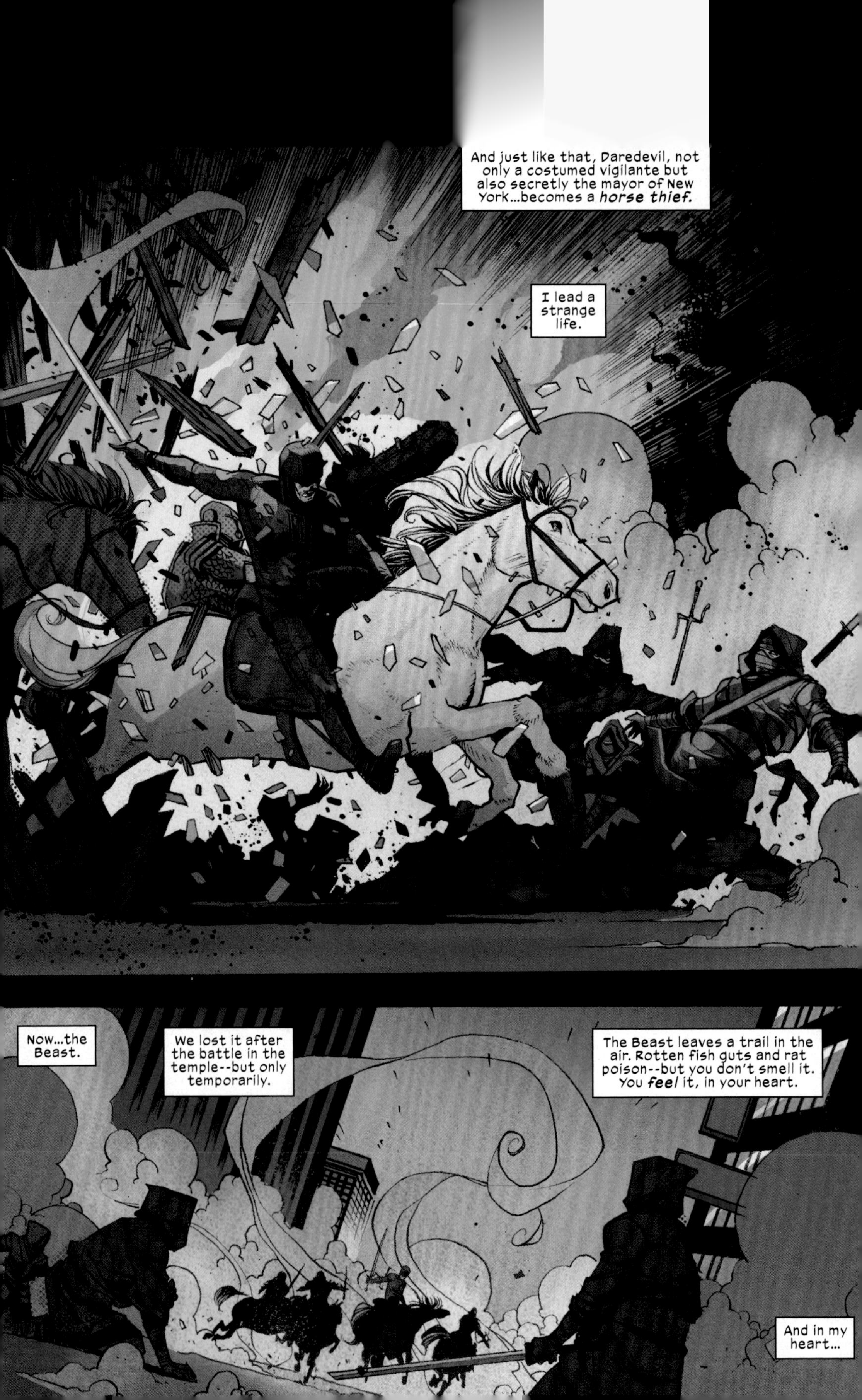
And just like that, Daredevil, not only a costumed vigilante but also secretly the mayor of New York...becomes a *horse thief.*
I lead a strange life.
Now...the Beast.
We lost it after the battle in the temple--but only temporarily.
The Beast leaves a trail in the air. Rotten fish guts and rat poison--but you don't smell it. You *feel* it, in your heart.
And in my heart...

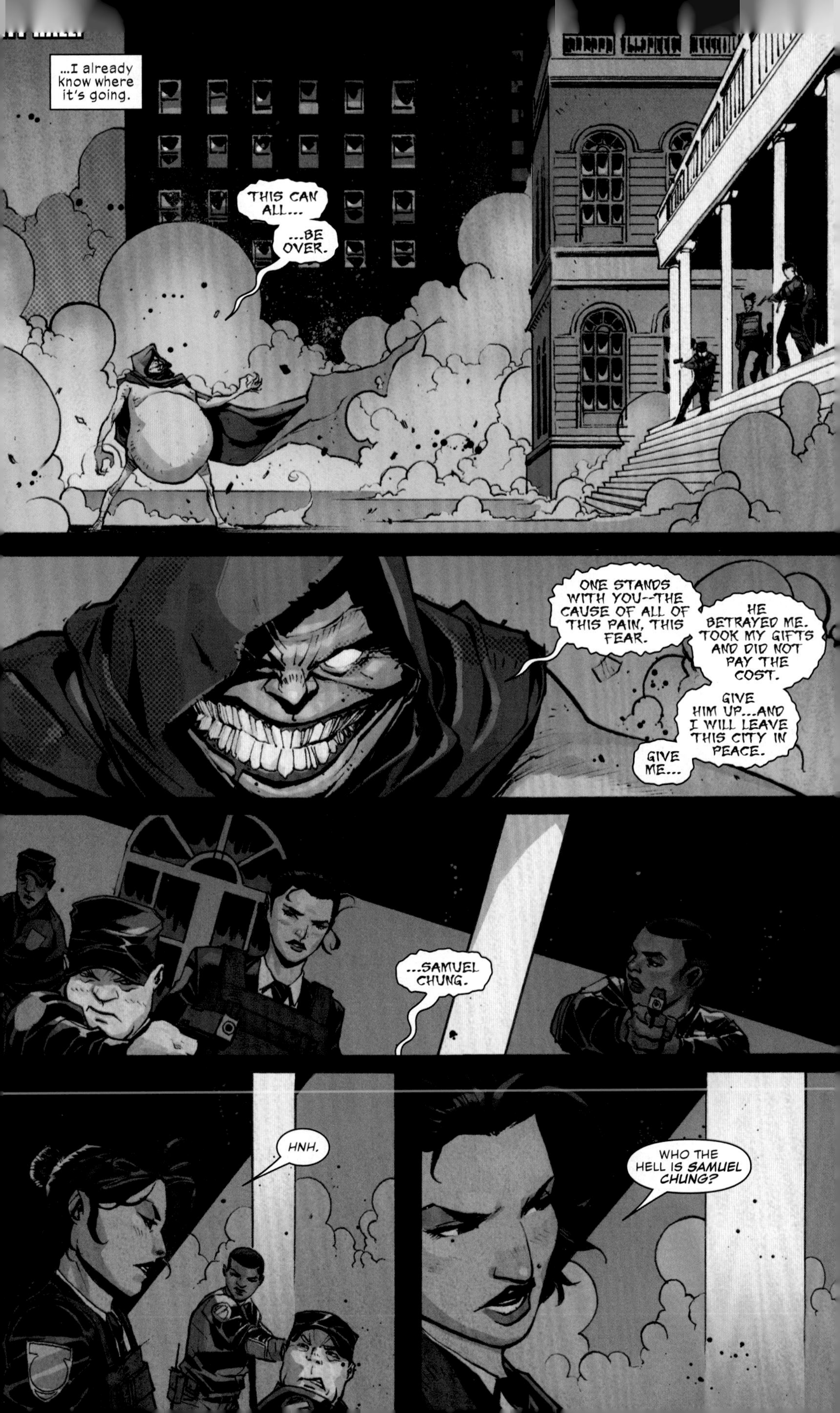
...I already know where it's going.
THIS CAN ALL...
...BE OVER.
ONE STANDS WITH YOU--THE CAUSE OF ALL OF THIS PAIN, THIS FEAR.
HE BETRAYED ME. TOOK MY GIFTS AND DID NOT PAY THE COST.
GIVE HIM UP...AND I WILL LEAVE THIS CITY IN PEACE.
GIVE ME...
...SAMUEL CHUNG.
HNH.
WHO THE HELL IS SAMUEL CHUNG?

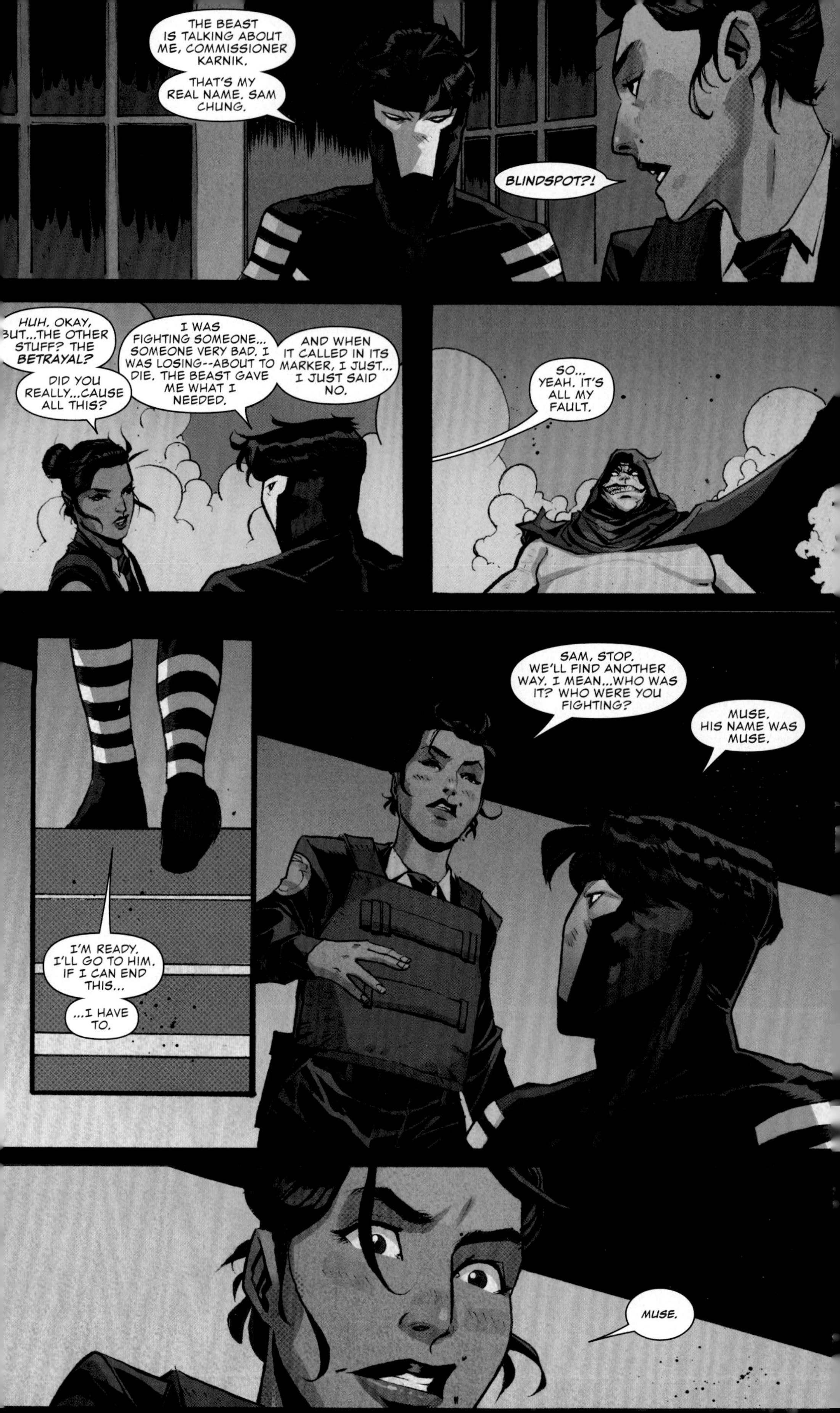
THE BEAST IS TALKING ABOUT ME, COMMISSIONER KARNIK.
THAT'S MY REAL NAME. SAM CHUNG.
BLINDSPOT?!
HUH, OKAY, BUT...THE OTHER STUFF? THE BETRAYAL?
DID YOU REALLY...CAUSE ALL THIS?
I WAS FIGHTING SOMEONE... SOMEONE VERY BAD. I WAS LOSING--ABOUT TO DIE. THE BEAST GAVE ME WHAT I NEEDED.
AND WHEN IT CALLED IN ITS MARKER, I JUST... I JUST SAID NO.
SO... YEAH. IT'S ALL MY FAULT.
I'M READY. I'LL GO TO HIM. IF I CAN END THIS...
...I HAVE TO.
SAM, STOP. WE'LL FIND ANOTHER WAY. I MEAN...WHO WAS IT? WHO WERE YOU FIGHTING?
MUSE. HIS NAME WAS MUSE.
MUSE.

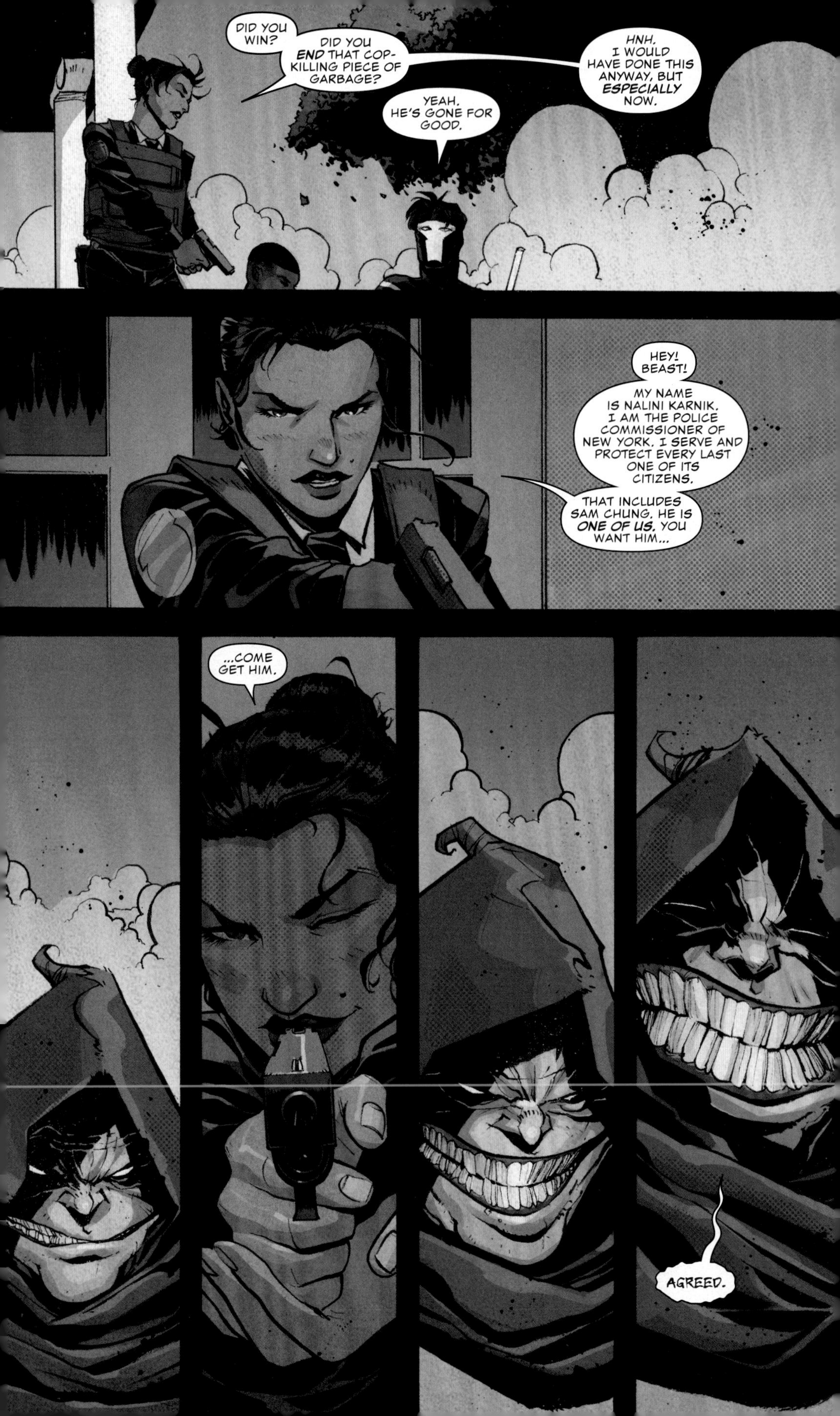
DID YOU WIN?
DID YOU END THAT COP-KILLING PIECE OF GARBAGE?
YEAH. HE'S GONE FOR GOOD.
HNH. I WOULD HAVE DONE THIS ANYWAY, BUT ESPECIALLY NOW.
HEY! BEAST!
MY NAME IS NALINI KARNIK. I AM THE POLICE COMMISSIONER OF NEW YORK. I SERVE AND PROTECT EVERY LAST ONE OF ITS CITIZENS.
THAT INCLUDES SAM CHUNG. HE IS ONE OF US. YOU WANT HIM...
...COME GET HIM.
AGREED.

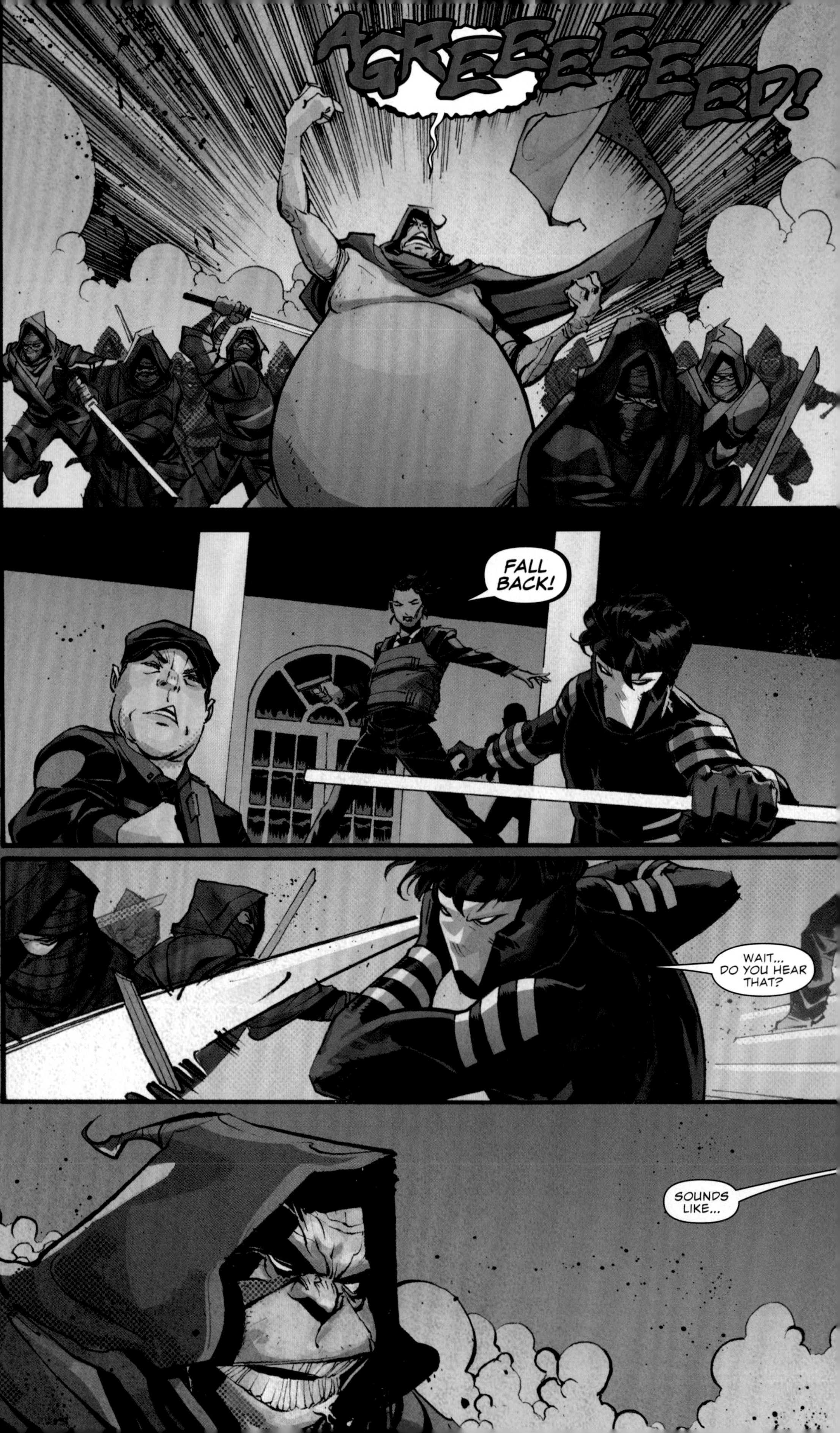
AGREEEEEEED!
FALL BACK!
WAIT... DO YOU HEAR THAT?
SOUNDS LIKE...

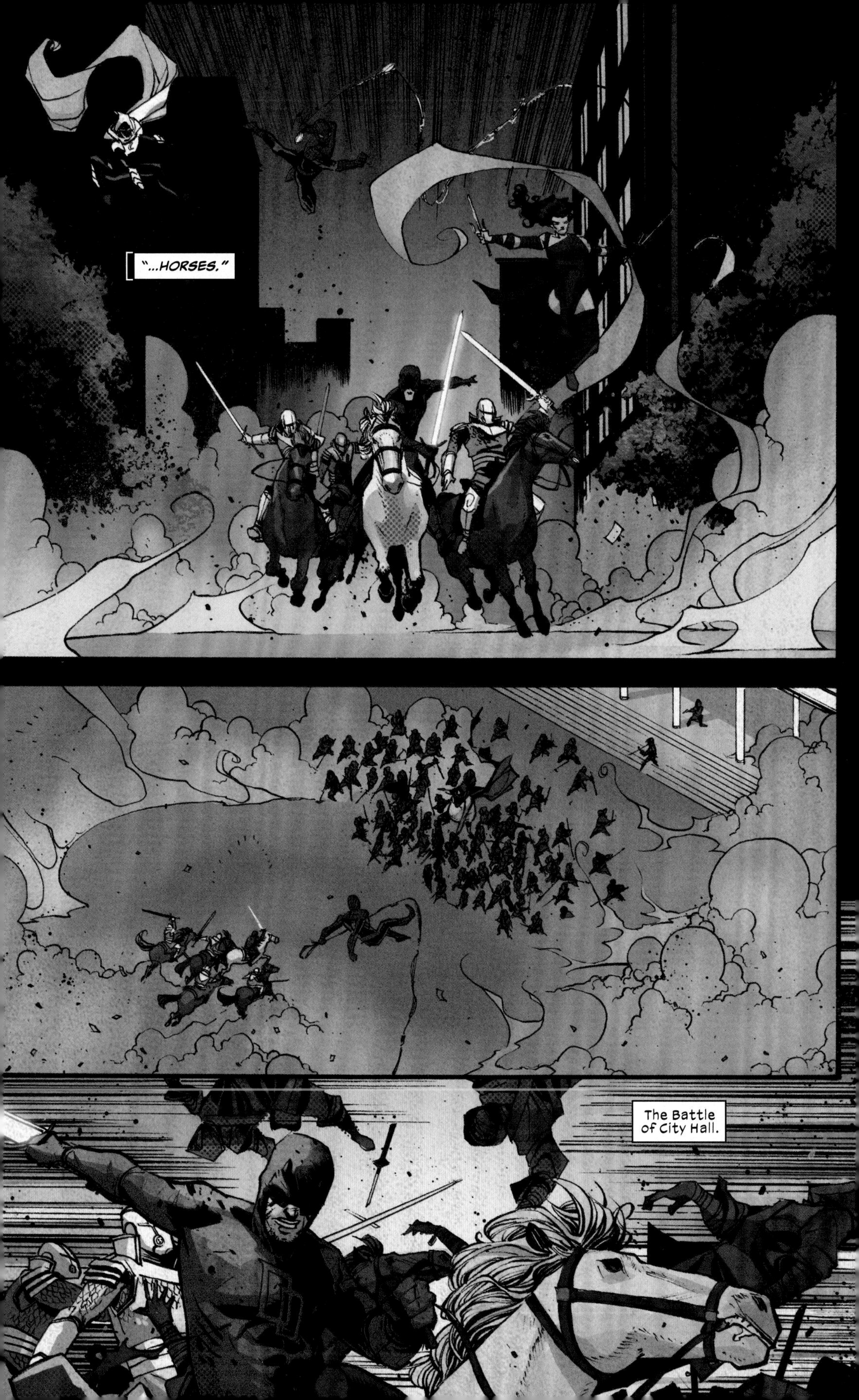
"...HORSES."
The Battle of City Hall.

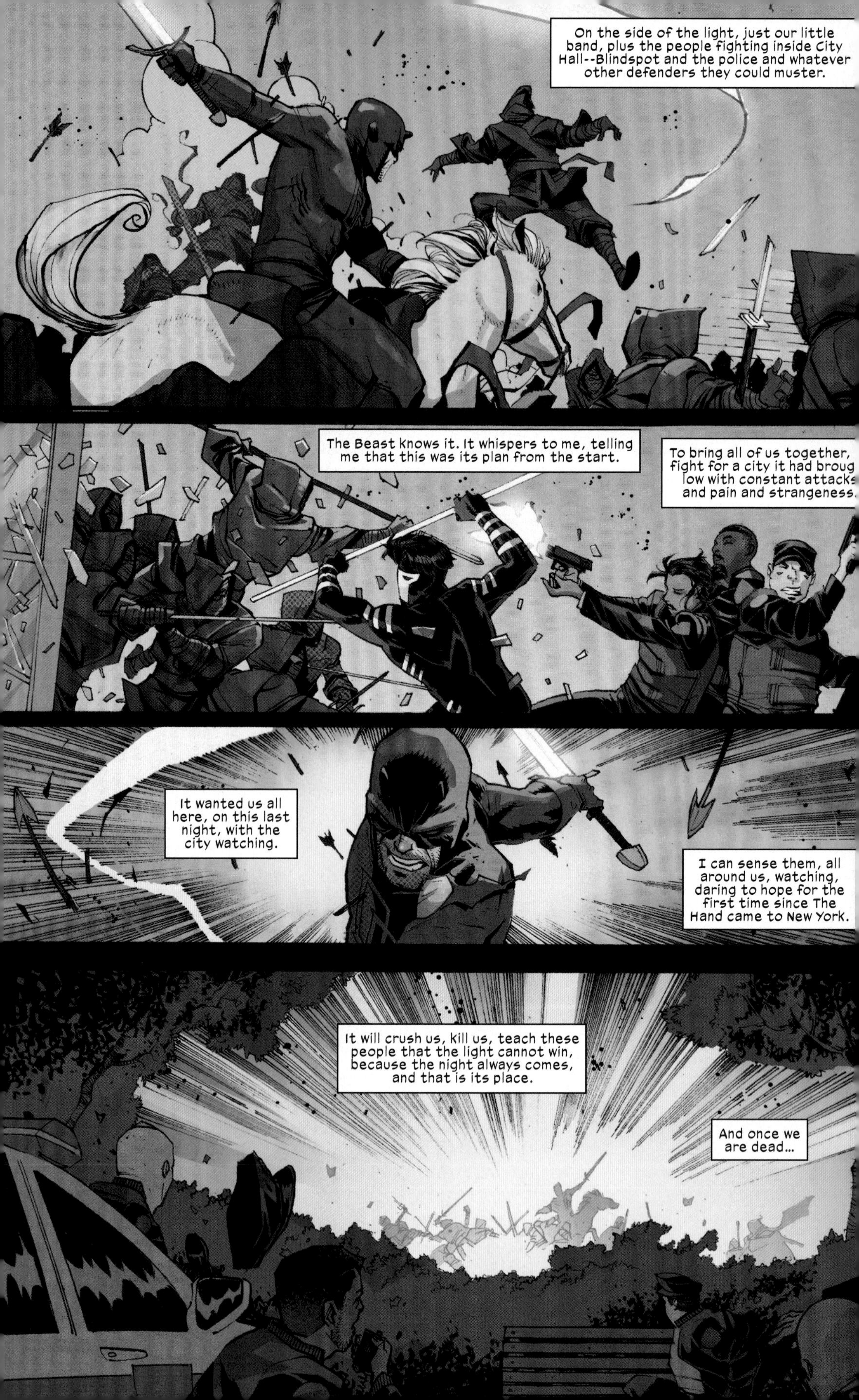
On the side of the light, just our little band, plus the people fighting inside City Hall--Blindspot and the police and whatever other defenders they could muster.
The Beast knows it. It whispers to me, telling me that this was its plan from the start.
To bring all of us together, fight for a city it had broug low with constant attacks and pain and strangeness.
It wanted us all here, on this last night, with the city watching.
I can sense them, all around us, watching, daring to hope for the first time since The Hand came to New York.
It will crush us, kill us, teach these people that the light cannot win, because the night always comes, and that is its place.
And once we are dead...

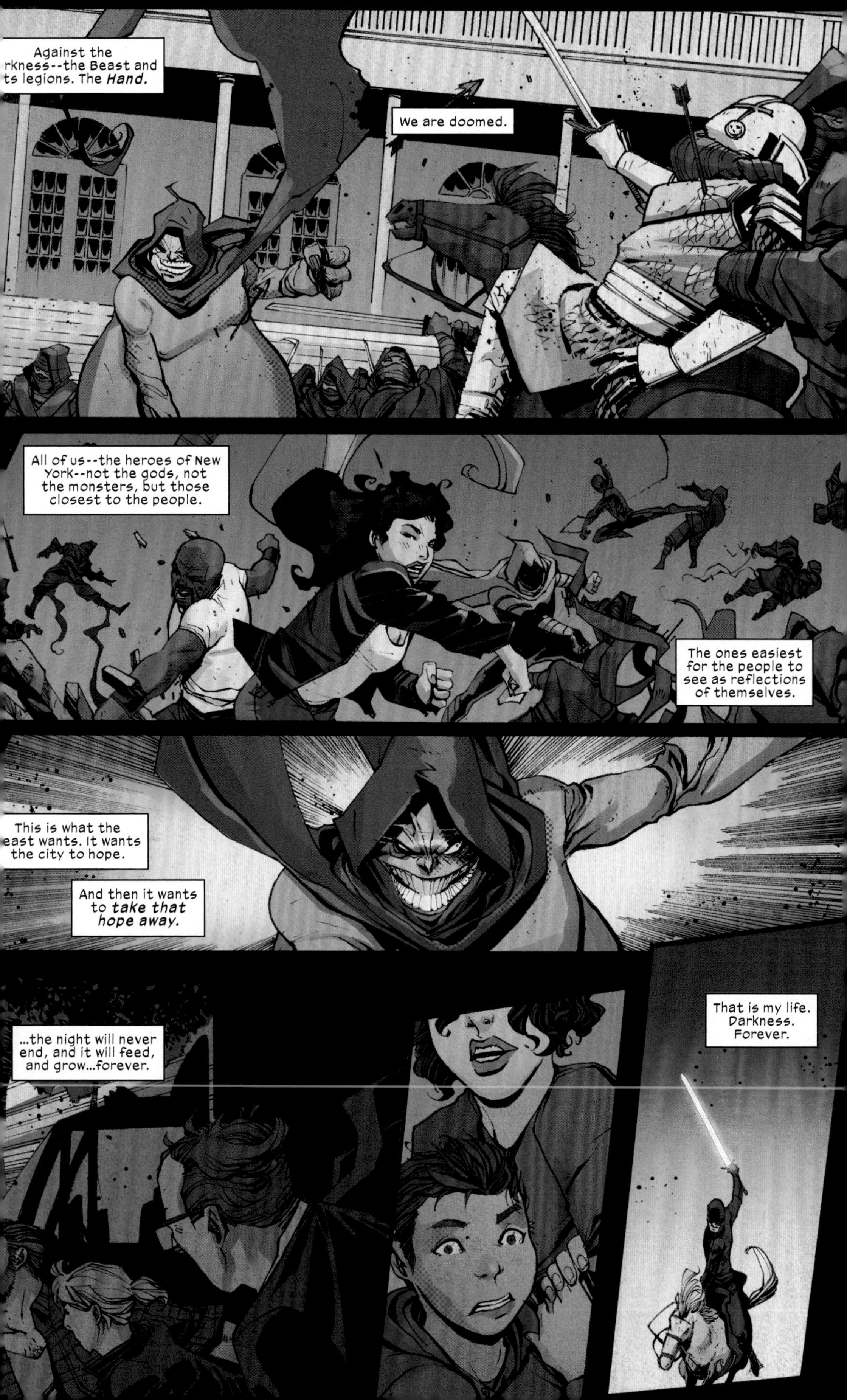
Against the rkness--the Beast and ts legions. The *Hand.*
We are doomed.
All of us--the heroes of New York--not the gods, not the monsters, but those closest to the people.
The ones easiest for the people to see as reflections of themselves.
This is what the east wants. It wants the city to hope.
And then it wants to *take that hope away.*
...the night will never end, and it will feed, and grow...forever.
That is my life. Darkness. Forever.

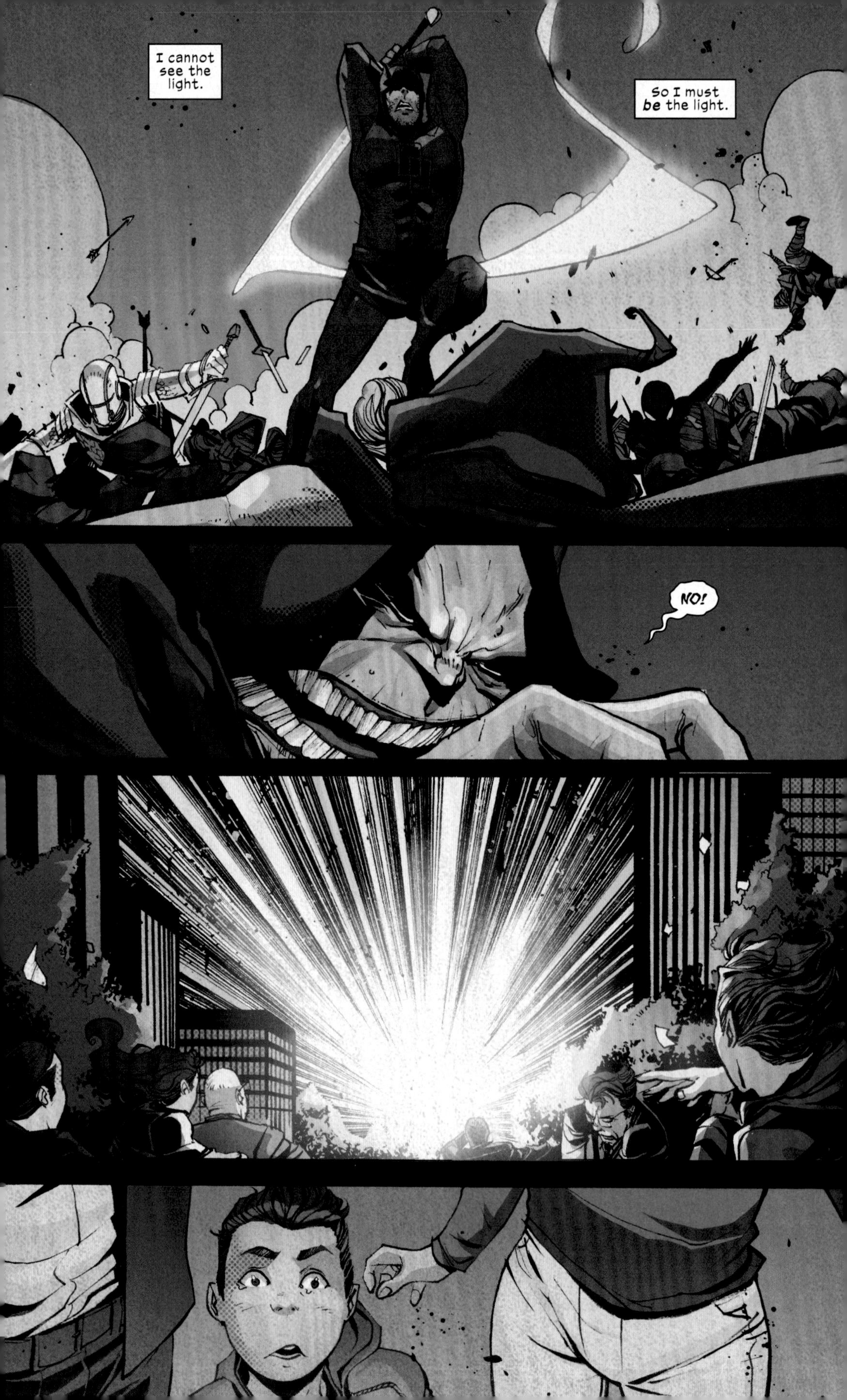
I cannot see the light.
So I must *be* the light.
NO!

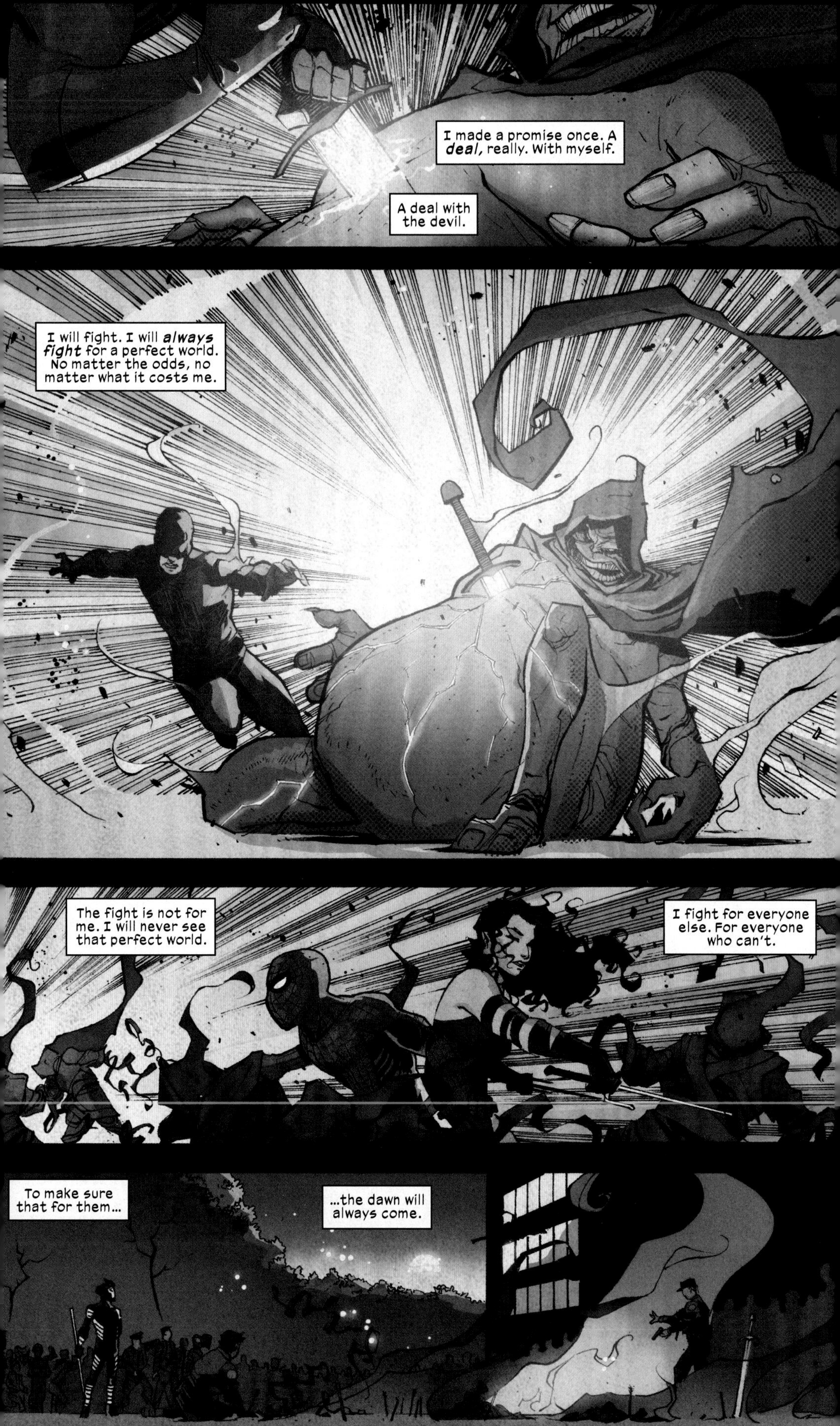
I made a promise once. A *deal,* really. With myself.
A deal with the devil.
I will fight. I will *always fight* for a perfect world. No matter the odds, no matter what it costs me.
The fight is not for me. I will never see that perfect world.
I fight for everyone else. For everyone who can't.
To make sure that for them...
...the dawn will always come.

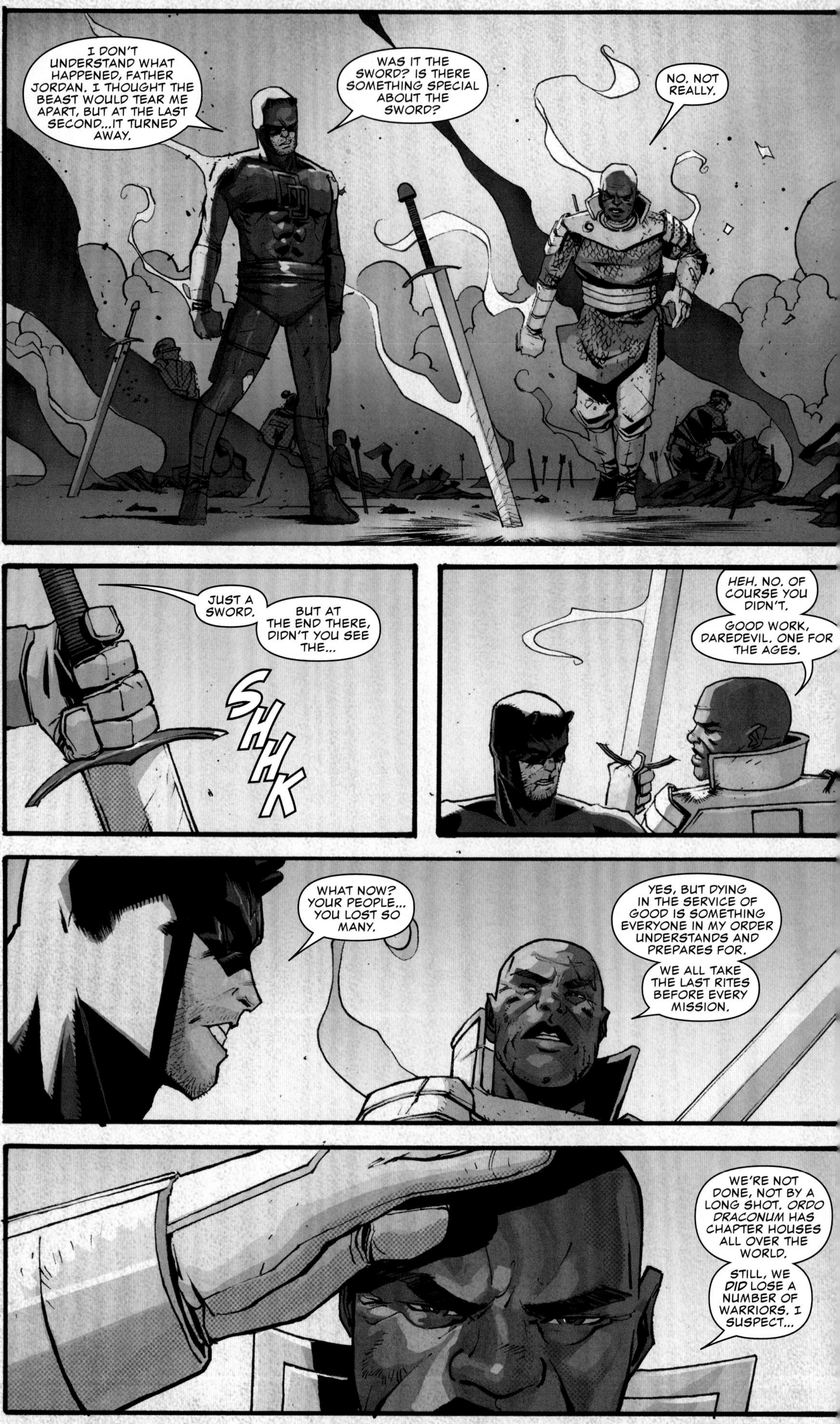
I DON'T UNDERSTAND WHAT HAPPENED, FATHER JORDAN. I THOUGHT THE BEAST WOULD TEAR ME APART, BUT AT THE LAST SECOND...IT TURNED AWAY.
WAS IT THE SWORD? IS THERE SOMETHING SPECIAL ABOUT THE SWORD?
NO. NOT REALLY.
JUST A SWORD.
BUT AT THE END THERE, DIDN'T YOU SEE THE...
SHHK
HEH. NO. OF COURSE YOU DIDN'T.
GOOD WORK, DAREDEVIL. ONE FOR THE AGES.
WHAT NOW? YOUR PEOPLE... YOU LOST SO MANY.
YES, BUT DYING IN THE SERVICE OF GOOD IS SOMETHING EVERYONE IN MY ORDER UNDERSTANDS AND PREPARES FOR.
WE ALL TAKE THE LAST RITES BEFORE EVERY MISSION.
WE'RE NOT DONE, NOT BY A LONG SHOT. *ORDO DRACONUM* HAS CHAPTER HOUSES ALL OVER THE WORLD.
STILL, WE *DID* LOSE A NUMBER OF WARRIORS. I SUSPECT...

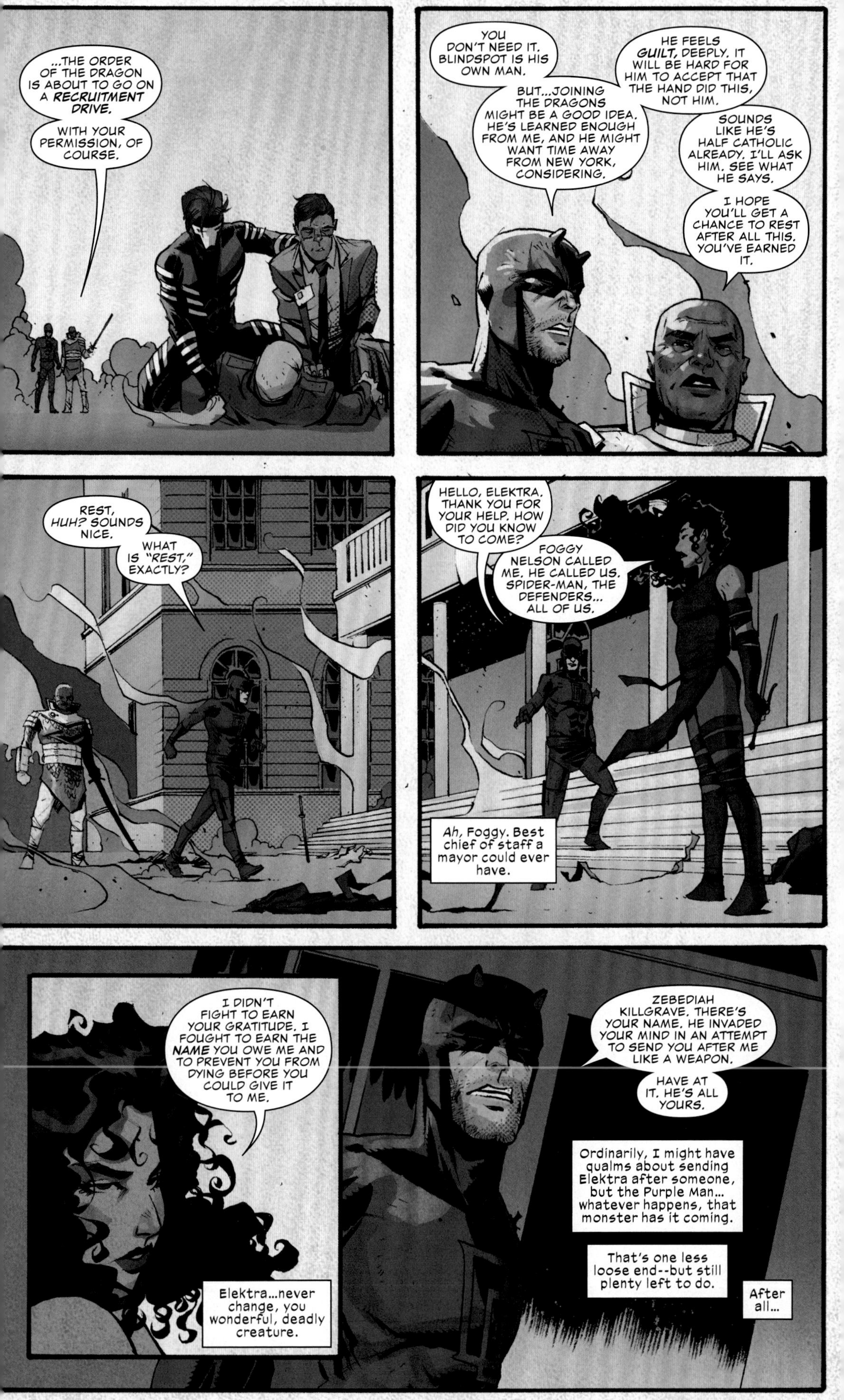

...THE ORDER OF THE DRAGON IS ABOUT TO GO ON A RECRUITMENT DRIVE.
WITH YOUR PERMISSION, OF COURSE.
YOU DON'T NEED IT. BLINDSPOT IS HIS OWN MAN.
BUT...JOINING THE DRAGONS MIGHT BE A GOOD IDEA. HE'S LEARNED ENOUGH FROM ME, AND HE MIGHT WANT TIME AWAY FROM NEW YORK, CONSIDERING.
HE FEELS GUILT, DEEPLY. IT WILL BE HARD FOR HIM TO ACCEPT THAT THE HAND DID THIS, NOT HIM.
SOUNDS LIKE HE'S HALF CATHOLIC ALREADY. I'LL ASK HIM. SEE WHAT HE SAYS.
I HOPE YOU'LL GET A CHANCE TO REST AFTER ALL THIS. YOU'VE EARNED IT.
REST, HUH? SOUNDS NICE.
WHAT IS "REST," EXACTLY?
HELLO, ELEKTRA. THANK YOU FOR YOUR HELP. HOW DID YOU KNOW TO COME?
FOGGY NELSON CALLED ME. HE CALLED US. SPIDER-MAN, THE DEFENDERS... ALL OF US.
Ah, Foggy. Best chief of staff a mayor could ever have.
I DIDN'T FIGHT TO EARN YOUR GRATITUDE. I FOUGHT TO EARN THE NAME YOU OWE ME AND TO PREVENT YOU FROM DYING BEFORE YOU COULD GIVE IT TO ME.
Elektra...never change, you wonderful, deadly creature.
ZEBEDIAH KILLGRAVE. THERE'S YOUR NAME. HE INVADED YOUR MIND IN AN ATTEMPT TO SEND YOU AFTER ME LIKE A WEAPON.
HAVE AT IT. HE'S ALL YOURS.
Ordinarily, I might have qualms about sending Elektra after someone, but the Purple Man... whatever happens, that monster has it coming.
That's one less loose end--but still plenty left to do.
After all...

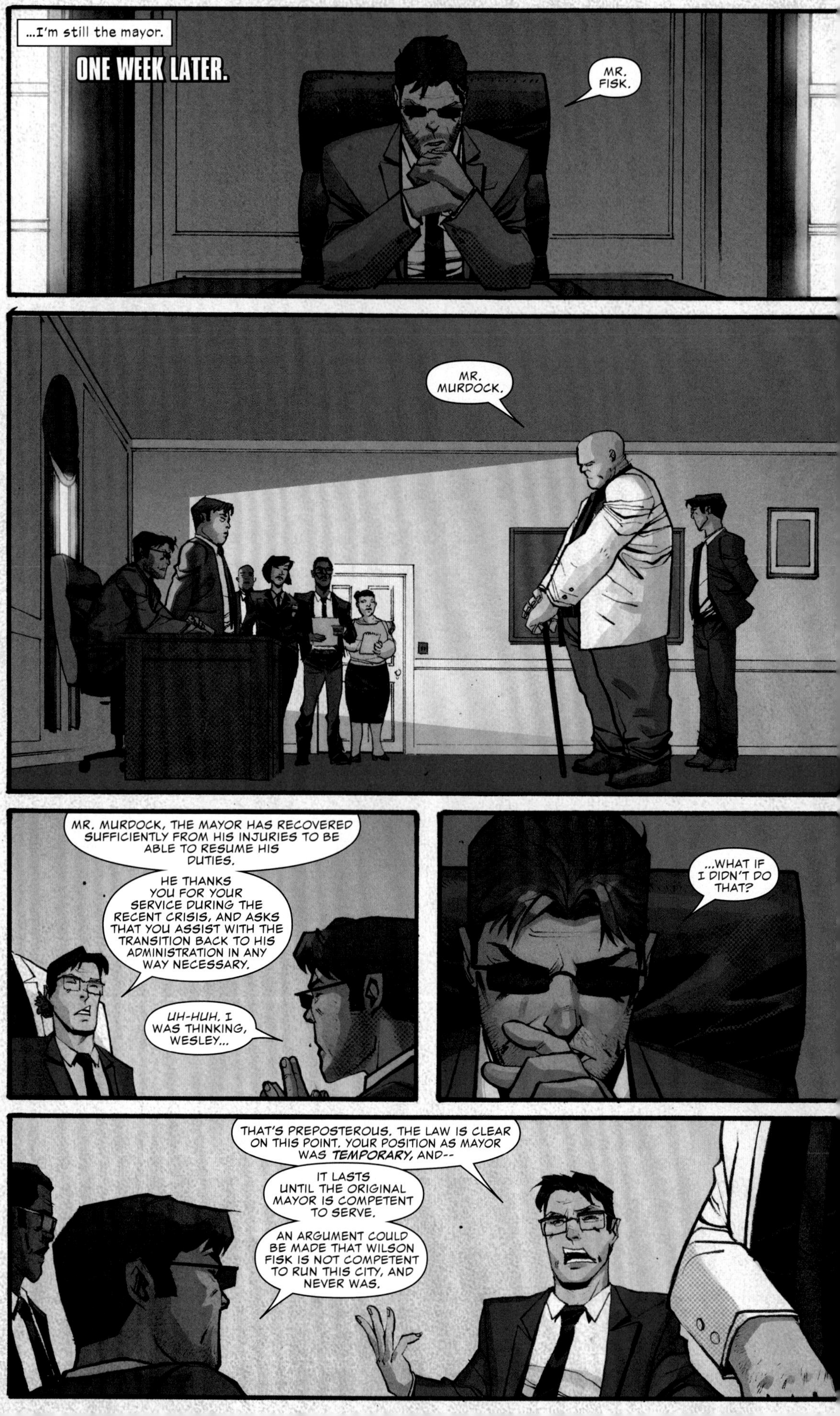

...I'm still the mayor.
ONE WEEK LATER.
MR. FISK.
MR. MURDOCK.
MR. MURDOCK, THE MAYOR HAS RECOVERED SUFFICIENTLY FROM HIS INJURIES TO BE ABLE TO RESUME HIS DUTIES.
HE THANKS YOU FOR YOUR SERVICE DURING THE RECENT CRISIS, AND ASKS THAT YOU ASSIST WITH THE TRANSITION BACK TO HIS ADMINISTRATION IN ANY WAY NECESSARY.
UH-HUH. I WAS THINKING, WESLEY...
...WHAT IF I DIDN'T DO THAT?
THAT'S PREPOSTEROUS. THE LAW IS CLEAR ON THIS POINT. YOUR POSITION AS MAYOR WAS TEMPORARY, AND--
IT LASTS UNTIL THE ORIGINAL MAYOR IS COMPETENT TO SERVE.
AN ARGUMENT COULD BE MADE THAT WILSON FISK IS NOT COMPETENT TO RUN THIS CITY, AND NEVER WAS.

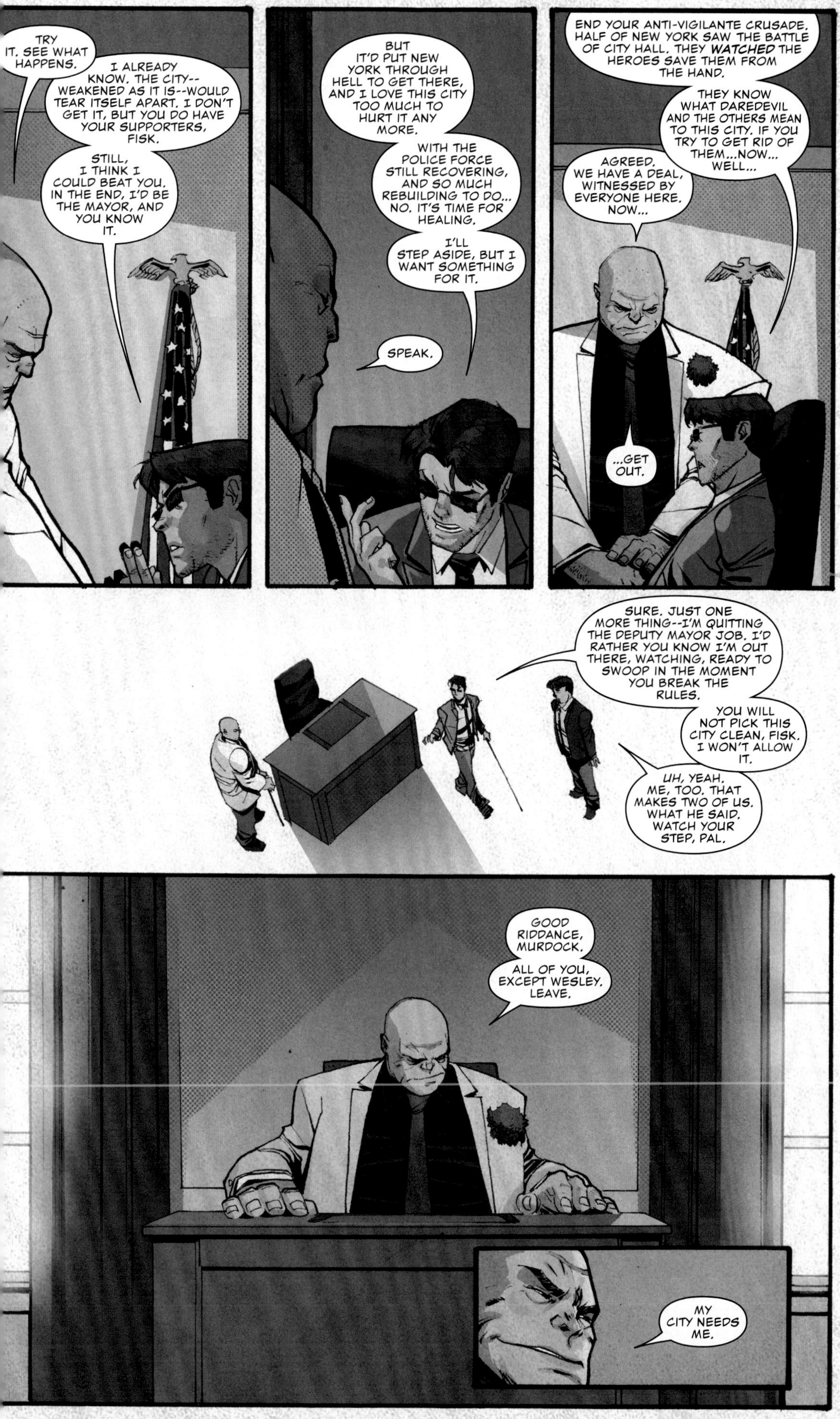
TRY IT. SEE WHAT HAPPENS.
I ALREADY KNOW. THE CITY-- WEAKENED AS IT IS--WOULD TEAR ITSELF APART. I DON'T GET IT, BUT YOU DO HAVE YOUR SUPPORTERS, FISK.
STILL, I THINK I COULD BEAT YOU. IN THE END, I'D BE THE MAYOR, AND YOU KNOW IT.
BUT IT'D PUT NEW YORK THROUGH HELL TO GET THERE, AND I LOVE THIS CITY TOO MUCH TO HURT IT ANY MORE.
WITH THE POLICE FORCE STILL RECOVERING, AND SO MUCH REBUILDING TO DO... NO. IT'S TIME FOR HEALING.
I'LL STEP ASIDE, BUT I WANT SOMETHING FOR IT.
SPEAK.
END YOUR ANTI-VIGILANTE CRUSADE. HALF OF NEW YORK SAW THE BATTLE OF CITY HALL. THEY WATCHED THE HEROES SAVE THEM FROM THE HAND.
THEY KNOW WHAT DAREDEVIL AND THE OTHERS MEAN TO THIS CITY. IF YOU TRY TO GET RID OF THEM...NOW... WELL...
AGREED. WE HAVE A DEAL, WITNESSED BY EVERYONE HERE. NOW...
...GET OUT.
SURE. JUST ONE MORE THING--I'M QUITTING THE DEPUTY MAYOR JOB. I'D RATHER YOU KNOW I'M OUT THERE, WATCHING, READY TO SWOOP IN THE MOMENT YOU BREAK THE RULES.
YOU WILL NOT PICK THIS CITY CLEAN, FISK. I WON'T ALLOW IT.
UH, YEAH. ME, TOO. THAT MAKES TWO OF US. WHAT HE SAID. WATCH YOUR STEP, PAL.
GOOD RIDDANCE, MURDOCK.
ALL OF YOU, EXCEPT WESLEY. LEAVE.
MY CITY NEEDS ME.

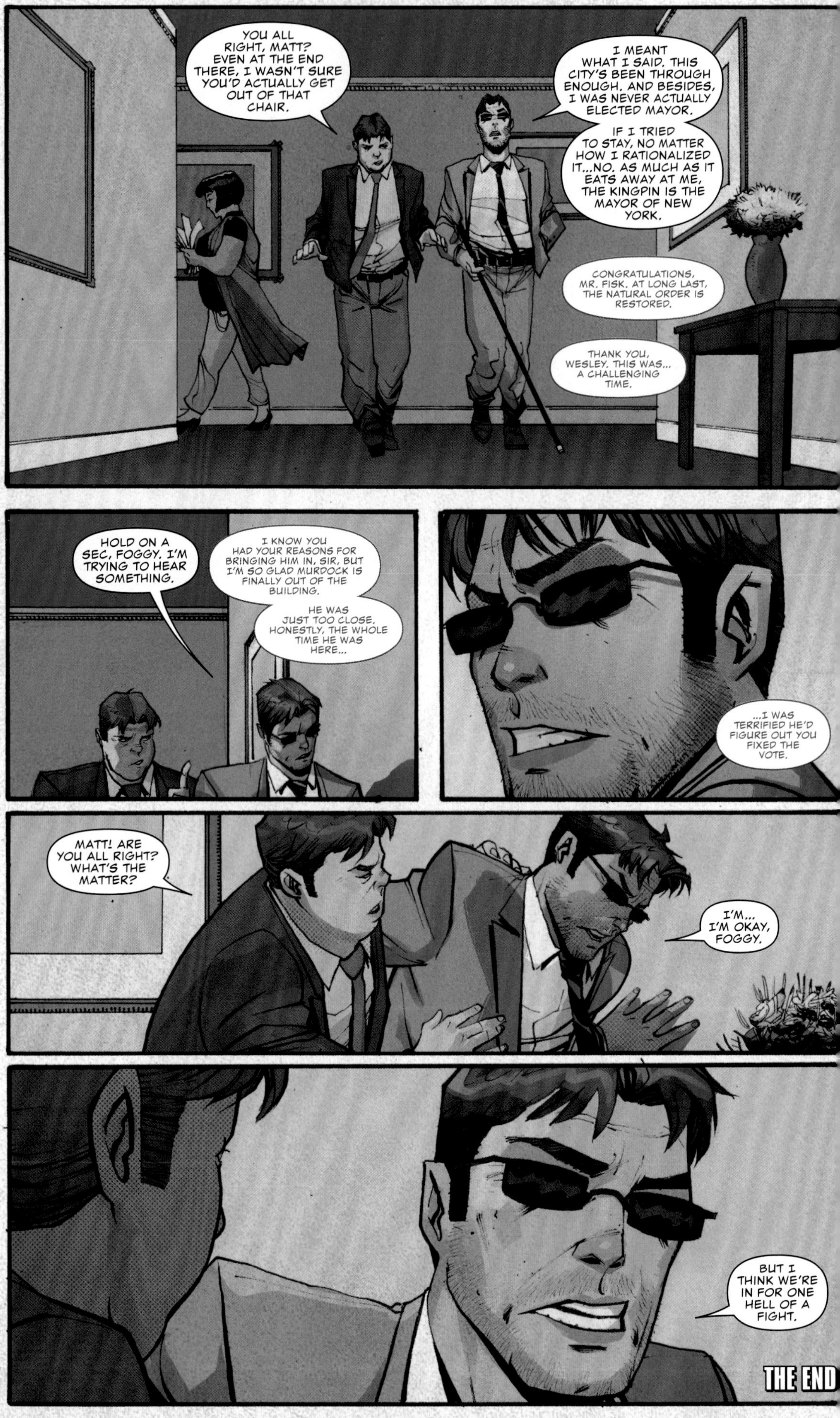
YOU ALL RIGHT, MATT? EVEN AT THE END THERE, I WASN'T SURE YOU'D ACTUALLY GET OUT OF THAT CHAIR.
I MEANT WHAT I SAID. THIS CITY'S BEEN THROUGH ENOUGH. AND BESIDES, I WAS NEVER ACTUALLY ELECTED MAYOR.
IF I TRIED TO STAY, NO MATTER HOW I RATIONALIZED IT...NO. AS MUCH AS IT EATS AWAY AT ME, THE KINGPIN IS THE MAYOR OF NEW YORK.
CONGRATULATIONS, MR. FISK. AT LONG LAST, THE NATURAL ORDER IS RESTORED.
THANK YOU, WESLEY. THIS WAS... A CHALLENGING TIME.
HOLD ON A SEC, FOGGY. I'M TRYING TO HEAR SOMETHING.
I KNOW YOU HAD YOUR REASONS FOR BRINGING HIM IN, SIR, BUT I'M SO GLAD MURDOCK IS FINALLY OUT OF THE BUILDING.
HE WAS JUST TOO CLOSE. HONESTLY, THE WHOLE TIME HE WAS HERE...
...I WAS TERRIFIED HE'D FIGURE OUT YOU FIXED THE VOTE.
MATT! ARE YOU ALL RIGHT? WHAT'S THE MATTER?
I'M... I'M OKAY, FOGGY.
BUT I THINK WE'RE IN FOR ONE HELL OF A FIGHT.
THE END

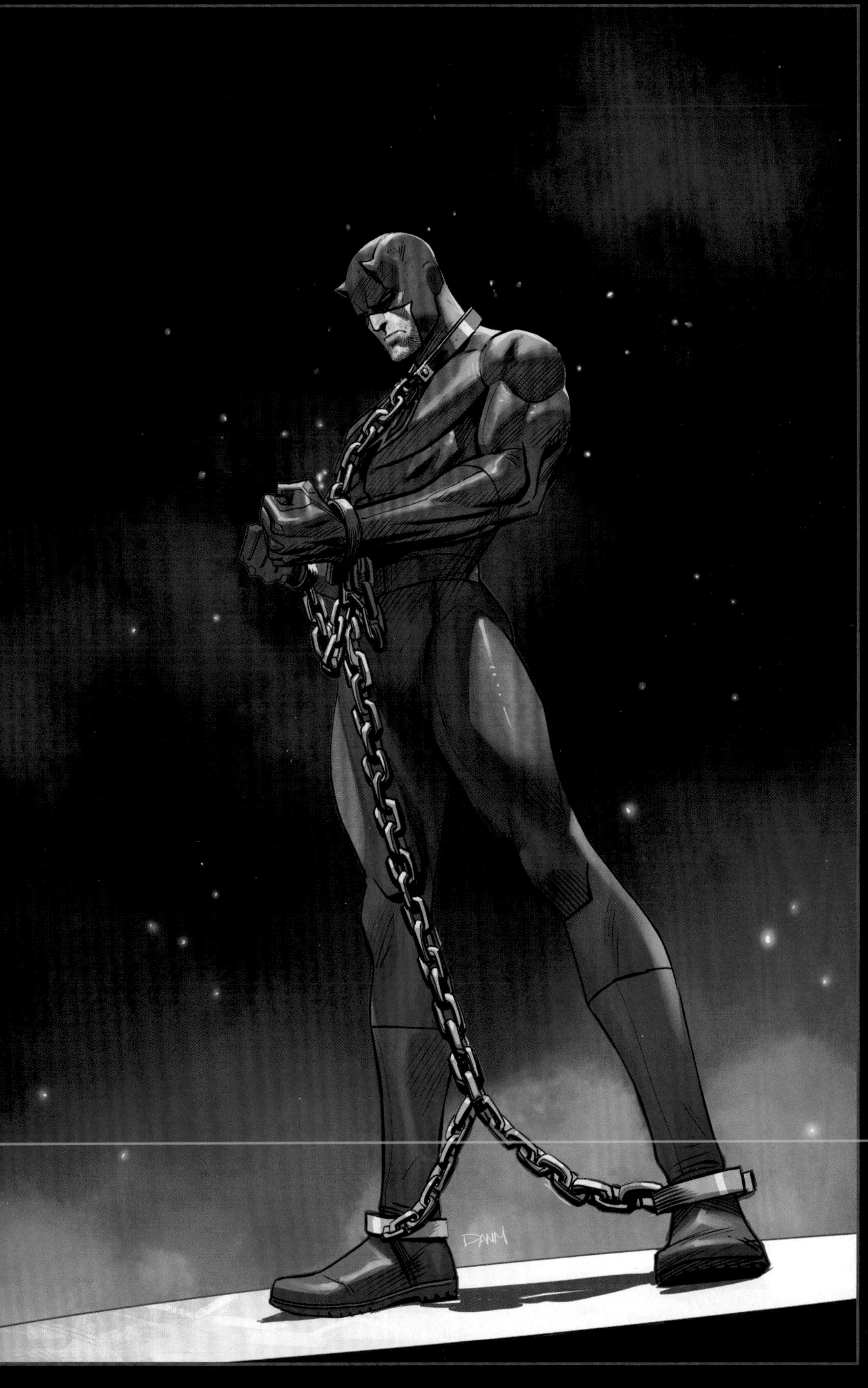

DANIEL MORA & ROMULO FAJARDO JR.

No. 601 VARIANT

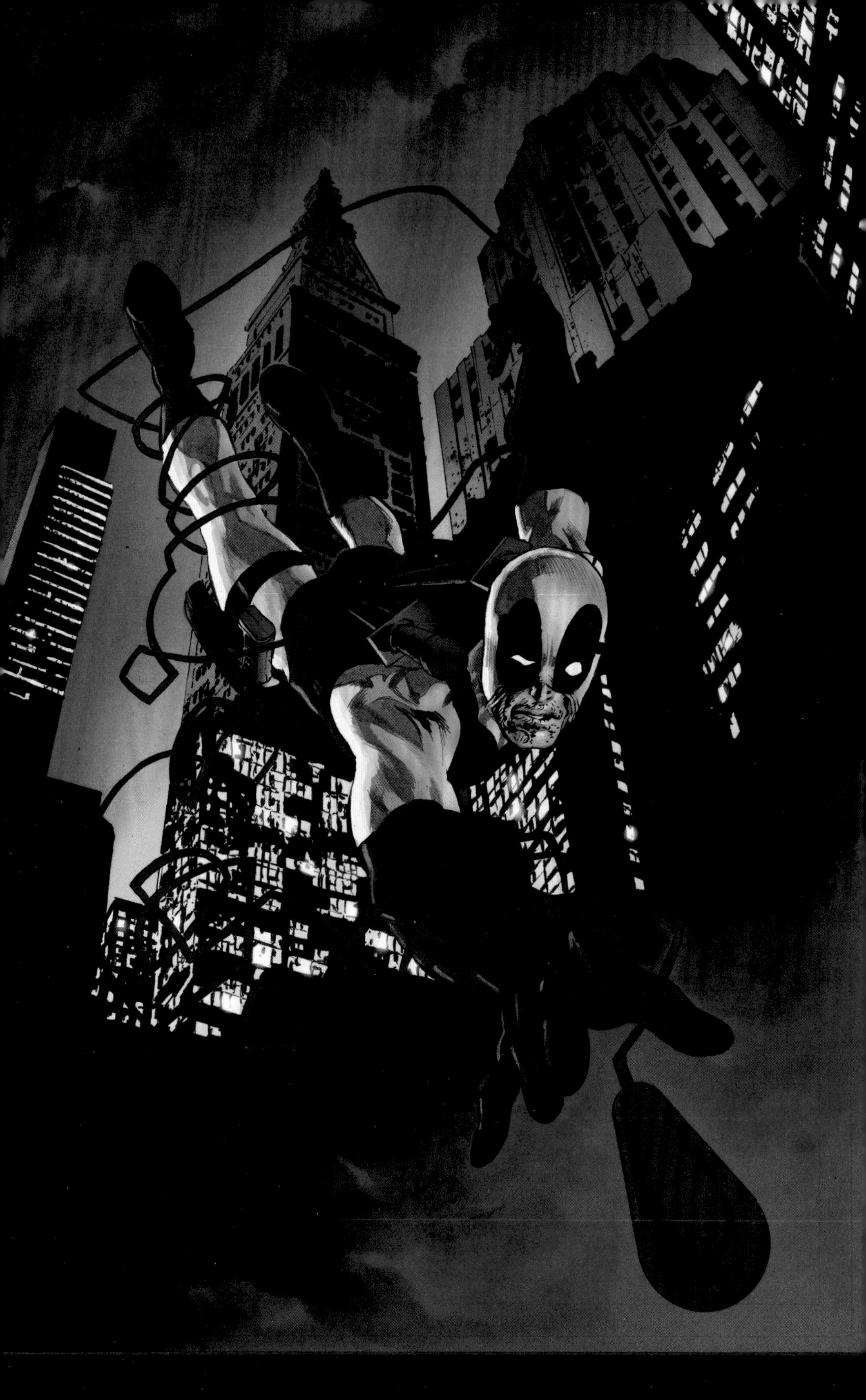

MIKE PERKINS & ANDY TROY

No. 602 DEADPOOL VARIANT